A Game with Dice

"The life of man is like a game with dice:
if you don't get the throw you want,
you must show your skill in making the
best of the throw you do get."

(Terence, *Adelphi, 1.739*)

A Game with Dice

Michael Arnold

HERONHILL BOOKS
PETERSFIELD HAMPSHIRE

HERONHILL BOOKS

PETERSFIELD HAMPSHIRE

First published in the USA in 2003
This second revised edition published in the UK in 2004

Copyright © Michael Arnold 2004

ISBN 0-9548232-0-6

Printed and bound in Great Britain by
RPM PRINT & DESIGN

Produced and printed by members of
THE GUILD OF MASTER CRAFTSMEN

Book Design and Typesetting by Cecil Smith
Typeset in Caxton

RPM PRINT & DESIGN
2-3 Spur Road, Quarry Lane, Chichester, West Sussex PO19 8PR
Telephone : 01243 787 077   Fax : 01243 780 012
E-mail : sales@rpm-repro.co.uk   Website : www.rpm-repro.co.uk

For my
children
and
grandchildren

Contents

Introduction

I had had an uneventful flight from Doha to Dhahran, in the Persian Gulf, in a little four-engined Heron. In the very early sixties, flying in the Gulf was still somewhat rudimentary, but the only way to get about. As Sales Manager for the local Shell marketing company, that is what I had to do.

In Dhahran I climbed into an ancient DC3, bound for Riyadh. The desert shimmered in about 100 degrees in the shade, and the informal activity at the small airport proceeded at its usual leisurely pace. The pilot and co-pilot, in faded khaki, were doing mysterious things in the cockpit. The passengers made their way into the aircraft: a few Arabs in white robes (dish-dashas), a European businessman, an Indian clerk. Last to come aboard was a burly Saudi policeman, handcuffed to a wild-looking man who was chained hand and foot.

"He's all right," said the policeman in Arabic, "just a little *majnoun*, you know, not quite right in the head. I have to take him to Riyadh."

They took the seat immediately behind me, and the policeman transferred his end of the handcuffs to the bar on the back of my seat. The madman sat gibbering quietly to himself. The propellers began to turn.

The engines roared, the tail lifted and we were off in a huge cloud of yellow-brown dust. As the plane banked and set course to the west, I could see the gentle curves of the sand dunes undulate towards the horizon.

I felt the madman patting me gently on the head. I turned to look. The policeman smiled, showing yellow, broken teeth. "He likes you," he said.

We flew on. Some twenty minutes later, we began our descent towards a small airstrip, serving a village in the middle of nowhere. We landed and taxied to a small hut. The engines went on running. The door opened and the heat hit us like a wall of fire; the temperature must have been well into three figures.

The first of the new passengers to board was a short, rather self-important Arab gentleman carrying a cardboard box. He was followed by two ladies, presumably his wives, indistinguishable under a pyramid of flowing black robes and in traditional masks; through the eyeholes I could see sparkling black eyes. The ladies were loaded with a large assortment of household goods, bundles and boxes. Finally came a ragged young boy dragging three goats, which resisted strongly.

The door closed, and we were off again. As we climbed, the atmosphere became cooler, and the passengers relaxed. The madman was howling quietly to himself, and giving my head the occasional pat. Presumably he still liked me. The family group chattered away, the goats were tethered at the back and the boy sat beside them on the floor.

The plane droned on. The madman decided he had to go to the toilet, so the policeman detached the handcuffs from the back of my seat and locked the end on his wrist, before getting up and escorting his charge to the rear of the plane.

Suddenly I smelt the pungent odour of charcoal smoke. Craning my head towards the back, I saw one of the Arab ladies squatting in the gangway lighting a charcoal brazier to make coffee for her husband. She poured some lighter fluid on the charcoal and flames gushed from the contraption. The goats seemed restless.

Just at this moment, the madman and his escort came out of the toilet. The madman stumbled, and fell, with a rattle of chains, onto the brazier. He howled and kicked, getting one of the goats in the belly. The goats, terrified, broke loose and ran up and down the plane; there was burning charcoal everywhere and the coffee lady screamed. The boy tried to crawl under the nearest seat. The policeman, in a reflex action, drew his revolver and the passengers piously implored Allah to protect them. The Indian clerk was wagging his head from side to side and muttering "Oh dearie me, oh dearie me!"

At this point, the madman began loudly cursing Allah, an unspeakable blasphemy and obscenity. The passengers, convinced that their last hour had come, uttered pious disclaimers and begged forgiveness on his behalf. The Indian clerk's voice rose by an octave.

The co-pilot charged out of the cockpit with a large fire extinguisher. He almost got to the burning charcoal when he was tackled by a goat, and fell, spraying the surrounding area with foam. The madman was rushing up and down, dragging the policeman behind him; one of the goats got into the cockpit from which there came a series of oaths. The plane wobbled. I wondered what my family would do without me.

Gradually, things got back to normal. The madman, frothing a little at the mouth, was again tethered to the back of my seat. The goats were recaptured and tied up in the back. The fire was out and the passengers managed to wipe off most of the foam. The husband agreed to wait for his coffee until we had landed.

This we duly did at Riyadh, about an hour later. I hurried to disembark, after a final pat on the head from the friendly madman. It had been an exciting trip, but not as exciting as the first one I took as a child.

But perhaps I should go back to the beginning ...

CHAPTER ONE

Poland

The winter of 1931-32 in Poland was a particularly cold one. I was told that, when I was born, there were some five feet of snow in the courtyard of the block of flats where my parents lived. The six-floor stone building, one of many in Sienkiewicza Street in Lodz, lacked any character or beauty, but was solid and warm during the long winters. It was built round a cobbled courtyard where later I was to play with my football. At the entrance, there was a dark and mysterious den where a wizened, ancient concierge lurked. I grew convinced she was a witch – *Baba Yaga* – and there was proof, since there was usually a broomstick leaning against the wall by the door.

I remember my father as a rotund, cheerful man with a friendly face. The buttons on his suit were always under strain and I wondered if they ever popped off. He was an editor with one of the big national daily papers, *Glos Poranny*, and travelled widely – to Paris, London and Berlin. A charming man, full of anecdotes and jokes, and never one to let facts spoil a good story. His hobby was playing the ocarina – a small, flute-like instrument – and my childhood memories always have the background of sweet, simple melodies which filled the flat when he was there. He died in Paris, when I was four years old, of a sudden heart attack. Sadly, I never knew him well enough to miss him as a person.

My mother was of a very different sort. She was the daughter of a millionaire industrialist who ruled his large family within a set of iron rules on the Victorian model. Although very wealthy, he firmly believed that his children were a subservient race and should have no more than was necessary for their immediate health and wellbeing. Thus his control of the family was absolute, and his quiet, gentle wife had no influence at all. She died after presenting him uncomplainingly with his brood of seven children. He married again after a decent interval, a lady whose attitude to the children whose stepmother she became was less than loving, though not actively unpleasant. My own dim memories of my grandfather show a stern, unsmiling man to whom I was regularly presented for approval. The formula required that I should identify myself as Isabel's son, and then enquire after my grandfather's health. He would reassure me on this, and then open the third drawer on the left of his desk (the interviews always took place in his dark, panelled study) and offer me a sweet from a battered tin he kept there. I would thank him and he would then touch his knuckles to my forehead in a curious sign of benediction, and I was dismissed.

My mother – known as Iza – and her younger sister Ina were a perpetual thorn in his flesh. While my other uncles and aunts exchanged their independence for the relative comfort of the huge family house ruled by my grandfather, Iza and Ina – blonde, shapely and extraordinarily beautiful – would have none of it. They could not accept the rigid discipline which forbade all make-up, all clothes other than drab and shapeless, all alcohol, tobacco and music (except for the better-known classics) – in fact, all that, in their view, in their youth and in the Twenties, made life worth living.

Ina was the leader, and my mother the follower. Thus it was Ina who somehow persuaded my grandfather that both sisters showed great promise as budding violinists ... she played him a Bach partita ... and that she should be sent to live with his brother, a businessman as rigid in outlook as my grandfather, in Leipzig to attend the Conservatoire and develop her musical talent. It seems he did not suspect where her talents truly lay.

Off she went, and nothing much was heard from her for a month or two. It was perfectly obvious to her that she had simply exchanged one prison for another, and so she absconded to Berlin and enrolled at the Conservatoire there. Panic in the family. Grandfather immediately stopped her allowance and delivered a series of ultimata on the 'or else' model. Ina defied him. The family watched agog. She then produced a trump card: she announced to Grandfather that she was earning a living by busking with her violin in Berlin street cafés (she had formed the *Ina Quartet*), and was managing nicely. Grandfather capitulated and, to the astonishment of the family (who had hitherto considered him wholly invincible), reinstated her allowance against a promise that she would try to behave herself. However, far from attending to her music, she plunged headlong into the social whirl of the decadent Berlin of the Twenties. She managed to conceal this from my grandfather and spun him a splendid tale of a newly chaste and cultured existence. She strongly suggested also that my mother should join her, on the grounds of there being safety in numbers. After some persuasion, he consented.

They had a wild time: strings of admirers, theatre, parties, fast cars, gifts of chocolates and orchids. They drank, smoked and modelled their looks on Marlene Dietrich and Greta Garbo. They were known as the Blonde Twins from Lodz throughout Society. My mother, under the name of Iza Norska, even starred in a film of the swooning, *femme fatale* variety. It was not a success.

But all good things had to come to an end. After grandfather realised what was happening, he cut off their allowances and gave them a final ultimatum to return to Lodz, or else. The two young sophisticates surrendered and came home.

My grandfather now had a serious problem on his hands: he considered the Blonde Bombshells as tainted, practically scarlet women. He feared contagion with their siblings, who regarded them with a mixture of envy, fear and a vicarious *schadenfreude*. It was obvious that the polite society of Lodz would not accept them back. The only answer he could think of was to get them married off in a hurry, preferably to husbands who would take them away somewhere. Anyway, they were in their late twenties, and it was past time.

Opportunely, there appeared a strange little man, who was to become my much beloved Uncle Max. He was an untidy, shy person, with a diameter of about five feet; almost perfectly spherical. He spoke a curious mixture of Polish, Russian and German but could speak none of them well. His antecedents were not known, beyond the fact that he came originally from the border country between Russia and Poland, that he was a highly qualified doctor (he had studied in Vienna) and had served as such with the Cossacks during the First World War. He had lived in the Hedjaz, in far-off Arabia, and then had moved to be the Royal doctor to Abdulla, the King of Transjordan.

Apparently he had been told by the King that it was time he got married, and that he should go on leave to Europe and come back with a wife. To this end, Uncle Max told me, the King had summoned a servant and told him to bring some jewels. The servant returned with a casket of unset gems and the King had plunged his hand into it and given Uncle Max a large handful, instructing him to buy "a really good woman." There were emeralds, diamonds and pearls, which Uncle Max put in his pocket and took to Lodz to find a wife.

After a whirlwind courtship during which many of the gems were set in pieces of jewellery, Uncle Max and Ina were married, and amid tears, cabin trunks and farewells, he bore her off to the mysterious deserts of Arabia, land of Rudolf Valentino and Sheherezade. The society and newspapers of Lodz had a field day, and grandfather reckoned that was one down and one to go.

There then, fortuitously, appeared my father. He was not at all what grandfather had in mind, but his assiduous courtship of my mother, full of a typically Polish passion and impulsive romance, together with grandfather's growing desperation, finally led to what turned out to be a very satisfactory marriage. My parents moved to their own modest flat and letters came from Ina, with unusual stamps, saying that she and Uncle Max had moved to Baghdad, where he had become the Royal physician to the Court and person of King Faisal I, brother of King Abdulla and recently enthroned King of Iraq.

My mother was a small woman, with delicate bones and small hands and feet. Her plunge into the film world during her Berlin escapade had affected her deeply. I realised fairly early that, in her own right, her personality was very vague. She was always playing a part: the Loving Mother, the Supportive Wife, the Brave Little Woman, the Cultured Hostess, the Beautiful Lady, and so on. Her passion for films made her view life and people as a procession of stereotypes. But she was a woman of great determination and courage.

It was not possible for me to see my mother as one person; she was a parade of characters, always changing, always relevant to the moment, with only her appearance to give continuity.

This appearance was also somewhat artificial, although very pleasing to the eye. She was, like Ina, a blonde. She treated her face as a canvas on which to paint the right picture: delicately pencilled eyebrows, a mouth of the right shape and colour, eyelashes to accentuate blue eyes, carefully pink cheeks. I remember my astonishment, on the few occasions I saw her in the early morning, unprepared, at how little there actually was, compared with the face I was used to. I believe that my father, who was wholly unconcerned with his appearance and had only one character, was rather bewildered at the variety of wives he seemed to have married.

The flat in which we lived, while modest by grandfather's standards, was adequate for our needs. The sitting and dining rooms were large and equipped with massive, dark furniture and heavy curtains. On the walls were reproductions of famous paintings, in particular a huge canvas of the Rape of the Sabine Women, which puzzled me, since I could not understand why anyone should wish to ride horses while wearing no clothes. Of particular interest was a small gilt Cupid, hanging by a chain from the chandelier above the dining table; this monstrosity had a button on its bottom which, when pressed, sounded a bell to summon the maid from the kitchen.

The flat had large windows, overlooking the somewhat drab street on one side, and the inner courtyard, with a small garden at the far end of a large cobbled area, on the other. These windows, which were double, would be closed in late October and the crevices stuffed with cotton wool. They would then not be opened again until the spring, when the worst of the cold was over.

I was born in very early 1932, two months prematurely. I had no fingernails and some trouble with breathing, but these problems soon passed. My father was delighted and though my mother, as was then the fashion, did not see a great deal of me, she showed me love when we were together. However, I did remain an only child.

The earliest memories are always difficult to distinguish from what I was later told, but some small fragments remain. I remember family gatherings in grandfather's house, with regiments of aunts, uncles and cousins. I remember the sunlight in my small bedroom and the stuffed animals sharing my bed. I remember being balanced on the convexity of my father's waistcoat, though seldom, while he played simple tunes to me on his ocarina.

My clearest and happiest memories are of Michasia. To my parents she was maid, cook and nanny; to me she was guide, friend and a never-failing source of care and food. Since my father was seldom around, and my mother busy with her own life, most of my time was spent with Michasia in the kitchen, curled up on the big tiled stove. Such a stove was, traditionally, a five-foot cube, with the tiles often decorated with country scenes. It was a warm and a comfortable place for a small person to be and from my perch I watched her cook and clean, and listened to her endless stories of witches, princesses and animals.

She came from the south of Poland, deep in the country. She was a jolly, rotund person of middle age, with black, braided hair always bound in a bright kerchief, and with long, dark dresses, covered when indoors by a large white apron. When she sang to me, her eyes would close and her hands would swing from side to side, following the tune.

There were bedtime stories and, on cold winter mornings, 'kluski na mleku' – small dumplings in hot, sweet milk. There were shopping expeditions and illicit portions of wild strawberries, when in season. There were walks in the park and the odd ice cream in the summer sunshine.

Once or twice a week, Michasia would prepare me for a formal appearance at a tea party my mother gave for her friends. This involved a sailor suit, so starched that incautious movements could be acutely painful, scrubbed face, slicked-back hair and, of course, best behaviour. I would be led into the sitting room where a group of very elegant ladies sipped tea and ate small cakes, to be embraced by Loving Mother, petted, fed, exclaimed over and finally allowed to return to the informal comforts of the kitchen.

Every summer, Ina would suddenly appear on a visit. She spent the three months of the summer in Europe, to escape the intense heat of Baghdad and to restock her wardrobe. She would spend some time in Paris, to buy clothes and hats from the leading fashion designers and then have a week in Vienna, to attend the opera. Since it was one of Uncle Max's duties to accompany the Iraqi Royal Court on their occasional official visits abroad, Aunt Ina also went as a Lady-in-Waiting to the Queen, and had to be suitably dressed. Of course, as a leading figure in Baghdad society, she had to be up with the latest fashions. I have a memory of a scented vision in furs, glamorous and exotic, who would tell her tales to a stunned family audience, an orchid in a garden of weeds.

She told us that Uncle Max had been elevated to the rank of a Pasha of the First Class (roughly equivalent to a Viscount). Since his surname was difficult to pronounce, he was known throughout the Middle East as Dr Max Pasha, a name he was to bear until his death. After a suitable interval, Ina would take her many trunks and hatboxes, and depart again for the Orient.

One day, when I was four, Michasia woke me, sniffling, and took me to see my mother in her bedroom, normally forbidden territory. Mother was in bed, weeping and prostrated. Sadly, my father had died suddenly of a heart attack, while on a visit to Paris. I was embraced by Grieving Widow and told that father had gone away to God for good and that now I was the man of the house. It was some days before I realised that the pleasant person who played the ocarina would never return. Somehow, my mother took over my father's job at the newspaper, and became the breadwinner in the guise, unusual for the time, of Career Woman. She wore suits and spoke in an efficient, clipped way.

School, when it started, was not very exciting and I do not remember anything about it except for one particular: the school hat, which we all wore, was modelled on a Polish officer's cap, khaki coloured, square-crowned and with a lacquered black peak. In place of the Polish eagle above this peak, there was a metal school badge. We were all immensely proud of the hat, and for the first week or two I insisted on going to bed wearing mine. This was, of course, forbidden, but I could usually get round Michasia.

During the summers, we always went with about a dozen other members of the family to a small village some seventy kilometres southwest of Lodz. There was my best friend, Ryszard, who was some sort of cousin, and the same age as I; three girls, aged between five and nine and a couple of teenage cousins: Marja, a pretty girl with long, blonde pigtails, and my 18-year-old cousin, Jasio, whom I worshipped. He was a tall, well-built chap, with broad shoulders and very fair hair. Assorted uncles and aunts, in groups of three or four, would be there to look after us and they would change every week or two, like a guard, replaced by a new lot coming down from Lodz.

We rented a group of four primitive cottages, standing alone in a field near some woods. They were quite old, made of wood and with thatched roofs. There was no running water or electricity and one of Ryszard's and my duties was, every morning, to bring up some buckets of water from the well at the back.

My cousins and I spent the long summer days in walks through the neighbouring fields and forests and in playing Indians in the woods. For us all, this was paradise after the town. I also well remember long walks with Jasio, collecting baskets of bilberries and wild strawberries in the forest. With his penknife (which I coveted), he would shape boats for Ryszard and me from chunks of pine bark, which we would sail on the series of ponds not far from the village.

Ryszard was my particular friend. He and I were inseparable, both at school and during our holidays. He was smaller than I was, with a mop of unruly blond hair, and a wonderful imagination: he could conjure up bears, monsters, bandits and ghosts for us to fight or run from. We often lay in ambush in the woods and jumped out of the undergrowth at the girl cousins, yelling and waving our arms, to see them scatter and run screaming for home, pigtails flying.

The forests were of pine and spruce, dark and cool and scented in the summer heat. There were tall sunflowers in the fields around, and we would always pick a ripe one each, and eat the seeds as we walked. The series of ponds, linked by a small stream, were mysterious and a wonderful setting for Ryszard's tales of adventure.

There were few people around, and the only regular visitor was a local peasant, Piotr, who brought us milk, butter and fresh, crusty bread every day. He was quite an old man, with a brown, weather-beaten face; he was usually dressed in a dark blue smock and huge, knee-high boots covered with mud. We could sometimes persuade him to stay a while and tell us stories of wolves and bears, though only the younger among us really believed.

In the evenings, the families would sit, all together, in the huge kitchen of one of the cottages and everyone had to tell a story. The wavering light of the kerosene lanterns bathed everything in a soft, golden glow. But the corners of the big room were dark, and we would invent blood-chilling tales to frighten the girls before everyone had to go to bed. Ryszard, of course, always had the most grisly and bloodthirsty ones. He would wink at me as the girls clung together in delicious terror.

The summer of 1939, when I was seven, started much like the others. I was unaware of the rumble of approaching war, though I sensed that the adults were tense and worried. There seemed to be more soldiers around than usual, and a number of uncles had gone into uniform, especially Uncle Tomasz, resplendent in the colourful uniform of the Polish *Uhlans*, the Cavalry Regiment.

On the first day of September the sky was a bright blue, with some fleecy white clouds. Yet we heard a distant rumble, which pulsed through the clear air and got louder and louder.

Ryszard and I snatched up our school hats (we always wore them) and ran out of the cottage to see what was making the strange noise.

"Get the children indoors," shouted Uncle Jan to Jasio, who herded us, protesting loudly, into the cottage where we rushed to the windows and craned out to see what was happening.

A dark band across the sky was approaching from the west. As it got closer, we saw hundreds and hundreds of airplanes which, to me, looked like swarms of flying ants.

"Look," said Ryszard, "there are thousands of them. What are they?"

"Bombers, German bombers," Jasio was hurrying by.

Hour after hour the throbbing bands of German planes passed overhead on their way to destroy Poland's cities. The rhythmic drone of the engines was overwhelming, terrifying and we could hear the crunch and crash of bombs falling on Lodz, many kilometres away. I did not know what to think. Destruction on that scale was too much for a boy's imagination and it was not until I saw the ruins that the full realisation of the terror hit me.

The following day, we were woken by a curious whistling sound, followed by a bang. We ran out of the cottage, but nothing was to be seen. The whistling and bangs continued. We were between the Polish and German forces, and the whistling and banging was the sound of artillery shells passing both ways over our heads. War had arrived.

My mother was in Lodz, and came rushing down to the village to collect me. She told us that things were going very badly and that we had to get back home as fast as we could. The family packed rapidly, and got into two ancient cars to go back to town. Ryszard and I managed to sit together in the back, all squashed up between other people, boxes, suitcases and overcoats.

"I don't want to go home yet," Ryszard complained. "There was no time to finish our special hiding place near the lake. Now it will just be school and all that stuff ..."

"I don't think it will be like before," I replied. "I hope our house hasn't been smashed by the bombs."

"Look at all those people," Ryszard was trying to see out of the open side of the car. He was wearing his school hat, the one which looked just like that of a Polish officer and which kept getting knocked off as he wriggled and squirmed. "Look, horses..."

I tried to put my hat on too, but mother snatched it away. "You should not be wearing that now," she said. "Take yours off at once, Ryszard," she ordered. Ryszard pretended to do so, but soon had it on again. Mother didn't notice; she threw my hat out of the window. I was horrified and protested loudly, but she took no notice. I began to cry. It had been my most precious possession and it was gone. Why had she done it? What possible reason was there? And Ryszard still had his. It was so unfair.

The journey was difficult and frightening. The Germans were advancing rapidly, and the road was choked with a stream of people going both ways. Cars, carts and wheelbarrows pushed and jostled in the thick dust, and occasional despatch riders on motorcycles dashed back and forth. There was an air of panic; rumours spread rapidly. The Germans were at the gates of Lodz; the Russians were invading from the East; the Treaty countries would not come to our aid; the Polish army and airforce were being destroyed.

Suddenly, the air began to scream. We pulled to the side and jumped out of the cars. From the sky, came wailing, howling dots which rapidly took on the shape of planes: *Stukas!* At the time, we did not know what they were, but when explosions, flashes and smoke began to come up the road towards us, we realised they were the infamous German dive-bombers. There was no opposition, and the pilots amused themselves by sowing death and destruction among the refugees on the crowded roads. Cars, carts, horses and people were obliterated in the explosions and great clouds of dust and smoke lay, like a pall, over the road. We were lucky; just before reaching the area where we cowered in the ditch, the planes flew away, and the people slowly emerged from their hiding places to take up again their weary trek.

Ryszard and I had been huddled together in the ditch. We thought it was the most exciting thing we had ever seen, although we were both absolutely terrified.

Then we saw our first Germans. Huge, grey tanks, with black German crosses on them, came rumbling down the road, scattering the other traffic, with soldiers clinging to the outside. The troops were laughing and joking, and occasionally would fire their rifles into the air. Our cars had pulled into the side, and stopped, and we had all got out again and were hiding behind them, away from the tanks, in a shallow ditch. Ryszard was still wearing his hat and I was very jealous. As he peered round the back of the car at the passing tanks, his hat must have been spotted by a German soldier and mistaken for that of a Polish officer. There was a bang, and Ryszard was thrown backwards. He lay next to me and there was a neat small hole in his forehead, slowly oozing blood. He didn't move, though I shook his arm. Mother quickly pulled me away and it was some time before I realised that suddenly Ryszard was not there any more. He was seven.

It was difficult to realise that he was gone. Uncle Jan and Jasio put him into the other car and Mother said I could not go with him. I thought it was extraordinary that it took such a short time to die, and that dying lasted such a long time. This was not like our games in the woods.

It took us the best part of two days to do the seventy kilometres back to Lodz. Mother and I climbed the stairs to the flat and she unlocked the door. We went in and saw a woman in the sitting room with a German officer. He had his jacket off, and I could see a large pistol in a holster on the table beside him.

"What do you want?" said the woman, getting to her feet. "How dare you walk in, just like that!"

"This is my house," said my mother. "Who are you, and what are you doing here?"

"Oh, no," said the woman. "This is not your house any more. Everything here belongs to me. Doesn't it, *liebling*?" she asked the officer. "I am a German, and we own Poland now; so you and your brat can get out."

The officer picked up his holster, and mother took my hand and we left. We now had nothing but the clothes we wore. The small suitcase of my summer belongings had to stay in the flat. Mother was crying angrily as we made our way down the stairs.

We walked across town to the flat of my Uncle Genio – my father's brother – and his wife, Aunt Lusia. They lived in a basement flat which I loved, because there was a mysterious cellar, reached by a trapdoor hidden under a rug on the floor.

Since they were childless, they were very fond of me, and we often used to visit. Mother collapsed into Lusia's arms, and told her what had happened. Genio immediately said that we should stay with them, and began to make plans to overcome the immediate problems of survival. It was clear that there would be a shortage of food, though few Poles at the time had any idea of the extreme brutality of the Germans or the real dangers to life which would quickly become apparent as the occupation of Poland changed from front-line troops to the Gestapo.

Those first few weeks are hard to remember. The women and I stayed indoors, while Uncle Genio made sporadic forays into the outside world. From one of these, to my great delight, he brought back four rabbits in a wicker basket, with a large bundle of greenery. These were installed in the cellar and were to be our emergency rations, though happily I did not understand the full import of this plan. For me, the rabbits were a constant joy. It was wonderful to climb down the ladder into the cellar and hold and stroke the little furry bodies. I had never had a chance to have any pets, and I sat for hours watching and playing with them.

It was during this period that tragic events overtook the family. My grandfather was killed by a German soldier, in the hall of his house, while trying to prevent three of them from coming in to loot and rape. He had only his old cavalry sabre in the umbrella stand, and was no match for a Schmeisser machine pistol. Uncle Tomasz died during the glorious charge by the *Uhlans*, with their lances, against a Panzer regiment of tanks. I do not believe there were any survivors among the two hundred or so horsemen, but a tank was disabled. Many uncles and aunts simply disappeared.

On one occasion, I persuaded my mother that I should accompany Uncle Genio on one of his expeditions. There was a strange feeling about the city: pedestrians scurried about on the pavements, keeping close to the walls, while Germans swaggered about, barging passers-by into the gutter. Many people had yellow badges sewn onto their clothes; Uncle Genio said they were Jews, whom the Germans particularly hated. In one small square, there was a scaffold, with bodies hanging on it – Uncle Genio hurried me past. He said that a German soldier had been killed in a nearby street by the Underground, and these were people who had been murdered in reprisal. We managed to get some bread, and a scrawny chicken in exchange for Aunt Lusia's silver teapot, and went home quickly.

It was now some weeks since we were with my Uncle and Aunt. My mother was getting more and more worried, since the newspaper (no longer being produced), of which she was an editor, had been a virulently anti-Nazi one, and we learned that she was on the 'wanted' list of the Gestapo. Thus it was with terror that we heard, early one morning, a loud banging on the door. Uncle Genio opened it, to reveal a young SS officer, in his black uniform and shiny boots.

The officer barged in, followed by a sergeant, and came into the sitting room. We stood up.

"Names and papers," he shouted.

We produced the documents we had, and Uncle Genio told him our names. The officer looked around the room. There was a silence. Then, from beneath our feet, there was a scurrying noise; the rabbits! By now there were seven of them.

"What's that noise?" the officer shouted. "What are you hiding under the floor?"

He dragged the rug aside to reveal the trapdoor, and drew his pistol. The sergeant cocked his machine gun.

"Open it!" the officer commanded, and Uncle Genio pulled the trapdoor up. The officer looked down into the cellar and grinned. "Hunting time," he said, and began shooting at the rabbits, which ran about in a panic. Happily, he missed them all, and we were very lucky that they provided a distraction, for he threw our papers on the floor and, with a sharp order to the sergeant, stalked out of the house. Perhaps he was upset at having missed. I was on the floor under the table having hysterics.

It was this incident which finally persuaded my mother that we must try to get out of Poland as soon as possible. It was very cold and the winter made food harder and harder to find. We had already bartered everything of value and she felt badly about living off my uncle and aunt. But where to go? The only relatives we had abroad were Uncle Max and Aunt Ina in Baghdad, and that was a very long way away.

Uncle Genio made enquiries, and found that the manager of the bank which my mother used was still in charge, although all accounts were frozen. Undaunted, my mother went there one day, and after much pleading succeeded in getting the manager to give her a little of our money. He risked his life to do so, and we were very grateful.

Then we had a stroke of amazing luck. Uncle Genio discovered that in the hierarchy of the German unit administering Lodz, there was an officer in the army who had known Mother and Ina during their time in Berlin.

With trepidation, mother went to see him. As it happened, he was a good man, and after many days of begging and persuasion somehow organised for us permits to leave Poland. These were very rare and precious documents, and we almost certainly owe our lives to him. On what curious coincidences can one's whole existence sometimes depend. Mother tried very hard to persuade Uncle Genio and Aunt Lusia to come with us, but they decided to stay.

So, one day, clutching a paper bag with some bread, a carrot and two raw potatoes, we set off for Baghdad. Mother had a blanket over her shoulders which Aunt Lusia insisted we take. I had one of Uncle Genio's woolly waistcoats on over my clothes. We never saw my Aunt and Uncle again.

To undertake the journey to Baghdad was a difficult and hazardous business. There was strict control by the occupying powers on the movement of people, and any German could – and often would – stop people and demand to see their papers. If these were not wholly in order, and sometimes even if they were, the people would be arrested and disappear. Public transport was virtually non-existent, and we had no information on the few trains that were still running or on any buses or trams. We knew little of the progress of the war beyond the rumour that Britain was fighting for her life on our side and that France had given up and been overrun. We knew only that we had to keep away from both Germany and Russia, and head south towards Italy, which had not yet officially entered the war. This meant that we not only had to get out of Poland, but also had to brave the dangers of Czechoslovakia and Austria, both firmly in Hitler's grip.

Thus we set out from Lodz, with Brindisi as our halfway goal, a distance of some 2,500 kilometres. As I said, Mother was a determined and brave woman, whatever her shortcomings. She told me that, no matter what it cost and however long it took, we would get to Ina and Uncle Max in the end. I found it hard to believe; the distance seemed enormous.

We made our way to the railway station and enquired about trains to Wroclaw, a town some 200 kilometres south of Lodz. One of the railway officials, an elderly Pole in a bedraggled uniform and with a huge walrus moustache, looked at us as though we were crazy.

"Wroclaw," he said ruminatively. He chewed the end of his moustache. "Why would anyone want to go to Wroclaw these days? Better to stay at home and keep one's head down."

The station was crowded, and there was an all-pervading odour of steam and steel: slightly sweet and warm and damp. The warmth was welcome after the snowy chill of the streets, but we felt uncomfortable with many German soldiers and officers, in their black and grey uniforms, pushing their way roughly through the crowds.

"Well, if you insist on going to Wroclaw," said the official, "you better be sure you have all the right papers, and enough money for the ticket. I can't tell you when there will be a train, and you must just wait and keep asking. There may be one today and then again, there may not. Things have changed ... "

Mother bought two tickets at a little window and we sat on a bench. I chewed on the carrot. The crowds ebbed and flowed around us and from time to time there was a 'toooot tooot' and a train came clanking in or out. We sat there for hours and hours, trying to be inconspicuous and avoiding at all costs any eye contact with Germans. We were approached only once, by a nondescript-looking man in a dirty raincoat and felt hat who demanded to see our papers. We noted that our friend with the big moustache was hovering nearby and nodding slightly. Mother produced our papers and the man scrutinised them carefully and gave them back somewhat grudgingly before disappearing into the crowd.

"You must be careful," said our friend. "There are many Gestapo around and also some traitor Poles who are helping the Germans."

"Why?" I asked.

"Never mind," said Mother. "We have more important things to think about."

It became dark, and the station looked even more depressing. Our friend suddenly appeared and said: "Quick, you must hurry. There is a train for Wroclaw on Platform six. Run ... "

We snatched up our few belongings and ran, pushing through the crowds and trying to avoid the German uniforms. The train was there, with a huge black engine, covered in pipes, tubes and grease, with smoke puffing gently out of the funnel. I wanted to stay and look at it properly; I had never seen an engine close up and it was very exciting. But mother dragged me along the train and pushed me into a carriage. Surprisingly, the train was very crowded, and we were lucky to find one of the last few places in the compartment to sit down, somewhat out of the way, in a corner. The carriage was a Third Class one, and there were wooden benches on which to sit. We could hardly see out of the windows, which were smeared with grime and condensation as well as being crowded with people trying to look out at the platform.

The train clanked, shuddered and slowly pulled out of the station. There was a general sigh of relief.

"How long will it take us to get to Wroclaw?" Mother asked the elderly man sitting next to us.

"Who can say," he replied. "In the old days it took about three hours but when I came to Lodz last week, it took – well – about ten. I shall be thankful if we make it."

I looked round at the people: it was a great mixture. There was a peasant sitting across from us, in a dirty smock, unshaven and with a large empty basket. Next to him sat a gentleman in a beautiful warm overcoat, though it was rather shabby and not too clean. He had a pince-nez on his nose and my eyes kept returning to it to see if it had fallen from its precarious perch. There were several women with babies and an old man with only one leg. But what I noticed most of all was that no one was talking and no one smiled. They seemed lost in their own thoughts and those thoughts did not seem to be very happy ones. The clickety-click, clickety-clank of the wheels filled the silence.

There was a little moonlight and dimly, through the smeary windows, I could see the snow covered fields of Poland. There were occasional woods, with the pines dark against the white ground. The carriage became hotter and hotter, and there was a smell of many unwashed bodies. The lights, little bulbs along the walls, blinked and flickered dimly and the people began to doze. The train went clanking on, sometimes faster, sometimes slower and, on occasion stopping for unknown reasons. There was always that sigh of relief when we started again.

Mother sat very upright, with her arm round me. Her face was grim and from time to time, tears would roll down her cheeks. There was no makeup any more and she looked not at all as she used to. We felt shabby and frightened and hungry. It was obvious I should not speak, so gradually I dozed off.

The train stopped. I was woken by the sound of the doors being wrenched open and voices shouting: "Out, everybody out; papers, papers!"

Many of the people looked frightened, but we all climbed down from the train. We were at what looked to be a small country station and the platform was short and well below the carriage steps. It was almost dawn, and in the dirty grey light we could see many German soldiers pulling people out of the train. Many fell to the ground.

"Line up on the platform," an officer shouted. "Men on the left and women and children on the right. Hurry, hurry!" He stalked up and down while his soldiers shoved people about with their rifle butts.

The crowd gradually formed two groups. We pushed our way towards the centre of the one on the right; it seemed safer not to be on the outside. In the middle, between the groups, a young couple clung together; he was dressed in a dirty-looking overcoat and had a cap pulled low over his face while the girl was in a flowery dress, with a thick, black shawl covering her head and shoulders.

"Leave us together, please, please ... she cried. "We were

married yesterday. Leave us alone ... "

A burly German sergeant, with one of his men, tried to pull them apart, but they clung to each other so strongly that he could not separate them. I saw him lift up his rifle and hit the young man in the face with the butt. The man fell down, with blood streaming from his head and the soldier wrenched the girl away and dragged her, screaming, towards our group. The young man was picked up by two soldiers who pulled him, stumbling, out of the station and to an army truck we could see on the road outside.

All the papers were checked carefully, and a number of people were taken to the truck. The rest of us were allowed to climb back into the train, and we started off again. I did not quite understand why, but there was an enormous feeling of relief. The compartment was quiet, except for the sobbing of the young bride, who was being comforted by an old country woman with a face as brown and wrinkled as a walnut.

We clanked slowly along. A watery sun came up and showed us fields covered in snow and the sharp outline of trees and bushes. I was very hungry and thirsty, but our supplies were for emergencies, mother told me. The well-dressed gentleman sitting opposite suddenly put his hand in his pocket and produced a large piece of bread. He offered it to me.

"Thank you very much," said Mother. "We couldn't possibly accept this. You, too, must be hungry ... "

"Ah, well," he replied. "I'll manage. After all, I don't have to grow any more!" He offered me the bread again and I looked at mother; my mouth was watering.

"Well, if you're sure ... " she said to him, "It really is most generous of you."

"Who would have thought that bread would ever be so precious," the gentleman smiled. "We have taken so many things for granted."

I munched up the bread. It was some days old but tasted wonderful. I tried to make it last, but it was soon gone. Mother refused to have any.

The train continued slowly on its way. People talked quietly and I could hear the occasional sob of the young bride.

Suddenly, the train stopped. There was silence. We all sat expectantly, waiting for something to happen, but nothing did. Gradually, some people pulled the windows open, and craned their heads out to see what was happening.

"Where are we? ... What's going on? ... Why have we stopped? ... Are we in Wroclaw yet? ... No, it can't be ... Can you see any Germans?"

Then we saw a man walking down the length of the train. It was the engine driver and he was calling up to the carriages: "This is as far as we go. I'm sorry, but the partisans have destroyed the track just up ahead, and we can't go through. It's hard luck but you will have to get out and go on on foot, unless you want to go back to Lodz. I'm going to back the train to the last station. Come on, make up your minds ... "

Mother looked at me and said: "We can't go back now. We'll have to walk."

I looked at her. "How can we walk to Uncle Max?" I asked. "It's much too far."

"No, no," she said. "We will try to get to Wroclaw and perhaps there will be another train; maybe even one to Vienna."

We gathered up our belongings and climbed down from the high step of the carriage, onto the gravel beside the line. There were people climbing down all the length of the train. It seemed very few wanted to go back.

It was now about midday. There was a pearly white light, and the train stood quietly, with wisps of steam wreathing the engine. There were lots of people milling about, not quite knowing what to do next. The fields stretched out in all directions, and there was a narrow dirt road a little distance away, running parallel with the railway line. A group of people began to walk towards this. We followed them.

We walked for hours, stopping now and then for a short rest. Gradually we dropped behind the group of people ahead, until they were out of sight. There was nothing to be seen except the fields and the sky. We had eaten all our food and I was very hungry and cold. Mother's face was grim and set as we plodded on.

Towards dusk, we sat beside the road and rested. Suddenly,

behind us, we saw a horse and cart approaching slowly up the road. We waited. Driving the cart was a very old man, dressed in a grimy smock and with a curious red rag wound about his head. The horse was small and looked thin and weary. The cart had two huge wheels and seemed to be empty; it stopped beside us, and the man examined us carefully for some time.

"Been walking long?" he asked. "You don't look very bright. Where are you headed?"

"Wroclaw," replied Mother. "We were on the train, but it stopped and couldn't go any further; so we decided to walk."

"Ah, yes," the old man observed. "The track is gone. Our boys did that," he added, with a certain amount of satisfaction. "Well, you have a pretty big walk ahead of you."

There was a long pause as we all stared at each other. "Perhaps you would like to ride with me," he said eventually. "I have a small farm some kilometres down the road in the direction you are going. At least it will save you some of the walking."

Mother thought about it. "I can't pay you anything," she said. "We have very little left, and we need it for train fares. We are going a long way."

"Don't worry about it," the old man replied. "We must all help each other in these times, with the krauts all around. Climb aboard."

We scrambled into the cart, which had a layer of dirty straw on the bottom. The old man chirruped to the horse, which started to walk wearily on.

"I am called Mietek," the old man said. "Who are you?"

"My name is Isabel, and this is Jedrek," Mother said. Surnames were seldom used in the country. "We are from Lodz, and we are going to Italy."

"Goodness gracious, that's a very long way. Of course, I don't blame you for getting out. Things are getting very nasty," the old man spat on the road. "The krauts are stealing everything. We can just about get enough to eat here in the country, what with potatoes and a few chickens. But I hear that in the towns people are starving."

The cart trundled slowly down the road. It had begun to

drizzle, a thin, vapour-like rain, known in Poland as *kapusniak* (cabbage soup), and soon we were all soaked through. The old man hunched over in his seat and hummed tunelessly.

He turned the cart off the road onto a narrow track, leading to a little wood. Beside the wood stood a small cottage, with rough wooden walls and a thatch made of grasses and reeds. It was painted a dingy white and had a small window beside the door. There was smoke coming from the little chimney on one side.

"Home," said Mietek with satisfaction. "You'd better come in and dry your clothes, and maybe the Old Woman will find you something to eat." He looked sideways at me. "I think young Jedrek could probably manage that."

My mouth was watering at the though of food, any food. Mother said: "Thank you very much. We would be happy to come in. But are you sure you have enough for us as well?"

"We'll manage," said Mietek. "We have a field of potatoes, and there is always food in the country if you know where to look for it."

He jumped to the ground. "Old Woman, Old Woman," he shouted, "Come out and see the people I brought." He turned to us,"You go on inside while I fix Mietek up for the night."

I stared at him. "You call your horse by your own name?", I asked. "Why do you do that? There are lots of good names you can call him."

The old man winked at me. "I call him Mietek, the same as me, so that when the Old Woman calls me to do something, I can always say I thought she was calling the horse." He chuckled.

An ancient woman appeared at the door. "Who are these people? Why did you bring them here?"

The old man told her what had happened and she led us into the cottage, while I saw Mietek leading Mietek to a ramshackle barn. He was still chortling.

The cottage consisted of one large room, which served as kitchen, bedroom, sitting room and everything else too. The outhouse was some yards away, behind the cottage, and there was a small well to one side. The wall at one end of the cottage was made of rough stone, and in this there was a large hearth, with a big wood fire. Hanging over the fire, on a sort of iron arm, was a big black pot, with something bubbling in it. There was a large bed in one corner, and, in the middle, a huge rough wooden table with benches on all four sides. Strings of dried wild mushrooms festooned the cooking area, spreading their pungent and wonderful fragrance throughout the room and mixing with the mouth-watering smell of hot potatoes and herbs coming from the black pot. There was a large bag of salt, and several sacks of potatoes stacked in the corner.

"Sit down, sit down," the old woman said. "You look frozen through." She ushered us towards the table. "Take off your wet things and I will dry them by the fire."

We shed our outside layers, and she spread them over the sacks near the hearth, where they soon began to steam.

The door banged open, and Mietek came in. He closed it tight, and then went to the window, which had no glass in it, and shut the wooden shutters. The room looked cosy in the leaping firelight.

"What do you have for us to eat today, Old Woman?" he asked. "The usual wonderful things, I suppose ... " He winked at me and tapped his nose in a conspiratorial sort of way.

"Don't show off," grumbled the old woman. "When you are hungry, everything tastes good". I nodded energetically.

Mother looked tired and strained. She sat slumped at the table, her head in her arms. The old woman looked at her for a moment, then gently laid a woollen shawl over her shoulders. I sat expectantly, hungrier than I could ever remember, with the marvellous smell from the pot an agony. It fought with an almost irresistible desire to close my eyes and sleep for a week.

Mietek sat down at the table opposite and, at last, the old woman produced some wooden bowls and filled them from the pot with a huge ladle. She gave us the bowls, which emitted a fragrant steam, and also a wooden spoon each.

I plunged my spoon into the wonderful soup and took a scalding mouthful. It was the most delicious food I had ever eaten; a sort of mixture of potatoes, herbs, mushrooms in a whitish, savoury liquid.

There was silence, except for slurping noises from Mietek.

"She's a good cook," he said with his mouth full, "There is not much to eat, but in the country you can always find something. We have a cow and some chickens, and we manage. I always said only fools live in towns."

I was really too busy to listen, and only began to slow down in the middle of my third bowlful. My stomach felt like a balloon, and I could no longer keep my eyes open.

Dimly, I heard a cock crow. Time to get up, I thought. Perhaps Jasio would come for a walk down to the ponds ...

I opened my eyes and saw the old woman bending over the fire. It was daylight, and the dream was gone; I was back in the farm, lying on some sacks in a corner not far from the big bed. Mother was still asleep next to me, wrapped in a motley collection of shawls and coats. Mietek was nowhere to be seen.

"Well," said the old woman, "so the young master has decided to wake up. Go and wash at the well then come and have breakfast."

I washed at the well, shivering, and put on my newly dried and warm clothes. Breakfast was frothing fresh milk, some rough bread, and an egg. AN EGG! It had been many months since I had seen one. I tried to make it last, but it was soon gone. Mother had had her breakfast, and it was time to go.

"So you want to go to Wroclaw," said Mietek. "I can take you some of the way if you like."

"Thank you very much," said Mother. "We have a long way to go and every little helps." She seemed to have recovered much of her strength, and I also was ready to go, though my legs were still rather stiff.

Mietek went out to harness Mietek to the cart, and we thanked the Old Woman for her kindness. She was very gruff, and interrupted us to say that thanks were unnecessary, and that we all had to help each other in these difficult times. "My son is with the partisans," she said. "Because of this, everything else is not important."

As we went out of the door, she pressed a small package into Mother's hand. "Just something to keep you going ... some bread and a piece of cheese ..."

We were both moved and climbed hurriedly into the cart.

Mietek chirruped to the horse, and we were off. My last sight of the Old Woman was her standing in the doorway of the cottage, and wiping her eyes with the edge of her apron.

The sun was dim and watery, but it was a little warmer than the day before. The horse walked slowly down the road; the fields stretched empty on all sides and there were occasional clumps of trees here and there. Mietek was silent, hunched over the reins.

After some time, he raised his head and, putting two fingers in his mouth, produced a shrill whistle. I looked up and saw, several hundred metres away, a line of men coming out of a small copse, and walking in single file, silhouetted against the grey skyline. The shrill whistle was returned, and one man raised a rifle above his head, and pumped it up and down.

"My son," said Mietek proudly. "They operate in this area and we see them sometimes. But it is dangerous, so he never comes to the cottage – we haven't talked to him for two months now ... "

We went on and on. At about midday, Mietek reined the horse and we stopped.

"This is as far as I go. If you follow the road, you will be in Wroclaw by nightfall. Good luck; go with God."

Mother said: "I have nothing to give you for your kindness."

"I don't want anything," said Mietek. "I am sure you will be able to help somebody else sometime, and when you do, think of us."

He turned the old horse round, and the two Mieteks went slowly back up the road.

We walked. As before, we walked for about an hour and rested for some minutes. Mother was anxious to reach Wroclaw before night. As dusk fell, we nibbled on some bread and cheese. It tasted wonderful.

Some houses appeared, and we made our way through the outskirts of the town. We asked the way to the railway station, and reached it just as darkness fell. The town was quiet, with few people about, and patrols of men in the grey uniforms of the German army in many of the streets. There was also the occasional menacing black uniform of the SS.

The railway station was crowded and noisy. There were two trains at the platforms with the remembered smell of hot steam and oil. People were hurrying to and fro in a determined sort of way, though it was hard to tell just where they were going, and why. Small groups of officials stood here and there, and German troops were scattered throughout the station.

We made our way to a ticket window, and joined a short queue. There were two young men in front of us, whispering together. The queue moved slowly forward and, just as the young men reached the window, three men in long raincoats and wide-brimmed hats appeared and grabbed them by the arm.

"You come with us," one of the raincoated men growled. "You'd better be ready to explain everything ..."

"We haven't done anything," one of the young men shouted. "Leave us alone. We were just going home. Let go ..." He struggled to free himself but to no avail. The raincoats dragged him and his companion away. The rest of the crowd pretended not to notice.

We were now at the little window, behind which stood a little old man with one eye, wearing the railway uniform and a cap.

"Where to?" he asked.

Mother pushed her face close to the window. "We are heading for Italy," she said. "Where are the trains running to now?"

"Well," said the little old man, "Everything is very uncertain and the trains go here one day and there the next. There is one which may go as far as Brno, and maybe even Vienna, but you can't be sure. That's the best I can do."

"That's wonderful," said Mother. "Can you give us tickets to Vienna? We may be lucky."

"Here you are," said the little old man. "But be sure you have the right papers – they are very tough at the borders. The Germans are everywhere."

"How much are the tickets?" asked Mother. We had very little money left.

The little old man brought his face close to the window, and crooked a finger. Mother leaned forward, and I craned my neck to hear.

"Forget it," said the little old man. "Good luck to you, and I

hope you get out all right. *Poland is not yet lost while we live...*"
These were the first few words of the Polish National Anthem.

"God bless you," said Mother, with tears in her eyes. "We will
always remember you."

The little old man winked his good eye and said loudly: "Get
on with you and stop wasting my time. Platform 3. Go now; the
train could leave at any time."

We hurried to the platform, and there was the train, puffing
and hissing in a cloud of steam. As we climbed aboard, a voice
said loudly: "Papers!"

There was a Raincoat next to us, with his hand out. Mother
gave him our papers which, much to his disappointment,
seemed to be in order. "Where are you going?" he asked. "And
where are you from?"

"We are going to my husband in Vienna," Mother lied. "We
were stuck in Lodz, and now we are going to join him."

"Hmmm.." said Raincoat. "All right, but behave yourselves."

Much relieved, we climbed onto the train, and found two seats
in a corner of the carriage. We sat there for nearly an hour, when
suddenly the train gave a whistle, a lurch and we were off.

I think I must have slept most of the way, since I do not
remember much of that day. In my mixed-up dreams there were
clankings and hissings, occasional peremptory commands of
"Papers!", the irregular swaying of the carriage, stopping and
starting. I was wakened from a dream of a food-laden table at
which I had just sat down, by Mother shaking my shoulder and
saying: "Wake up, Jedrus, we've arrived ..."

By some miracle, the train had passed through Brno, and
gone on to Vienna, across two borders. Mother said that
everyone had had to show their papers several times, but
because there was an important German military mission in the
first class carriage, the Gestapo was unable to hold the train up,
as they would certainly have done otherwise. Of course, being
able to speak fluent German, Mother had a big advantage.

We wandered round the railway station in Vienna, with its
ornate decorated columns and crowds of clean and well-fed
people. There was a very big difference between them and the
ragamuffin starvelings in Poland's stations. Certainly, Mother

and I looked out of place in our ragged clothes and muddy, cracked shoes.

"We will get something to eat," said Mother. "But we are running out of money, so it can't be anything special." We bought a loaf of wonderful fresh, amazing-smelling bread and I was given a glass of milk. It was a feast I have always remembered; the best for a year.

Mother discovered that there was, supposedly, a train direct to Milan, through the Tyrol and Innsbruck. We had only just enough money for the tickets. If the train did not go through as planned, well, it would be more walking. There could be trouble at the frontier. Mother said that the buffoon Mussolini was a friend of Hitler's, and would certainly join him in the fighting soon. She said that a buffoon was a fat fool.

The trip was uneventful until we reached the Italian border. The train stopped. Here, the Gestapo, the frontier guards, the soldiers, everybody wanted to check that no precious inhabitant was escaping their embrace.

It was early morning, and there was a grey drizzle which made everything damp. The lights on the border platform glowed orange in the mist. Everyone looked half-asleep and miserable. We could see the lights of the Italian post a little way down the line; we had almost made it.

There were the usual shouts of "'*raus,'raus*!", but more muted than usual, perhaps the guards were worried about the sleeping military delegation in the first class coach. The passengers lined up in the murky light in two rows: men and boys in one long line, and women and small children in another. I hung onto Mother's hand; were they going to separate us and kill us when we had almost succeeded?

"Don't make any noise, and don't look in their eyes," Mother whispered. We had found that if you kept your eyes on the ground and did not look Germans in the face, they let you go more quickly.

But the lines were not for separation and killing; they were done so that the passengers could be thoroughly searched for any valuables which they may have tried to take out of the country. I knew that Mother had a tiny pair of gold earrings sewn into the hem of her coat; they were the very last things we had now that all our money had gone.

Three large women in uniform began a thorough and brutal search. They looked everywhere. They made me take off all my clothes, and even looked inside my shoes and socks. They tore open the seams in Mother's dress and, of course, found the earrings. Surprisingly, they did not make any fuss about it, or beat us, but quietly pocketed the earrings, and told us to move on. We were shivering in the cold and damp, and quickly climbed back into the train, after getting our papers checked yet again. A small group of people were pushed to one side, and I could see through the window that the Gestapo were loading them into a lorry. There was a small, old man who was crying. Before the war, I had never seen a man cry.

At long last, the train jerked and clanked its way over the border, and stopped, panting and hissing, in Italy! A lovely Italian soldier, smiling broadly, came into the carriage: "*Benvenuti, benvenuti a Italia!*" he said.

I asked Mother what he meant. "He says we are welcome," Mother was crying. "We did it! We are in Italy. Now we can go to Ina in Baghdad and never again see the Germans," she hugged me so hard it hurt.

After a quick look at the papers, the Italians allowed the train to go on, and some hours later we pulled into the grimy station in Milan. We were dirty, tired, hungry, thirsty and we did not have any money. Our clothes were ragged and our shoes coming apart.

"Come along," said Mother briskly. "We have to send a telegram to Ina to tell her we are here, and ask her to send us some money so we can come to Baghdad."

We marched along to the nearest post-office, which was not far from the station, and went up to the telegraph counter. After establishing that the clerk could speak a little French, Mother explained that we wanted to send a telegram to Baghdad, but that we had no money. "The lady to whom I am sending the message will pay," Mother told the clerk.

"I'm sorry," said the clerk, a rather prim little man with slicked-down hair and a tiny moustache. "I cannot send anything unless you pay."

Mother argued and argued, but to no avail. We were in despair.

We left the post office and wandered down the road. There were lots of people hurrying about, and cars, and it all felt very strange without the German uniforms and the constant fear. We did see a couple of Blackshirts strutting down the pavement, but people seemed to take no notice; certainly there was not the same cringing away as from the Gestapo.

Suddenly Mother stopped and said in a very loud voice: "They will not win!" She grabbed my hand and marched into the ornate entrance of a grand looking hotel we were passing. The doorman tried to stop us, but Mother, dragging me by one hand, swept by him and up to the reception desk, manned by a very suave young man in a spotless suit.

"I am the Princess Woltowska of the High Tatra," said Mother loudly in her impeccable French. "I have just arrived from Poland and have lost my belongings in an accident. I desire your best suite. Immediately."

The desk clerk, now joined by an older gentleman, also impeccably attired, gaped at Mother, who looked like a tramp.

"Have you any identification …" asked the older gentleman.

"You will address me as Your Highness!" interrupted Mother loudly. "I am not accustomed to being interrogated by clerks."

At this time, apparently, many members of European aristocracy were leaving occupied Europe, and some were passing through Italy. The hotel people could never be sure who was real and who was pretending, and were seriously worried about offending some important person, thus losing them and their friends forever as clients.

The older gentleman made his decision. "Your Highness is very welcome," he said, bowing. "We do have a suite free for just two days, and Your Highness will be very comfortable there. But I must beg that other arrangements be made for the day after tomorrow."

Mother smiled graciously, and we swept upstairs to the suite.

The very first thing Mother did was to have a bath, and ring down for some food. I also had a long, hot soak in the tub, and we were careful both to be in the bathroom when the food arrived; we could not give the waiter a tip, since we had not a single note or coin of any sort.

The food was delicious; the bed was soft. It was warm and dry and quiet. All things which used to be normal but which we had not experienced for a long time. We slept.

When I awoke, sunshine was pouring in through the window, and there was a fragrant smell of coffee and fresh bread. For a moment I was completely lost then, with a rush, I remembered. Here we were in a grand hotel in Milan, clean and safe, no more Germans or guns or walking endlessly down wet dark country roads, or sitting in damp smelly trains. It was strange: the changes were too rapid and I could not keep up. It all seemed unreal.

Mother came in from the bathroom and said: "Good morning, good morning. Come on, get up and have some breakfast; you must be hungry."

I jumped out of bed and tucked into the delicious things on the tray. Mother, in the meantime, rang for the maid, who proved to be a handsome young Italian girl, with flashing eyes. She wore a black uniform, with white collar and cuffs.

Mother chatted with her in a mixture of French and German, with a lot of waving of arms in an Italian sort of way. It turned out that the maid's name was Carlotta, that she came from a village north of Milan, that she was engaged to be married to one of the waiters in the restaurant and that she disliked the Germans. This final characteristic persuaded Mother that Carlotta was to be trusted, and thus Carlotta was told part of our story, somewhat embellished to increase its dramatic content.

She stood there, her eyes wide, as Mother told her of our escape from our ancestral castle, how the Germans had murdered her husband the Prince, how I was the last remaining Prince Woltowski of the High Tatra, and how we were escaping to mysterious Baghdad, out of reach of German assassins. The upshot was that Carlotta, dazzled by Mother's story, lent us the modest sum we needed to send our telegram to Aunt Ina, asking for funds and telling her where we were.

Mother went out to the main Post Office to send the telegram to Ina, since we could not, discreetly, send it from the hotel, and returned. We still had not a penny, so all we could do was go for walks, then return to the hotel for meals. I felt awful: my hair was almost down to my shoulders, my clothes were ragged, I could not understand the language. Mother was snappy and short-tempered, worried about the race between money from Ina and being thrown out of the hotel and reported to the police for non-payment of our fast increasing bill.

We went to bed that night in a very worried state. It was the last night agreed by the hotel manager and we would have to move, and pay, the next day.

At seven o'clock there was a knock at the door. "Surely they can't throw us out so early," Mother muttered. "At least until noon ..."

She opened the door, and there was a bell-boy, in his little pill-box hat, holding a small tray with an envelope on it. "Telegram for Your Highness," he said. Mother thanked him in a grand way, but still there was no money for a tip, so he put his tongue out at me as the door closed.

Mother looked at the envelope. It was addressed to Her Highness, the Princess Woltowska of the High Tatra. She ripped it open and read the telegram. Ina was ecstatic to have heard from us (she had had no news for many months) and could hardly wait to see us. By some extremely influential magic, Uncle Max had arranged a large sum of money to be available to Mother at a Milan bank and both he and Ina urged us to waste no time in coming to Baghdad.

Mother heaved a huge sigh of relief. "Our troubles are almost over," she said. "Now we can begin to live again." She gave me a hug. "The most urgent thing now is to make ourselves look good. How wonderful that will be!"

The next two days were a great whirl of activity, and impressed on me for the first time how important money can be, and how it becomes more and more important as one has less and less of it.

Carlotta was repaid, with a large bonus. Mother vanished for the entire morning, and came back as I remembered her: wonderfully elegant, with beautifully coiffed blonde hair, sweet-smelling, exquisitely made-up and followed by a small caravan of bell-boys bearing new and heavy suitcases, which turned out to contain a whole new wardrobe for Mother.

"Now it is your turn," Mother said to me. "We'll go and get you back into proper condition."

We went downstairs. The Manager and staff of the hotel, dazzled by the butterfly which had emerged from the grubby chrysalis of two days earlier, bowed low to Mother and somehow found that we could remain in our suite indefinitely; the telegram had given us the required cachet, and Mother's appearance had confirmed her aristocratic claims.

I was taken, in quick order, to a hairdresser for a short back and sides and a clothing store, where I was equipped with several new outfits, including another foul sailor suit.

Mother said that Italy would soon enter the war on the side of the Germans, and that we must get out and go to Baghdad, to Aunt and Uncle. Thus, some days later, we took the train down to Brindisi, a very different affair from the last train journey. This time it was First Class, with our own private compartment, splendid food, and a conductor who just could not do enough for the glamorous *Principessa* since Mother had thought it amusing to keep up the fiction as long as it worked.

In Brindisi, the port on the heel of Italy, Mother booked us on the first available ship to Beirut, which was leaving in two days' time. We stayed at a small hotel and I spent much time looking at the sea, which I had never seen before. Mother was very short-tempered and brittle, and this was strange, since I thought our troubles were pretty much over. Still, her moods swung between euphoria and misery and the best thing was to stay out of her way.

On the second evening we boarded the ship, a small and nondescript mixed passenger and cargo vessel, and set off for Beirut. I stood with Mother at the rail and watched the lights of Italy gradually disappear together, I hoped, with the horrors of the past year.

CHAPTER TWO

Baghdad

The wake of the ship, in the clear blue of the water on this sunny day, led back to Italy; the prow pointed at Beirut. It was hard to remember, when I woke each morning, that there was no more danger, that there was plenty to eat and that the Germans were a long way behind us.

The ship was nothing very wonderful, I suppose, as ships go; but to me it was a whole new world. It seemed amazing that something should be so completely self-contained, and afloat, and able to go wherever it wished. The rust, and the peeling paint and the all-pervading smell of cabbage and wet clothes were not important. What was important was the gentle rise and fall of the deck, the smoke coming out of the single grimy funnel and the visit I was allowed to make to the bridge, where the captain (as a great favour to the *Principessa*) let me sound the hoarse, loud and wonderful siren, not once but twice! Mother, in the meantime, seldom left our cabin, and lay on her bunk with various tragic expressions on her face whenever the somewhat bedraggled stewardess brought her trays of light foods and drink.

My first sight of Beirut could not have been more exciting: it was twilight when we sighted the mountains of Lebanon on the skyline, a faint blue-green haze at the limit of vision. Then, as the daylight faded, we saw the bright pin-pricks of lights garlanding the hills and a mass of what looked like a sparkling heap of broken glass between the mountains and the sea. By the time we tied up at the jetty, it was dark and not far off midnight.

Mother said that we would sleep on board and disembark the following morning.

"*Principessa, Principessa*," the stewardess was banging on the cabin door and her voice was very excited. "There is a wonderful gentleman who has come to visit you ..."

"Go away," said Mother. "It is much too late for wonderful gentlemen."

"No, no; he says you have to come now and he was sent by a Minister and he must see you and ..."

"Oh, very well," said Mother wearily. "Please ask him to wait."

We dressed and went out on deck. The 'wonderful gentleman' turned out to be a rotund, fussy Iraqi Consulate official, who had received instructions from Baghdad to meet and entertain us, and finally see us on to the coach for Damascus.

Monsieur Baba, for so he introduced himself, was overwhelmingly hospitable, and this was the problem. In spite of Mother's reiterated assurances that all was well, that we were very grateful, that Monsieur Baba had done his duty impeccably and that we wanted to go back to bed, he insisted that we go into Beirut to sample the night life.

We had barely escaped from the Germans with our lives; we were both completely exhausted; I was eight years old; it was one in the morning; no matter, Monsieur Baba was taking us to a nightclub. We gave up and followed him down the gangway to a waiting limousine.

Even at that unearthly hour, the quayside in Beirut, the melting pot of the Middle East, was fascinating. A crowd of a dozen different nationalities, dressed in all sorts of strange clothes, pushed, jostled and elbowed their way through the press: the white robes of the Arabs, the baggy trousers of the Druse, the ragged loincloths of the porters, the suits and ties of the officials, the khaki police uniforms ... A feast of new experiences for me. The floodlights were very bright and the noise of a dozen languages, the hooting of cars and the rattle of machinery were deafening. There was also the smell of fruit, garbage, oil and sweating humanity as well as unidentifiable Eastern odours.

The limousine, driven at high speed through crowded streets, took us to the nightclub. I remember little of it, except that Mother and I took it in turns informally to fall asleep, much to Monsieur Baba's irritation, and that the atmosphere was thick with smoke and the jangling of a sort of music, to which plump, oily ladies gyrated their middle sections, while waving their arms in the air. I drank a sticky lemonade which tasted very pink.

We eventually made it back to the ship, and having thanked Monsieur Baba profusely, said yes we would mention the wonderful evening when we got to Baghdad, fell into our bunks.

We were woken early in the morning, after only a couple of hours' sleep, and told to get up or we would miss the coach to Damascus, where we had to go in order to catch the monster cross-desert Nairn bus. Monsieur Baba was there, looking fresh and bouncy, to make sure that all was well. Our small pile of luggage was easily absorbed by the boot of the limousine and we said goodbye to the Captain and left the harbour.

The coach was a somewhat dirty and dented affair, standing in a palmy square, with the rather grand sign proclaiming it to be the "Cross-Desert First Class Special Luxury Nairn Connection to Baghdad – Damascus Section". Monsieur Baba made sure we had seats, that our baggage was loaded, and gracefully said goodbye, kissing Mother's hand and pinching my cheek, to my great and inarticulate fury. He also made guttural threatening noises at the driver, presumably instructing him, on pain of unspeakable Eastern tortures, to ensure we were comfortably transferred to the Big Bus in Damascus. And thus we left Beirut, waving to Monsieur Baba as we rattled and swayed our way out towards the hazy, blue mountains we had to cross.

The road between Beirut and Damascus was well-travelled and therefore had a poor surface. It was not very wide, and in many places the edge abruptly became a precipice, which provided a magnificent view from the window if only one had the courage to look. The driver, behind whom we sat, was a merry soul, puffing away at endless cigarettes and waving his arms about. He also sang from time to time, a curious wailing melody to which he kept time, beating his hands on the steering wheel. It was an exciting drive, but I noticed that Mother had her eyes shut most of the time and one of her 'how I suffer, death is nigh' expressions on her face.

Our fellow travellers were a mixed bunch: a businessman and his wife, presumably returning to Damascus from a Beirut visit; a couple of young French soldiers; two sinister looking Druse, who muttered to each other behind their hands while glaring at the soldiers; and a small family group who chattered non-stop. None seemed likely to be making the connection to Baghdad.

After some three hours over the mountains, we descended into a valley and drove into Damascus. Mother said it was one of the oldest inhabited cities in the world and much involved in the Crusades, about which I had read. But the impression which remains with me of that first visit is one of sand-coloured buildings and all-pervasive sandy soil and dusty atmosphere. True, there were gardens, and palm-trees and colourful domes on the mosques, but sand was the main ingredient of every scene. Also, it was hot and dry, under a cloudless, pale blue sky. We stopped, and there was the Nairn Bus!

Certainly it was the largest vehicle I had ever seen, bigger even than a German tank. Semi-articulated, on vast tyres taller than me, with a corrugated silver skin and a ladder leading up to the driver's cabin perched high in the front, it was an awesome beast. At the time, it was the normal way of travelling to Baghdad, if one could afford it, since the alternative was to go by small, non-air-conditioned buses, dusty, dirty and slow. The Nairn (so called after the Scottish brothers who owned the line), was a specially constructed bus, with air-conditioning, a toilet, and tiny windows with dark glass. The route followed was that of the oil pipeline, and stops were made for simple meals at the periodic pumping stations.

As we stood and waited to board the bus, the hustle and bustle of Damascus swirled round us. There were rickety, hooting taxis; small donkeys pattering along, some with fat men balanced on their backs; a squad of French soldiers marched by, in their round hats with a piece of cloth at the back; and of course, the inevitable gallery of assorted spectators of all ages, who stood and gaped at whatever was going on.

We mounted the bus and found two seats towards the back. Our meagre luggage had been stowed in a cavernous, cupboard-like cavity in the lower part of the huge beast, together with assorted cargo for Baghdad: wooden cases of fruit, jerrycans of unknown liquids, a bale of cloth and a number of rolled-up carpets.

There were only two other travellers on the bus: a French army officer and a prosperous looking Arab gentleman, in a suit and a bright red tarboosh (or Turkish hat shaped like an upside-down flower-pot, with a black tassel), who sweated a lot and chain-smoked flat, perfumed cigarettes. The driver hooted, and off we went.

Ours was by far the largest vehicle on the road and, as such, had right of way. The driver, perched in solitary splendour in his separate cabin on the tractor unit, kept his foot on the accelerator and his fist on a very loud hooter, and we fled along the road towards the desert at high speed, scattering cars, donkeys, pedestrians and the occasional camel before us. The small mud houses of the outskirts flashed by, and we were in the open, on a barely discernible track, heading east.

I do not remember very much about our desert trip; there was a mounting excitement at the thought that we were about to reach the end of our journey, which had been so strange and so long. Through the little dark windows of our bus, I could see a monotonous brown landscape, with rocks and bits of scrubby plants. Occasionally there were sand-dunes, and the feeling of a real desert.

For most of the journey of nearly two days, we followed, between Palmyra and the K-3 Pumping Station, the oil pipeline from Iraq to the Mediterranean. We stopped at other Pumping Stations for meals and to stretch our legs, and as a break from the bumping, roaring progress along the undulating track which was the main road between Iraq and Syria.

We reached Al-Hadithah just after dawn, on the second day. This small village was where the oil pipeline struck off north-eastwards towards the oilfields of Kirkuk, while the road, slightly improved, continued into the fertile, and legendary, Mesopotamia (or land-between-rivers) in the middle of which lay the fabled city of Baghdad.

The landscape changed: there were now groves of dusty date-palms in enclosures divided by low mud walls; small patches of very green grass with spiky shrubs dotted about; everywhere there were channels with slow-flowing muddy water, brought up from wells by patient, blindfolded donkeys going round and round, turning a horizontal wheel which was geared to bring up an endless belt of buckets.

We had been following the Euphrates river for many miles now ... a wide, turgid body of water, the colour of milk chocolate. There were some small boats on the river, with brown, triangular sails, and also some very peculiar-looking coracles called *gufas*, perfectly round and with a diameter of some six feet; very difficult to propel and steer. They were made of palm branches, thickly daubed with natural asphalt, and looked unsafe, though much used.

We passed Lake Habbaniyah: a large and placid sheet of water, where flying boats landed, coming from Europe. There was an RAF base there, but we did not stop. On we went, on to Baghdad.

Through some small villages, and a small town called Ramadi. Then there were the western outskirts of Baghdad: the suburb of Khadhmain, with its glorious golden mosque, a paved road, cars, people, donkeys, shops ... we were there. The bus shuddered to a halt in a little square, the engine growled and died. Our journey was over; we had made it.

The door opened. A great gust of hot, dry air filled the interior of the bus. The other passengers grabbed their belongings and pushed their way out. Mother just sat there.

"Come on, come on," I said. "Let's get out; we are in Baghdad!"

Mother stared blankly at me, and slowly got up and moved towards the open door. I followed. We went down the steps onto a bare, dusty platform. There was a loud squeal:

"Iza, Iza!" A beautiful, elegant creature, dressed with care and taste, threw herself at Mother. "I never believed you would arrive ..."

Mother clutched her, and sobbed, without saying anything. I

stood beside the two sisters and looked around. There was a small crowd of interested spectators, mostly in Arab dress, though some wore trousers and shirts and curious black forage caps. Then I noticed a smallish, round person, with huge, horn-rimmed glasses, dressed rather untidily in a black coat, waistcoat and trousers, in spite of the heat. He was grinning the most enormous grin I had ever seen, nodding and patting his large stomach slowly with both hands, as though beating a drum. It was my Uncle Max.

Aunt Ina then pounced on me, making Polish aunt noises. She was dressed in a bright green dress, with some sort of vague floral design, and a broad-brimmed white hat. She smothered me to her perfumed bosom. "Come, we must go home. You must be exhausted," she said. "Ahmed, Ahmed!" she shouted to her driver, "Come and get the luggage!"

Uncle Max came diffidently forward, and embraced us in a rather shy way. He mumbled something unintelligible; he could not actually speak any language properly. He could make himself understood in Polish, Russian, German, Italian, French, English and Arabic; but in none of these languages was he able to speak grammatically or with anything approaching a correct accent. What was worse, he mixed the languages, and the resulting communication tended to be puzzling.

Aunt swept us to a huge, bright green car; I was told it was a Chrysler, with lots of shiny chrome and a white canvas hood. The wheels had white sides and inside everything was of white leather. We were ensconced in the front seat with me in the middle and Aunt behind the wheel. Uncle Max had climbed into the back of a smallish, black Ford, and Ahmed, the chauffeur, drove him away to the clinic. Uncle Max had never learned to drive and had no wish to do so, Aunt Ina said.

With a loud blare of the many-toned horns we were off in a cloud of dust. Mother sat there, sobbing quietly; I peered out of the windscreen at the houses, streets and people flashing by; Aunt Ina babbled her pleasure and delight at our arrival, honking loudly at suicidal pedestrians, donkeys, black carriages with thin horses and a few other cars. She constantly changed gear with great flourishes of her elbows, which I mostly managed to avoid, and wound the enormous white steering wheel to and fro with abandon.

In twenty minutes or so, we arrived at the house. We skidded to a halt inches from grey-painted metal gates, set in a high, mud wall, and honked musically. The gates swung inwards, and we drove into a small courtyard, centrally placed in a grove of date-palms, with a dusty lawn and some beds of rather garish, false-looking flowers. The gates swung shut behind us. Aunt Ina turned off the engine. We got out and faced a line formed by the domestic staff, on parade to greet the new arrivals from the war in Europe.

At the head of the line was a distinguished looking, gray-haired person, tall and slender, dressed in a black suit. This was the majordomo and butler, Hussein, an Iranian who had served my aunt for some ten years.

Next to him was Ali, the cook. Without having any great expertise in the kitchen, he nevertheless could reliably produce a number of fairly sophisticated dishes when required. His history was somewhat chequered, as there was always a state of open warfare between him and Aunt; he was periodically fired or resigned. After a week or two of a new cook, and after he had spent that period with a new employer, both he and Aunt, through some form of telepathy, would decide that the devil they each knew was better than the new devil, and they would be reunited for a further turbulent period. I was worried by Ali, who seemed to take a great delight in cutting the throats of the chickens he was about to cook and serve; but, to do him credit, he would always give me the ice-cream making machine to scrape out when he had removed the contents before a party.

The third personage was a short, rather squat person in a white gown, whose task was to clean the house, scrub the floors and do the coarser tasks in the kitchen. He was always grinning and it took me a long time to communicate with him. He was generally known as "Entah", this being 'you' in Arabic.

The fourth, and last person was Ibrahim, the gardener. He was a very ancient person who had, in the middle of his mouth, one solitary tooth, which was fascinating and attracted the gaze of anyone who spoke with him. His job, other than constantly watering the garden and keeping it tidy, was to harvest the dates, when they were ripe, from the palms in the garden, and to look after the many animals frequently arriving at the house, as payment in kind from Uncle Max's poorer patients. There were always chickens, goats, sheep and, on one memorable occasion, a gazelle, brought to us and kept in a corner of the garden, much to my delight. Sadly, it lived for only a short time. Ibrahim also doubled as the night-watchman and thus could be found asleep very often, both during the day and night.

The driver, Ahmed, whom we had seen on arrival, completed the domestic staff. He spent his time driving Uncle Max around, and looking after the two cars.

The house itself was not large, by Baghdad standards. It was beige in colour and had two storeys as well as a flat roof; there were a number of balconies and terraces, floored with multicoloured tiles. Inside, there was an air of great opulence: Uncle Max was a collector of oriental rugs, and these were everywhere on the floors, and sometimes on the walls, glowing with wonderful rich colours and patterns. The furniture was fatly overstuffed, and there was much satin, plush and brocade; silver ornaments, trays, jugs and boxes were everywhere, mostly of Persian manufacture and decoration. The main salon, into which I was forbidden to go unaccompanied, had, on the wall facing the door, a full-length, life-sized portrait of a decoltée Aunt Ina, in a shimmering evening gown of gleaming peacock-blue and a somewhat idealised face. I found it rather frightening, as though the portrait was left to guard the house when the corporeal Aunt was out.

The dining room was relatively modest, though it could be dressed up with great elegance for a formal party, not least by the use of massive, solid silver under-plates. When the King or the Prince Regent came to dine, solid gold ones were borrowed from the Palace.

Upstairs were the bedrooms and bathrooms, five of one and two of the other. I had my own small room, with a bed, a small chest of drawers and a bookshelf; after all, I had no possessions. There was a large fan on the ceiling, which rotated solemnly all the time, not cooling the air but just moving it from place to place.

The worst thing was the nightmare. It was always the same one, night after night, just as terrifying each time. I was strapped down on a table in a cellar, unable to move. There was only a dim, red light and the slow beat of a drum. From the corner of my eye, for I could not move my head, I could see the bottom of a steep staircase, and I knew something was coming down. I did not know what it was, but it had an air of indescribable menace. I always woke up just before it became visible, in a cold sweat and terrified. Certainly, for the first six months or so, I could not get to sleep without having a light on.

I soon settled down to a simple routine. Mother had vanished into one of the bedrooms on arrival, and I was told that she had to be left alone to rest for several weeks; she was too ill to see anyone, including me, but with all the new things to explore I cannot say I missed her very much. Aunt Ina was very busy about her own affairs and Uncle Max was out from very early morning to late night. The servants spoke only English and Arabic, so there was a problem in communication, though, through necessity, I soon began to pick up essential phrases in both languages.

I discovered that the best time of my day was to get up very early, at about 5am, and join Uncle Max, who would have his breakfast alone at about that time. Aunt Ina would breakfast in solitary splendour in her bedroom, seldom before 10am. Uncle Max was, I think, somewhat lonely, and appeared to welcome my company. We would sit there solemnly, facing each other across the table, while we ate the cottage cheese, flat Arab bread and jam, with strong, sweet, black tea, drunk out of little decorated glasses, which was invariably his daily breakfast. It was difficult to have a conversation with Uncle Max; it was obvious he wanted to converse, but his mixed up languages were hard to understand. Gradually, we evolved a sort of *lingua franca* which meant we could communicate: it was a weird mixture of Polish, Russian, German, English and Arabic, but it worked.

We talked of many things in those early mornings: I told him all about life in Poland, and our escape, and my friends. He told me that it was important to be a doctor, and how he had established a free clinic for the poor and sick which he paid for by curing rich, important people and making them pay a lot of money. He told me that he was the doctor of the King and the whole Royal family and that he would make sure that I would meet them all. He told me tales of riding with the Cossacs during the First Great War, and the early days in the Middle East, and camels and bedouin Arabs and the desert. Breakfasts passed quickly and then he was gone, to return only at about 5pm for a very late lunch, eaten alone, though I would always join him if I could.

The weather was getting hotter. In Baghdad, winter temperatures frequently went down to freezing, while summer, principally in August, could be as hot as 120° Fahrenheit in the shade. It was marvellous, therefore, to be introduced to the Alwiyah Country Club, very much an expatriate enclave about a mile from the house, where, apart from the normal Club activities of a restaurant, bridge drives, dances, tennis and so on, there was a wonderful swimming pool, which became my home from home. I would walk there along dusty streets in the morning, and return to the house when the pool closed at six. I was given a small sum of money to buy a sandwich for lunch.

I had two problems: I could not swim, and I spoke only Polish, and thus was unable to talk to the handful of other boys of my age who frequented the pool. They were all mahogany-brown, could swim like porpoises, dive from the highest board and had known each other for years.

But I learned fairly quickly. When the others found that I took the inevitable duckings and practical jokes in good part, they set to and began to teach me both English and their aquatic skills. In a month or so, I acquired a tan and could more or less swim. The boys were the sons of English expatriates, who managed the rudimentary industries of Baghdad and worked in the Embassy. There were some foreign boys, sons of other members of the diplomatic corps, but a state of armed truce existed between us; I instinctively identified with the British.

My best friend was Barry, a skinny ten-year-old whose interests very much coincided with mine: cowboys and Indians, Tarzan games and such. His elder brother, Bendy (he was remarkably pliable), was, at fifteen, much more interested in girls and other boring subjects. It was odd, but there were no girls about, except on Saturdays when they came with their parents. Since they did little but giggle in groups, splash in the shallow end and gape at Bendy doing double somersaults from the high board, they were of no interest to us.

There was also a boy called Henry. He was my age and very quiet. His parents were, I think, part Indian, and thus tended to be ostracised by the normal Club membership. Barry and I liked him and he was certainly part of our tribe, but this was my first experience of the snobbery and rigid discrimination of an expatriate British community.

Thus my life came to revolve round the Club and my meals at home with Uncle Max.

Mother appeared after some weeks, looking much as I remembered her in Poland: golden hair, delicately pencilled eyebrows, painted nails and some dresses hurriedly adjusted from Aunt Ina's wardrobe. I recall seeing, during one of my very rare visits to Aunt's dressing room, a whole wall of wardrobes with what seemed to be hundreds of dresses, shoes, hats, furs and so on. Mother seemed mostly recovered, and, I realised later, was beginning to think in terms of attracting a suitable husband to look after us; we could not exist forever on Uncle Max's bounty, though I am sure he would not have minded. He and Aunt were childless, and he made me feel like his beloved son. I am not too sure about Aunt, though she was usually kind.

It was high summer, and very hot. And it was now that I was forced to become acquainted with the curse of the belly-band. In those days it was fairly widely believed, mainly by expatriates in the Middle East and India, that sunstroke and heatstroke could be avoided by wearing, next to the skin, a wide band of white flannel round the midriff. I do not know who promulgated this evil fiction, but, in spite of my protests, I was obliged to don the horror whenever leaving the house, and inspected as I went through the door. Naturally, I tore the band off as soon as I was out of sight, but on the relatively rare occasions when I went out accompanied by Mother or Aunt, I had to suffer the torture of the band and the resulting prickly heat. Since I also had to wear a *sola topi*, or pith helmet, it came as a surprise to all when I got heatstroke, and lay in a darkened room for several days, with a temperature in excess of 103° F. It was with great relief and pleasure that I heard Uncle Max say loudly, just outside my door, that the belly-band and the pith helmet were nonsense, as he had always maintained, and that "the boy should be left in peace to build up his own natural defences". Thankfully, Mother and Aunt gave up, and I was not thereafter obliged to wear either object.

A notable and, to me, unexpected event occurred when the weather really took the bit between its teeth and temperatures during the day soared to more than 120° F. in the shade, if you could find any. One morning, Aunt announced that from that night we would all sleep on the roof. I had been on the roof many times; it was flat, tiled and with a parapet all round it, reached by an extension of the stairs. It was not overlooked and was open to the sun and stars.

With a feeling of excitement, I mounted the stairs at bedtime, in pyjamas, dressing gown and slippers. On the roof, I saw, on one side, my bed, with four posts on the corners, supporting a white net to keep the mosquitos out. I also noticed that the legs of the bed stood in small tins which were full of kerosine, presumably to keep the ants out. There was another bed in a further corner of the roof, presumably for Mother, and two more, close together in a third corner, for Aunt and Uncle Max. Aunt cautioned me always to give my slippers a good shake before putting them on, since there was always a chance that a scorpion, with which Baghdad was infested, would be hiding there. I did, indeed, find a scorpion in my slipper on the third morning, after which I took the simple precaution of taking my slippers into bed with me, under the tucked-in net.

It is hard to describe that first night on the roof. It was not my first night under the stars; after all, during our adventures in Poland we had often been obliged to sleep in the open. But there the stars were faint, it was cold and there was, as often as not, a drizzle.

Here it was quite different. If one stuck one's head out from under the netting, the stars blazed down with a brilliance and brightness that is hard to imagine. The impact of this first night was unforgettable. The air was clear, there was no moon, and the sheer number of stars was truly breathtaking. I lay there marvelling long past the time when the adults came up, climbed into bed, and Uncle Max's snores grumbled across the roof, mixing with faraway howls of dogs and jackals.

The roof was to become a very useful place; in the summer, it was a splendid vantage point from which to observe the formal and very grand parties given, in the garden, by Aunt, sometimes with royalty present, in the person of Crown Prince Abdulilah, the Prince Regent. The cream of Baghdad society, with the men in tails and clanking with assorted decorations, and the ladies in brightly coloured evening dresses, remodelled for each party by local seamstresses over whom the ladies fought a vicious and neverending battle. Having hung around in the kitchen until bribed by Ali with assorted goodies from the forthcoming feast to go away, I would take my loot to the roof and there sit on the parapet, dangling my legs, eating and watching society cavort below.

Summer gradually turned to autumn, then winter came and, with the closing of the swimming pool, time hung heavy on my hands. It was then that Aunt got the appalling idea that I should go to school. In 1940, Baghdad was not what one might call a town which offered many facilities or distractions to the foreign community. For foreign boys like me, almost nine years old, there was really only the one school: the inaccurately named "American School for Boys". There was nothing even remotely American about it; the teachers were Iraqi, with the exception of two somewhat ancient Europeans, a Romanian and an Englishman/Italian. The actual teaching was either in strongly accented English (history, English books, geography) or in Arabic (mathematics, Arabic, French and science). The discipline was very strict, with punishments ranging from a literal rap on the knuckles with a wooden ruler, to a sentence of 'silence', sometimes lasting a week, during which it was forbidden to communicate with anyone at school for any reason whatever.

I was taken to school by Ahmed, the driver, in Uncle Max's car, which he would send back for me after being taken for his early morning visit to his clinic. We would drive slowly through the town, already, at 8am, bustling with *arabanas*, horse-drawn carriages pulled by starved-looking, miserable beasts which the drivers would lash with their whips with evident enjoyment. This was my first introduction to Arab treatment of animals: cruelty and disregard in the case of 'working' animals and pampering and cossetting of those animals kept for pleasure or sport, mainly horses and falcons, since domestic pets were virtually unknown in Arabia. I found the different attitudes confusing.

Baghdad was dusty, dirty and crowded. Street vendors loudly selling goods ranging from fruit and sweetmeats, to unsavoury looking lemonades, all in clouds of flies. *Coolies*, or porters, staggering along under unbelievable loads, which hung on their backs from a thick strap round their foreheads; I once saw a *coolie* with an upright piano on his back. They staggered along in a straight line, calling "*baalak, dir baalak*", "careful, watch it"; the load was too heavy for them to take avoiding action.

There were also many donkeys, trotting haphazardly in all directions, some with large men perched on the very end. The donkeys had no bridles, but were driven along by a constant pounding on their rib-cage by the heels of the rider, and steered by means of a small stick. The cars and small buses, greatly overcrowded, inched their way along, with horns permanently blaring. Women wearing shapeless black *abbayas*, all-covering shawls, skulked along the pavements, hugging the walls. There was a lot of noise.

The school building was a two-story concrete block construction, with a small paved courtyard where we were allowed to play, mostly fight, during the short morning break. We were given a mid-day meal in a dark hall at the back, seated at a long table in absolute silence. The whole school, some 40 boys, ate together. The meals were rather strange to me at first: usually a plate of rice, with some *mulukhiyya*, (a gluey sort of green vegetable) and, now and again, a piece of indeterminate meat. There was also the option of yoghurt slopped over the mixture and a large, flat, round unleavened bread called *khobus*, good to eat and useful in mopping the plate. After this, there was a fruit: an orange, or banana or a handful of dates. I had never had any trouble with eating and soon was quite enjoying the tastes of what was, I suppose, a fairly healthy diet. At mid-morning, one could have a glass of *shineena*, some yoghurt mixed with water, and slightly salted; very refreshing on a hot day.

Since my Club friends were being tutored at home, and my schoolmates were Iraqi, my Arabic improved by leaps and bounds, though the vocabulary was that of a nine-year-old. I remember being greatly impressed by the richness of the Arab system of cursing and swearing; very much more imaginative than in western languages. Certainly I managed to startle Aunt's domestic staff on many occasions. I do not remember any particularly close friends, except for one, al-Gailani, a fat and jolly chap who said he had an important father. I said I had an important uncle, which made us quits.

I was curious about Uncle Max's clinic, and asked Aunt if I could visit it one day.

"I don't want you going anywhere near it, the nasty dirty place. You never know what you may catch there. I can't think why your uncle bothers with it," was the answer.

But I was determined to see the clinic, and during one of my early breakfasts with Uncle Max, asked whether I could go with him one morning and go on to school directly from the clinic. I didn't mention my conversation with my aunt.

Uncle Max beamed, and patted his stomach with both hands, beating his drum, while going pop-pop-pop with his lips: a sign of being inordinately pleased.

"Of course, of course, if you really want to see it, although it isn't much to look at. There are all these poor people, you see, and the other foreign doctors are too busy with their big patients to do anything like this. So I spend the middle of the day with the rich ones, who pay for the poor ones morning and evening. Makes a good balance, pop-pop-pop. What about tomorrow morning?", he asked. "Just don't talk about it here."

I agreed at once, excited by both the visit and the deception. Uncle Max said nothing more, but winked at me and played his drum when he came in for his usual, very late lunch.

The following morning we got into the car together, long before Aunt or Mother stirred, and Ahmed drove us across the town to the clinic.

We drove into a part of the town which was new to me: the buildings and shops became more and more dingy and shabby, until we came to a narrow, unpaved road with undecorated concrete block, single story buildings on each side. In the middle of the road, which was unpaved, was an open sewer with dogs and children playing around. Some way down the road there was a large crowd outside one of the buildings; it was about six in the morning.

"There it is", said Uncle Max. "Lots of customers this morning..." We got out of the car, and the crowd pressed close to us. They were mostly in rags, old men, women with small babies, some bandaged, some crippled but all trying to touch Uncle Max. The closest ones tried to kiss his hand. He pushed his way unceremoniously through with me bobbing along in his wake.

"It's all right, it's all right," he was saying in Arabic. "There is time, you will all be helped, be patient ..."

Inside, there were three or four rooms: a sort of first aid room, presided over by an Indian man in a spotless white uniform and turban, introduced to me as Babu, who appeared to be Uncle Max's medical factotum; Uncle Max's own room, with a desk and chair, a bench and a sort of couch affair; and a small room which acted as a pharmacy. There was also a large person in khaki who kept order and ushered in the patients one by one.

"Oh, your Uncle Pasha is a most saintly man," said Babu to me while Uncle Max plunged into his doctoring. "He is alone saving many people from bad life and dying and doing for nothing. Oh, yes, small Sahib, a very most saintly man."

It was obvious Uncle Max was busy now, so, after some time, Ahmed took me to school. I will never forget those patients and the look on their faces when they gazed at my uncle.

Oddly enough, Aunt and Mother never did find out that I had seen the clinic, and it remained a secret between my uncle and me. He would sometimes wink, and play his drum in a happy sort of way. He enjoyed, as I did, the extra bond between us and the feeling that we had outwitted authority. Not, I suppose, the proper sentiment to instil in a growing boy.

The winter of 1940 came. In Baghdad, it got cold in the winter months and kerosene stoves abounded in the house, which was permeated by the distinctive smell. This was also the principal social season, and Aunt, as the accepted doyenne of the social set – though there were some aspiring rivals who never lasted very long – swung into her winter routine.

Thursday afternoons were musical: Aunt on the violin, Professor Hertz, later my piano teacher, on the grand piano, Sayyid Arshad, the Mayor of Baghdad, on the cello and Jens, the Swedish Embassy attaché, on the viola. Later, Mother was to join as second violin. Mozart, Beethoven and Brahms were elegantly slaughtered in the salon, with everyone sawing and tapping away with expressions of artistic agony on their faces. At half time, tea was taken, with minuscule sandwiches, as far as I was concerned not worth bothering with, small cakes and massive silver tea-sets with porcelain cups. The event was always reported at some length in the following day's *Baghdad Times*, the only English language newspaper, to the fury of Aunt's competitors. I was not permitted to attend the music in the salon, and Uncle Max always took great care to be elsewhere during the critical time.

Tuesday was Ladies' Day. Here, Aunt invited lady friends to lunch, always with one or two interesting strangers. At this time there was a growing flow of people passing through Baghdad, mostly connected with the various armies: British, Indian, Polish as well as the Red Cross and Red Crescent, and other welfare organisations. Aunt and her cronies, very dressed up, would partake of a light luncheon while lionizing a transiting famous Polish painter, poet, musician or dignitary, temporarily in uniform, but a prize nonetheless. Naturally, Uncle Max and I were thankfully excluded, though Mother was given the opportunity to expound on her escape and suffering.

Wednesdays were devoted to bridge: Aunt would arrange anything up to four tables, manned by diplomats, professionals and local dignitaries, with their wives. Play would start at about five o'clock, break for an hour – a splendid buffet dinner was served – and continue until eleven or so. This was not very expert 'social' bridge, for the most part, though the good players would try to end up at the same table and not infrequently voices were heard throughout the house, irritably enquiring why trumps had not been led, or that the spade lead showed signs of minimal intelligence. The sums gambled were very small and the evening was taken by most guests to be no more than a chance to gossip and have a splendid meal, often with mounds of caviar (Uncle Max had many Iranian friends), esoteric cold meats, salads and always spectacular puddings. I could always have some of what was left over, though the players had voracious appetites.

Naturally, there was a lot of going out as well. This was a constant battle between Aunt and Uncle Max, who loathed dressing up and going to parties, and grudged the time spent away from his patients. Time after time, Aunt and Mother would be ready, dressed up to the nines, at the appointed time, only to be told on the telephone that there was a life-or-death situation which Uncle Max had to attend, and 'why didn't they go on ahead and he would join them when he could.' Naturally, he never did, and I would sometimes hear him creep in after midnight to face an enraged Aunt. On occasion, however, encased in his dinner jacket or tails, with medals a-clank, purple faced and sweating, he would have to go along with his ladies. His greatest test, he told me, was the meeting at the party of his great rival, the British doctor, whom I shall call George.

Sir George Pasha, as he became known, was everything Uncle Max was not, and almost nothing of what he was.

Being British was, of course, a great advantage, and Sir George was a favourite of the British Embassy, the British community and the anglophile group of Iraqis. He was the Chief of the University Medical School and also was called in sometimes, by courtesy, to the Royal Family, when it was not anything very serious. He was a tall, distinguished looking man, with long, silvery wings of hair and a most accomplished charm and bedside manner. He played, successfully, at being an Edwardian gentleman, but most people, I suspect, saw through his courtly, pompous and sycophantic style.

Uncle Max disliked him intensely, though the worst thing I ever heard him say about Sir George was that 'he is interested more in healthy important people than in sick poor people'.

Christmas came and went. I did not find it very exciting, since it was geared to adult merrymaking, with an accelerated tempo of parties, including a marvellous fancy-dress affair, given by Aunt. I do not remember very much about it, apart from the procession of unlikely pirates, Chinese mandarins, witches and a magnificent Louis XV. It was not done to appear in Arab costume and the sight of a portly Arab gentleman dressed as an egg was very wonderful. Mother and Aunt wore identical, multicoloured Polish peasant dresses, with ribbons, lacy underskirts and cute bonnets. They were always much complimented, and did look rather handsome, but I thought perhaps the costumes would have suited wearers some two decades younger.

We did have a family Polish dinner on Christmas Eve, with *barszcz*, baked fish and *makowiec*, the traditional poppy-seed cake. There was a splendid tree, with real candles, which I was forbidden to approach, and a very formal exchange of presents… one each. I received from Aunt and Uncle Max six lead soldiers of some unknown foreign regiment, and from Mother an incredibly boring colouring book of different sorts of houses. My best present was from Ali, the cook, who smuggled up to my room my very own small cake, with a lot of cream. I devoured this secretly, after going to bed. I had no means of buying anything, so I gave to each adult some dates from the garden, wrapped in paper.

There were more parties, including one, for adults, at the British Embassy, on New Year's Eve. This was a full dress affair, and Uncle Max was forced to go, bursting out of his tail-coat, and with all his medals, ribbons and stars on display. These were from the King of Transjordan, the Shah of Persia, the King of Iraq and the Free Polish Government in Exile. They were very colourful. He was proud of them, and they helped him bear the hated social activity in which he was forced to participate. Aunt and Mother were consciously beautiful in splendid long dresses and furs.

By now, eight months had passed since we arrived in

Baghdad, Mother was as I remembered her in Poland: her hair was spun gold, her makeup perfection itself, her wardrobe both elegant and flattering, and her attention again concentrated on her appearance and social activities. I rather missed the close rapport we had established during our flight from Poland.

My ninth birthday was in February, 1941, notable only for my first glimpse into Uncle Max's 'Aladdin's Cupboard'. I had been given six more lead soldiers by Aunt and another colouring book by Mother. I also was allowed to invite two friends to tea, a stilted affair in best clothes and with closely supervised games. There was a cake with nine candles.

That morning, however, when I got up early to have breakfast with Uncle Max, he suddenly whispered in a conspiratorial way: "Come with me and don't make any noise."

He led me upstairs to his dressing room, where there was an enormous shiny wooden cupboard. He produced a large key-ring and unlocked the door. When he opened it, I could see shelves and shelves of boxes, of loose pens, watches, scent bottles, cigarette cases and lighters and heaps of gold and silver ornaments.

"These are presents I get from my friends and patients," Uncle Max stood back and played his drum happily. "Since they are presents to me, I will give a present to you, because you are a whole year older, and that is important."

He scrabbled about in the cupboard, and produced a magnificent gold stop-watch, with day, date and, most marvellously, the phases of the moon. It was certainly the most wonderful thing I had ever seen in my life.

"This is for you," said Uncle Max. "I hope you like it."

I was speechless, and embraced him. For the next seven hours I could barely keep my eyes off my watch, pressing buttons and adjusting ceaselessly. Sadly, Aunt spotted it after lunch and took it away. I never saw it again, and Uncle Max and I felt too unhappy about the whole episode to mention it. I suppose Aunt was right, but at the time it was a calamity for me. To do her justice, some days later she gave me a sturdy steel watch, on which I could tell the time with a minimum of glamour or excitement. It had, I remember, a loud and companionable tick.

Time passed; I enjoyed school very little and I did not learn much. The weather was too cold for swimming and there was not a great deal to occupy the time.

In March, I could feel there was a sort of tension building up among Aunt's friends, and at their weekly meetings there was a lot of low-voiced discussion and relatively little playing. Something was wrong politically, though I did not know what it could be. I asked Uncle Max, but he said that it was a lot of nonsense, without going into any detail.

At the end of the month, on the 30th, I was sitting in my room in the evening, playing in a desultory way with my few soldiers, when there was a sort of muffled scream from Mother downstairs.

"Oh no, not again! I can't stand it. Oh please God we shall all be murdered! Oh oh oh …"

There were consoling noises from Aunt and someone else. I went downstairs in a hurry, to find Mother prostrate on the settee in the sitting room, with Aunt stroking her wrist and Jens, the handsome Swedish attaché, hovering about in a worried sort of way.

It seemed that there was a revolution in the country, and we had to rush over to the British Embassy for safety, as soon as possible. We then entered a period of great turmoil, with Mother wailing that we would all be slaughtered, Aunt snapping curt orders at the bewildered staff (especially Entah, tossed like a cork between the conflicting waves of instructions from Aunt, butler and cook) and trying to decide which series of dresses and accessories to pack, to say nothing of her enormous jewel-case. I was handed a small bag, which contained almost the entirety of my modest wardrobe.

Uncle Max was not yet at home, to Aunt's fury. He did arrive, though, just before we were going to leave.

"Where have you been, you heartless man?" Aunt shouted. "Don't you know there are riots in town, and that we are going to be attacked any minute? Monster who doesn't care about women and children," she pointed dramatically at me. I shrugged my shoulders, trying to tell Uncle Max that this was not my idea, and I did not know what all the shouting was about. Mother leaned on the arm of the Swedish attaché.

"I came as soon as I got a call from the Minister of the Interior, who said that it may be wise for foreigners to go to the British Embassy and the American Legation for a day or two," said Uncle Max. "There are no riots, and I think there is no danger. But if you want to go, that's fine. Perhaps Jens will be kind enough to take you in his diplomatic car, because I am already late for the clinic."

"Heartless man," said Aunt in a cold voice, "It will serve you right if they kill you and burn the house. We are going now. This may be our last goodbye!" Mother gave a muffled shriek and raised the back of her wrist to her forehead in a tragic gesture.

"To escape from death in Poland with my baby only to die in the sand of faraway Baghdad," she said. "Come to me, my darlink!" she pulled me to her perfumed bosom. I fought, but she was still stronger than me. "We will always go together," she said dramatically.

Uncle Max gave a disgusted snort and disappeared into the dining room. We piled into Jens' large car and departed for the Embassy.

The British Embassy compound was an area of several acres of gardens, containing the main large Embassy building, a number of outbuildings and lots of palm trees. It was on the river, on the far bank, and we drove into town, over the old pontoon bridge across the Tigris, and through the large iron gates of the compound. There had been no riots that I could see, though the streets were unusually deserted.

In the compound, there were many people milling about, the cars were being neatly parked, and men with red armbands were giving orders to the newcomers as to where they should go, to which room they were allocated and that there was a general meeting, to be addressed by the Ambassador, at eight o'clock.

There were two or three hundred people at the meeting, sitting where they could, mostly on the floor. I recognised a number of Aunt's friends, notably a famous author, Freya Stark, but none of my own. I discovered later that they had sought sanctuary at the American Legation. There were some children, but unfortunately they were mostly girls, and younger boys. I was the eldest.

The Ambassador, an immensely tall and distinguished looking gentleman, came and stood before us. The gist of his speech was that the Iraqi Government had been seized by some pro-Nazi Colonels, led by a fellow called Rashid Ali al-Gailani (who turned out to be the father of my fat school pal). The King had been driven north to safety by his intrepid English Nanny, called Miss Borland, while the Prince Regent had escaped to the RAF station at Habbaniya, hidden under a carpet in the back of the American Minister's car.

After the buzz of comment had died down, the Ambassador continued: "I don't know how long we shall all have to stay here, but we must make the best of it. We are organising dormitories for everyone, and I shall ask you all to help in various ways. We have had all our radios confiscated (except one), and we are unable to get messages out to our people in Habbaniya, where we have aircraft and men – but they do know what is happening. There is no immediate danger, we have plenty of food and there are Iraqi troops guarding our gates against any mob action. Now please listen to the various activity organisers, and they will tell you what to do next."

I was sitting on the floor at the front, and his eye fell on me. He walked towards me and I stood up, with my eyes level with his thighs.

"Who are you, young fellow?" His voice floated down. "I don't remember meeting you before."

"I am the nephew of Dr Max and Aunt Ina, Your Highness," I replied, thinking that a local reference was better than an unknown Polish one.

The Ambassador laughed. "You don't have to call me that," he said. "I know your Uncle and Aunt and I am going to ask you to do a very special job for me. I want you to take charge of all the children here and to be responsible for keeping the grounds clear of rubbish. I am going to make you a sergeant, and you can salute me whenever we meet."

Naturally, I was most thrilled at this distinction, and when I was given a set of stripes on an elastic band the next day, I immediately put them on my arm, and began to bully and harass the other children. I gave each of them an area of responsibility and patrolled the grounds to make sure they picked up all the rubbish. Some of the younger girls objected, but I threatened the most terrifying punishments by the Ambassador and they submitted. My proudest moment was that afternoon, as I casually saluted the Ambassador when our paths crossed. To Mother's amazement he returned the compliment with a grin.

One of the people with us was Uncle Max's rival, Sir George Pasha. He spent his time charming the Ambassador and the more important people and playing bridge. On one occasion, when I fell down the steps and skinned my knee, Mother and Aunt wanted to take me to him to be looked at, but I felt that this would be a betrayal of Uncle Max and absolutely refused to go. It made Mother and Aunt angry, since they could not understand my feelings.

The Embassy, and its temporary inhabitants soon settled down to a calm routine, typical of the British under stress in a foreign land. Aunt and Mother were in a ladies' dormitory, which they hated, while I was in a room with five small boys, over whom I soon established sufficient dominance to get uninterrupted sleep. The food was not exciting, but plentiful, since the Iraqi Foreign Ministry, anxious to hedge its bets, arranged for daily deliveries of bread, rice, beer and any other staples which were necessary. We were given daily bulletins of news by the Ambassador, who told us that the whole uprising had been sponsored by the German Ambassador, a man called Dr Grobba, who was reputed to be 'quite a decent chap, just doing his job'. Hitler and the Nazis thought that their successes in the North African desert would culminate in the capture of Cairo, as they nearly did, and thus control of the Middle East, and an uprising against the Allies in Iraq would be a springboard for the control of Iranian and Arab oil, and the subsequent destabilisation of India.

In the Embassy, we were not bored. There was something happening all the time.

There were always two men, acting as sentries, who lay behind their Bren light machine-guns beside the drive and facing the wrought-iron gates. It was part of my duties to take them their mugs of tea at ten in the morning, and I sometimes sat and watched with them for a bit. On one occasion, there was a sudden shouting and yelling just outside the gates, where stood a huge bronze statue of General Maude on horseback, and a sizeable mob of unkempt and bedraggled rioters appeared and swarmed over the statue, smearing it with excrement. They were soon chased away by the Iraqi army detachment who guarded the Embassy, but I was told to 'leg it to His Nibs and tell him what's going on'. My English was very rudimentary, and I assumed that 'His Nibs' was yet another honorific for the Ambassador.

I rushed to the main building and burst into the room where the Ambassador was having a meeting with two or three people.

"Your Nibs," I panted, "I am sent by the machine gunner man to tell you that people are smear the statue with …", I did not know how to say it in English, "with *khara*." I used the Arabic word. "But is all right, the army chased them away." I remembered to salute.

The Ambassador looked at me calmly. "Please don't call me Your Nibs, and knock before you come in next time, Sergeant," he said mildly. "But thank you for the message".

There was a sort of sea-wall on the river bank, where the lawn sloped down to the waters of the Tigris. An Iraqi police boat patrolled up and down, to make sure that nobody escaped, and that no messages were passed to the outside. But when there were no officers looking, the policemen were quite amiable, and I often sat on the wall in the evening, exchanging friendly insults with the men in the boat.

On a couple of occasions they even gave me a fish, locally known as Tigris salmon, which I proudly bore off to the kitchens. In exchange, I sometimes stole some English cigarettes to give to the policemen.

They also told me a curious, but true story. Apparently, Hitler wanted to show the Iraqi Colonels that he was pleased with them, so he sent them, as his personal envoy, Major Axel von Blomberg, the son of the famous German Field Marshal. As the Major's plane was landing at the airport in Baghdad, and the troops below were celebrating his arrival by firing their rifles in the air, in a *feu de joie*, a stray bullet hit the guest of honour, and the envoy was quite dead when the plane landed and the door was opened.

During the early days of the siege, there were some excitements, notably the bombing of Baghdad's Rashid airfield by antique British planes from Habbaniyah, clearly visible from the Embassy. The Gladiators and Oxfords of the RAF came burping and growling overhead, very slowly, and dipped over the airfield, casually laying their explosive eggs, which were designed more to impress than to destroy. Eventually, the Germans, who could ill spare them, sent three Messerschmidt 110's and a Heinkel 111, but these modern aircraft were so fast that they inevitably over-ran the British fighters, which could fly at some 60 mph and turn on the proverbial dime. It must have been very frustrating for the German pilots and their Iraqi supporters on the ground.

What was more serious, potentially, was an attack on the RAF Station at Habbaniyah by a large armoured force of the Iraqi army. This force could very easily have overwhelmed the camp, full of women and children refugees from Baghdad, but for some unexplained reason the Iraqis just sat round the camp. Meanwhile, Mr Churchill let it be known that he wished the garrison to hold fast, and some Gladiators dropped a handful of bombs and grenades on the dug-in Iraqis, who promptly retired without a fight.

In the Embassy, we had no means of communicating with the outside world, and thus knew little of what was going on locally. A moment of great excitement occurred one morning (I happened to have unobtrusively climbed to the flat roof, from where I could observe the surrounding area, but which we were forbidden to do), when suddenly a Gladiator came burbling over the palmtops, at about 150 feet, and dropped a package, attached to a long red ribbon, onto our lawn. The police in the boat on the river managed to get off a couple of shots with their pistols, doing no damage, and I could clearly see the grinning face of the pilot, in his leather helmet, as he cheerfully waved from the open cockpit.

The package contained the latest news, which included the

information that a relieving British force was on its way from Basrah, the Iraqi port on the Persian Gulf, and that we were not to worry. Sadly, this was the only occasion that a message was delivered in this way, as the authorities considered the exercise to be too dangerous.

Everyday life must have been boring for the adults, although I found that there were things to do and happenings to be excited about every day. Mother and Aunt played bridge, helped with the rudimentary cooking (a very far cry from parties at home), and tried to blend, unsuccessfully, with the typical British expatriate ladies by whom they were surrounded. On the one occasion I asked about Uncle Max, Aunt snapped that he was probably dead and she did not care. Later she said she did not mean it.

The end of the siege came after a month. On the last day, the Ambassador called us all together for the last time. He said he was glad that the emergency was over, and that we were all safe. He said that everyone had behaved very well and he thanked us all for our co-operation. Mother and Aunt packed their large cases and my small one, but I insisted on wearing my khaki shirt and shorts, with the sergeant's stripes prominent on my arm. I also took great care to say goodbye to the Ambassador and to salute him for the last time. We then got into the car which Uncle Max had sent for us, and went home.

We drove back over the pontoon bridge and through the city to the suburb of Alwiyah, where the house was. There was not much damage visible, though there were some burned-out houses which Aunt said belonged to Iraqi Jews. Hitler's evil seemed to have a long arm.

At home, everyone was lined up to greet us, and Uncle Max stood there playing his drum. He told us that he had been perfectly all right and had, indeed, been given an escort by the rebels as he drove around the town to visit his patients. Aunt and Mother told him about the dreadful hardships we had endured for the whole month, and how he was a selfish man who only thought of himself. I was very glad to be able to tell him, at breakfast early the next morning, that there were no hardships and that I was glad he could go on helping people during the troubles. I also told him that Sir George Pasha, who had been locked up in the Embassy with us, had been very busy with the important people there, but had been too scared to go out. He smiled.

Life slowly returned to normal. My friends and I, now reunited at the Club swimming pool, exchanged lurid stories of our respective imprisonments in the British Embassy and the American Legation, which owed little to fact and a great deal to our active imaginations. Mother and Aunt, who quickly re-established the weekly programmes of entertainment, competed with each other and with their guests, in much the same way, in their stories of their own captivity. Uncle Max, as always, went his own quiet way and seldom allowed himself to show his amusement at the tales he heard.

The Prince Regent and the King returned to Baghdad, now that it was safe, and the King's stalwart Nanny Borland, a tough lady of about sixty, was much feted and praised for her bravery in spiriting His Majesty, aged six, away to safety in North Iraq. The Prince Regent's craven flight in the footwell of the American Minister's car was conveniently forgotten and not mentioned.

It was also this summer that Toby entered my life. One day, I heard a banging on the gates and Entah going to open them. This was a common occurrence, since not infrequently poor patients would come to the house seeking Uncle Max. or sometimes bringing what gifts they could afford to thank him for treating their ills.

I took no notice until there was a knock at my bedroom door and Entah appeared with a small. wriggling black and white bundle in his arms. He placed the bundle on the tiled floor and it was transformed into a small and enthusiastic spaniel puppy. I was stricken dumb and stood transfixed, while the puppy, after a brief reconnaissance of available floor space, promptly made a large lake beside my bed. I was enchanted, while Entah, more practical, rushed off for cleaning materials and made good the damage.

"Young Master," he said, "Some low Bedu brought this for you and said that Doctor Pasha had told them to find one like this. I don't know where he comes from, but I think maybe he was stolen." A ghastly thought occurred to us both at the same time.

"What will Memsahib say?" lamented Entah, while I panicked at the probable wrath of Aunt and Mother.

"Take him to the garden behind the kitchen, and don't let anyone see him," I asked Entah. "I will talk to Memsahib about him." This sounded much braver than I felt.

Gathering my courage, I went downstairs, where Mother and Aunt were having coffee, and discussing the afternoon's musical get-together.

I strolled into the room and casually said: "By the way, I have been wondering if, after all the riots, it would not be a good idea to have a guard dog, don't you think? I could look after him, and he would not be any trouble."

"No," said Aunt. "No," said Mother. They went on talking.

I retired to think again; I had lost a skirmish but still hoped I might win the war. After some time, I had another idea, and went back into the room.

"The garden has a lot of rats and things in it, and it might be a good idea to have a dog so that he can chase them away and they won't bother you during parties," I said.

"No," said Aunt. "No," said Mother. They went on talking.

The situation was now serious, and I determined to ask Uncle Max for advice. After all, the miracle appeared to have been his doing.

When Uncle Max arrived that afternoon for lunch, at about four, I was waiting for him.

"Uncle Max, Uncle Max," I cried when he appeared. "There is a little dog, a black and white dog, very small, who has come and Entah said maybe you did it!"

Uncle Max smiled broadly, and played his drum. "So, " he said, "A dog, huh? Well, well ..."

"Yes," I said, "But Aunt and Mother say I can't have a dog. They don't know he is here. If he has to go away I shall kill myself." I meant it, too.

"Na, na," he made a comforting noise. "Let me try to speak to them about it." He paused. "You can't call him it," he said, "He must have a name."

"I don't know any dog names," I said. "I have never known any dogs."

Hussein, who was serving lunch, suddenly said, "Entah has been saying that the small dog is very leaky, and is wetting his clothes all the time. He says he has to give the clothes to the *dhobi* (laundryman) to wash. You should call the small dog Dhobi, for Entah's sake."

Uncle Max nodded, and I tried the word out, "Dhobi... Dhobi," and it sort of tasted right. "From now, he is Dhobi," I announced.

I do not know what sort of magic Uncle Max wrought with the ladies, but the next morning Aunt said that Dhobi could stay, "on a trial basis, you understand", and if certain strict rules were observed. These were, mainly, that Dhobi was not allowed in the house under any pretext, and especially not in my bedroom; that he was not to be overfed; that I was to bathe him at least once a month; that he was not allowed to have fleas or ticks; that the staff was not to be pestered to help me with him.

Naturally, I agreed to everything and rushed out to tell Dhobi the good news. My cup was full when Uncle Max, coming in for lunch, diffidently presented me with a splendid collar for Dhobi, in leather, and with a little silver plaque attached saying "Dhobi"! Dhobi hated it at the beginning, but got used to it after a while.

I now knew true happiness. Here was a creature, not my property but my friend, who understood everything, was not complaining, could keep a secret, and exchanged with me the sort of unconditional love which only rarely is one privileged to experience. In short, there was no more loneliness.

I told my friends at the swimming pool about Dhobi, and they shared my joy, with one proviso.

"You can't call a dog Laundryman," said Barry. "Sounds silly, and anyway, you should give a spaniel a proper English name, not an Arab one." I was not sure that I agreed with the sentiment, but had to be discreet, in order to maintain my precarious position in the gang.

"What can I call him?" I asked. "He is used to Dhobi now."

"I know," said Bendy, after a moment of thought. "Call him Toby, like Mr Punch's dog. Now that is a good English name, and sounds like his old one, so he won't mind."

Henry and Barry both thought it was a good name, so I

agreed. That evening, I explained to Dhobi that he was to be re-named, and carried out the ceremony by pouring some water over his head (he objected) out of an egg-cup, and pronouncing solemnly: "You, who were Dhobi, are now and forever Toby, a good English name." Entah was very puzzled, and remained so, even after my explanation.

Toby and I lived together for about six months. He was quite well behaved, and it became a happy routine for me to sit with him on the back terrace, when I got home from school, and tell him what had happened that day, while he told me what he had been doing. There was one anxious time, when he was bitten by a scorpion, but Uncle Max gave him an injection and some powder dissolved in his water bowl, so that he got better. Even Aunt seemed not to mind him staying, though Mother would have nothing to do with him. Ali, the cook, was fond of him, and would give him titbits.

One day, in the autumn, I came home and there was no normal ecstatic greeting from Toby. I looked for him, but he was nowhere to be seen. In fact, there was no one about at all. I went to the back of the house, and saw Entah sitting on the back terrace, crying.

"Young master," he said. "Dhobi is dead. He ran out of the big gate into the road, and a car hit him and killed him." He took a shuddering breath, "It is my fault, for I left the gate open. You may kill me as well."

It took a little while for me to understand that there would be no more wagging tail, no more cold nose, no more love. There had been feelings I had never experienced before I held the warm, furry body of Toby in my arms. Now he was buried, alone for good, in a corner of the garden. Naturally, I forgave poor Entah, who was desolate for a long time. The family sympathised, especially Uncle Max, who understood enough to say: "Of course, no more dogs for a long time. You cannot replace a friend." Aunt said she was sorry, and even Mother sighed and said that one should always be prepared to lose the ones one loves and that they were hostages to fate. I did not understand this.

I felt a big emptiness in me for some time, and had to learn all over again that it was all right to be by oneself. Uncle Max resolved that I needed something new to think about, so he decided to take me to an Arab desert feast, to which he had been invited.

The occasion was the birth of triplet sons to the youngest wife (Number Four) of the Paramount Sheikh of the Southern Tribes. Since the birth of a son is a reason for rejoicing, and three sons in one go was an unprecedented event and concrete evidence of the Sheikh's virility, the feast was certainly warranted. Add to this the fact that the Sheikh was some seventy years old while wife Number Four (I never heard her name) was but fifteen, and a very special feast was called for.

Uncle Max and I, driven by Ahmed, left early in the morning in Uncle Max's black Ford. We had some seventy miles to drive, mostly on a rough desert track. But Ahmed knew the way well, since Uncle Max was an old friend of the Sheikh's and had, on one occasion, saved his eldest son from death by sitting beside him in his tent and giving him constant attention and medicines for three days and nights non-stop. Hence the invitation as to an honoured guest and full permission to bring me along.

We drove over the pontoon bridge, and out of Baghdad through the garden suburb of Karradat Myriam, southwards to the desert. We went through date palm groves and gardens of vegetables, separated by low mud walls, and with ditches full of muddy water irrigating the slightly raised beds. Soon the gardens became fewer, as we left the river behind us, and the soil became more and more sandy, until we were driving through beautifully sculptured sand dunes, towering high over the car, and lining the sandy track on which we kept up a fair rate of speed.

As we drove, Uncle Max told me stories of his experiences in Baghdad over his twenty odd years there. One sticks in my mind. It was an invitation to a desert feast, such as the one we were going to, but years ago, in honour of a new British Ambassador. Apparently, the Ambassador was a World War I hero, and had lost an eye at Ypres. He therefore wore a glass eye and being a man with a sense of humour, was embarrassed when, at drinking parties, his good eye would get more and more bloodshot, while the glass eye remained pristine. He therefore had acquired a series of progressively more and more bloodshot glass eyes, to keep pace with his good one, in a velvet-lined case, and would change the glass eye from time to time during the party. The last eye, brought out only on special occasions, had a little Union Jack instead of the pupil.

The Ambassador had never been to the Middle East and had no knowledge or experience of Arabs, so some cronies had told him to beware the traditional Arab joke of offering the guest of honour an eye of the roast sheep at the feast.

Thus, when the climax of the feast came, and the Sheikh leaned forward and plucked the eye from the sheep's carcass in front of him, and offered it to the Ambassador. The Ambassador, nothing loath, plucked out his glass eye and offered it to the Sheikh, who was aghast.

Uncle Max leaned back in his seat and chortled, beating his drum like anything, with his lips going pop-pop-pop. He was very pleased with himself, for he had made me laugh after many days of sadness, and this was the point at which I put the pain of losing Toby behind me.

We reached our destination close to midday, and I was startled at the size of the tribal encampment. A huge tent, big enough to accommodate several hundred people, stood at one edge of the camp. On three sides, and covering a large area, were small, family tents, including several, more luxurious than the others, close to the big tent. These were for the Sheikh's wives and children (I was told he had about thirty sons; it was not thought relevant to count daughters, and few Sheikhs knew how many they had). Then, outside the village of tents, I could see flocks of sheep, groups of camels and horses, and lots of people, in typical Bedouin clothes, milling about. I noticed that the women, traditionally veiled in the cities, were bare-faced in the desert. Uncle Max said that the Bedouin were the pure-bred Arabs, who despised the town-dwellers and called them mongrels. The feelings were fully reciprocated.

We went up to the big tent and were greeted by Sheikh Mohammed, the host. He was a tall, white-bearded man with a large, hooked nose and bright black eyes. He was dressed in a *thaub* (a long, white gown) and a brown woven *bisht* (an outer robe, edged with gold embroidery). On his head was a black and white *qutra* headcloth held in place by the typical Iraqi double square gold *aghal*. He also wore a beautifully worked leather belt with a gold-handled dagger in a gold sheath.

He embraced Uncle Max, kissing him on the nose, and calling him *Hakim* and *Habib* which meant learned and respected doctor and friend. He patted my head and said *"Ahlan wa sahlan bi ism ammak"* or welcome in the name of your uncle. Turning to Uncle Max he said *"Walad qawi, 'audhbIllah"*. This meant, Uncle Max said, that I was a strong boy, may God protect us. This last was always said after praising someone, most especially a child or a domestic animal, so as to prevent the effect of the evil eye from jealous people or devils.

In the big tent, which was completely open on the desert side, there were lots of people, but I noticed there were no women or girls or babies; just men and a few boys of my age and upward, though they were all Arabs, and eyed me suspiciously. There were few foreigners: some diplomats, bankers and major shopkeepers. But the Prime Minister was there, as were most of the Cabinet and the Mayor of Baghdad. These were all known to me from parties at Aunt's house, and when they came to greet Uncle Max, they mostly had a word or two for me.

The tent had a series of Persian carpets spread on the canvas floor, and after a short time we were invited to sit down with our backs to the tent wall, facing the open desert. Uncle Max was seated three or four places from Sheikh Mohammed, and I sat next to him, trying to remember what he had told me of Arab etiquette, such as not using the left hand to receive cups and glasses or eat, and not to let the soles of my sandals be visible. I was dressed in my formal clothes, namely a white bush-jacket, white shorts, and Indian-style *chapli* sandals. Uncle Max was in his plain gray suit, with his tie under his ear, as usual, and his waistcoat showing signs of strain, especially since we all sat cross-legged on the carpet.

"Remember," said Uncle Max, "right hand only and never refuse anything. When they give you coffee, accept two cups, then waggle the empty cup to and fro. This means 'no more, thank you'. It's no good saying it, because they will take no notice."

At this point, with everyone sitting down in a line some fifty yards long, servants appeared with huge copper coffee-jugs and holding, in their right hands, a nest of six or seven little egg-cups. The biggest servant went to the Sheikh, and having poured coffee in an amazingly clever way from a height of two feet into the tiny egg-cup, offered it to the Sheikh. The Sheikh took it, and gave it to the Prime Minister, who was seated on his right, and who politely indicated 'no, after you'. This went on for half a minute or so, and the Sheikh won, taking the second cup. The other cups were then distributed to the next four guests, and the other servants continued the line. After the second serving, the guest would waggle his cup, and the servant would proceed to the next unserved guest and fill the cup again, and so on until everyone was served.

I did not much enjoy the coffee, which was a clear green colour, with a strong taste of cardamom seed and unsweetened. I was told it was refreshing and the best drink in the desert, by my neighbour on the other side, who was one of the Sheikh's sons, about three years older than me. He also purposely jogged me with his elbow when I drank and made me spill the coffee on my white shorts, which would lead to problems with Mother.

When everyone had been served, the Sheikh shouted loudly, and at once a procession of servants came staggering round the corner, every four bearing a huge round brass tray, some five feet in diameter, heaped with food. On a hill of rice, there was, on alternate trays, a baby camel or an adult sheep, roasted. I discovered that within each animal, there was a lamb, within the lamb two or three chickens and within each chicken, a hard-boiled egg. All round the centre-piece, there were arranged more chickens, partridges, pigeons and eggs, and the whole was sprinkled with nuts and ripe dates.

There were also smaller platters of sweetmeats, fresh tomatoes and lettuces, and the local thin, twisted cucumbers, often up to three feet long. In between the platters were heaps of *khubus*, the local unleavened bread, round and plate-sized, to be used, in fact, as plates. There was no cutlery and no napkins.

Uncle Max looked at me with a broad smile: "Don't worry. Just do the best you can," he said.

I watched my neighbour, and saw him take a handful of rice and cram it into his mouth. He then pulled a chunk of meat from the camel in front of us and put it on a bread round, which he handed to me.

"Take it," he said in Arabic. "Eat it and be happy in my father's house." I thanked him and took the meat in my right hand and ate it. It was delicious. We all tucked in, and I noticed the servants hovering about, each with a knife, cutting up the animals and putting the pieces on bread 'plates' for the guests. I did not much like to see them get bricks and break the skulls of the animals so as to get at the brains and tongues, but the rest of the food really was very good and I ate too much. I got on well with the Sheikh's son, and managed to stuff a hard-boiled egg down the back of his robe in revenge for the coffee; but we parted friends. Although I watched very carefully, I did not see anyone offering or eating the sheeps' eyes.

After quite a long time, when everyone seemed to have eaten their fill, the trays were still heaped with food, though the best bits had gone. At a sign from the Sheikh, the servants took them away, and my young neighbour said: "Now the women and children will eat, and what is left after that will go to the servants, and the poor people. My father is a generous man, thanks be to Allah."

Now some men appeared with ewers and basins and clean, white cloths so that the guests could wash their hands, somewhat greasy after the meal. The water was scented with attar of roses and cool to the touch. Finally, more men came with incense holders, mostly 'oudh, an aromatic bark, slowly smouldering in the receptacles. Those with beards put their headdresses over the holders, and lifted their beards over the smoke. The beardless ones, like me, just wafted some of the pungent, sweet smoke over our faces.

There were some polite belches, and a murmur of traditional phrases which were always said by guests and the host, the one praising the hospitality and the quality and quantity of food, while the other disclaimed the praise and offered apologies for

70

the unworthy skimpiness and shabby standard of food and entertainment. I had yet to learn the proper things to say, so I just smiled.

I did not see any signal given, but there was suddenly the sound of muted thunder, and a long way away, in the desert, we saw an approaching dust cloud. The thunder grew as the cloud approached, and after a short time, we could distinguish a mass of Bedouin horsemen, charging towards us on beautifully caparisoned horses. As they approached within shouting distance, we could hear them shouting *"Allahu akbar, Allahu akbar"*, Allah is great, as they galloped, and waving their rifles. Then they started shooting in the air, and distracted us to such an extent that we did not notice a second wave of riders, this time on camels, at full stretch, coming up behind them. By now we were all standing, and from the tents around us came the shrill, piercing ululating of the women. I could feel the hair on my neck standing up, and I instinctively grabbed Uncle Max's hand.

As the horsemen got to within some ten yards of the tent, they pulled up their steaming mounts, and made them rear and pirouette before us. The camel riders arrived, and made the animals turn round and round. They were all firing in the air and shouting, the women were still making their shrill noise and there was dust and the smell of horse sweat everywhere.

Uncle Max bent over and shouted in my ear: "You are very lucky to see this. It is the greatest honour the Sheikh can give to the visitor. It is called the tribal ride and it is for the Prime Minister. It is not done very much now, so try to remember."

This was the climax, and soon afterwards we thanked the Sheikh and got into the car to go home. I thanked Uncle Max for what was a wonderful feast, and, although excited, found that the great quantity of food had made me sleepy so I remember nothing more until we were driving through the gates at home.

Aunt and Mother were waiting for us and wanted to hear how it all went. As I was recounting the story, Mother suddenly noticed the large green stain on my best white shorts. As always, when suddenly angry, her pale blue eyes got paler, her fine nostrils distended and somehow her ears went back, like those of a wolf. Since I could do this too, it did not frighten me, but people who did not know us very well used to get worried when they saw it.

"What have you done to your shorts, you awful boy?" she cried, "You can never be careful about anything."

I had learned the lesson that it is never worth explaining anything, so I just muttered I was sorry, and went to my room. I presume Uncle Max finished telling the ladies what we had been doing, and also explained about my shorts, the staining of which, and the cause, he had witnessed. Anyway, Mother sort of apologised later, and the stain came out, so all was well. It had been a memorable day.

Life rolled on uneventfully, until one day Uncle Max said to me: "Well, I have been talking with your Aunt and your Mother, and we think that it is time I took you to meet the King. He is younger than you, but he is lonely and I think you could be friends and play well together. So I must tell you how to behave and what to do, then we will go there."

Iza Norska

Mother as film star
Iza Norska

My loving mother
with me

My father,
Henryk Kronman, and I

On sledge in Lodz

My school cap
of which I was so proud

Dr Max Makowski,
my uncle

Aunt Ina
dressed for a party

Mother in her Indian
Red Cross Officer uniform

Aunt Ina
in wartime Baghdad

King Faisal II of Iraq,
1943

CHAPTER THREE

The King
and other people

There were two principal Royal palaces in Baghdad: the *Qasr al Zuhur*, or Palace of Flowers, where the young King lived, with his Nanny and staff, as well as the Queen Mother, and the *Qasr Abyiadh*, or White Palace, where the Queen's sisters and, sometimes, the Prince Regent, the King's uncle, lived.

His Majesty King Faisal II was six years old, three years younger than me, and, like me, had no father. He was the third Hashemite King of Iraq. His great-great-uncle, Abdullah, King of Transjordan, had been Uncle Max's first Royal patient, in the 1920s, and had been the King to give Uncle Max the handful of gems which helped in the marriage to Aunt. One of Abdullah's sons was given what was to become Jordan, and he became the grandfather of King Hussein; while the other was given Iraq, and became King Faisal I. When the latter died, his son, King Ghazi I, became King.

King Ghazi, young and handsome, married a kind and lovely lady, who became the mother of Faisal II. Unfortunately, King Ghazi, one of whose principal hobbies was the acquisition of fast sports cars (he had a marvellous collection), was killed in a high-speed motor accident, leaving an inconsolable young widow, and a baby. The running of the country was taken on by the Queen's younger brother, Crown Prince Abdulilah, who was to rule, as Regent, until his nephew was eighteen years old.

The great day came for my first visit to the King. Aunt and Mother were very nervous, and unceasingly instructed me to behave, to call the King 'Your Majesty', not to pick my nose or scratch, not to speak first but only to answer and so on. All Uncle Max said was: "Don't worry. He is a nice boy and you will have a good time."

At two in the afternoon I waited for the car, uncomfortable in my white bush shirt (very ironed), white shorts (heavily starched, and with a painfully sharp crease), white socks and highly polished sandals. Uncle Max's car arrived, and I got into the back, with Mother insisting on yet another combing of my hair, slicked down with some preparation or other.

Off we went, into town, across the bridge and south along a beautiful, flower-lined road, to the Palace. This could be seen from some distance: a large white building, with a few towers and minarets. The white was really dazzling and shone, like a pearl, on an island of greenery. As we got nearer, I could see a high wall encircling the gardens and Palace.

We drove up to ornate iron gates and stopped. A sentry with a rifle approached, and scowled ferociously, as he pointed the weapon at the driver, whom he recognised.

"How are you, Ahmed, you son of a goat?" he said, the scowl changing to a grin. "Where is Doctor Max? I wanted to ask him about a belly-ache I've got. And who is the small person you bring today? We've got one inside and don't need any more." Both he and the driver laughed loudly.

"This is the nephew of Dr Max coming to greet the King," said Ahmed. "It's all been fixed up."

"Fine. Go on in and welcome." The sentry looked at me. "Be nice to the King," he said. "He doesn't get many visitors, and those who come are not much fun."

The gates were opened, and we saw a large garden full of flowers surrounding a palace which looked even bigger close up. We drove up to a portico of huge columns flanking a wide staircase. Everything was a shining white and looked like marble. If this was the Palace of Flowers, how much whiter could the White Palace be! There was a broad strip of red carpet in the middle of the staircase.

As we drew up, an amazingly resplendent personage appeared at the top of the stairs. He looked down his nose at me as I hopped out of the car, and climbed the stairs, being careful not to step on the carpet. The personage stared at me in a haughty manner. He wore bright red puffy trousers, a dark blue jacket with gold piping and round his ample middle was stretched a wide band of gold cloth. On his head he had a dark blue hat with a white cloth wound around it. I noticed he had remarkably small feet.

"Are you of the House of Dr Max Pasha?" He stared at me unblinkingly and put his hands behind his back. "Are you come to pay humble greetings to His Majesty (may Allah protect him)?" His Arabic was formal and flowery and I understood only the gist of his questions.

"Yes, Your Highness," I answered, mindful of my instructions to be extra polite. At that moment, Ahmed drove away, leaving me marooned; I gave a gulp. "My uncle Dr Max Pasha has sent me to cheer up the King," I said.

"You may call me Sayyid Ali, not Your Highness," said the personage, relaxing slightly, and nodding his head in a haughty greeting. I bowed from the waist in reply. "I am the majordomo," the personage continued, "and I have come to show you the way, because of your Uncle, who is a great man."

We entered the grand doors of the Palace, and were in an immense hall, with a high ceiling decorated with gilt curlicues, a polished marble floor and brilliantly coloured Persian carpets. The walls were white marble, and had patterned hangings between the many open doors. There was an arcade of slim white pillars down the two sides of the hall, about ten feet from the walls. Through the open doors, I could see vast rooms, with more carpets and with polished furniture, not unlike Aunt's. There were also huge chandeliers hanging on long chains from the ceilings, with myriad cut-glass pieces winking and trembling in the slight draft.

I followed, as the Sayyid pattered across the hall and through one of the open doors at the far end. In this room we met three huge soldiers: two privates and a sergeant. Since I was of equal rank, I felt much more at ease and greeted the sergeant in a friendly way. He came over and looked down at me from his height of, probably, some six foot six. Like the others, he was dressed in a khaki uniform, very spick and span, and even his moustache, which formed a black bar projecting some way beyond his cheeks, was waxed and spiky.

"Peace be with you, Sergeant," I said in Arabic. "I also am a sergeant, appointed by the Ambassador during the Great Embassy Siege."

The big man grinned. "On you be peace, oh small sergeant," he said in a deep voice. "It is clear to me that you are a notable warrior and a leader of men." He winked. "Like me."

"Quiet, there," he suddenly roared at his two companions, who were trying to stifle their giggles. "Do you not see that this person is of great value, being not only an important member of the House of Dr Max, but also a military man in his own right; he will be a good friend of the King, (may Allah protect him), and they will spend good times together."

He suddenly noticed Sayyid Ali, who was standing nervously behind me. "Go, painted man," the Sergeant growled. "This small sergeant is now in my care." Sayyid Ali walked out, very fast, on his twinkly feet. I called "Thank you," after him, but I doubt that he heard me.

The Sergeant touched his hat. "I am Sergeant Abdullah," he said. "The King's life is my life and I am his servant and friend. Those two insignificant hangers-on try to help me but we don't need to bother about them. Their names are Hamad and Hameed. They are not important."

Hamad and Hameed, who looked very alike, nodded and smiled. All three were armed, with big revolvers at their waists, with cords from the butt running to a loop round the shoulder; a cartridge belt stuffed with bullets and a Thompson sub-machine gun. I recognised this from a war comic I had.

"But come, small sergeant," said Sergeant Abdullah. "I will take you to His Majesty, who is free to see you and has spoken to me of you."

I had to trot to keep up with the Sergeant's long strides as we went into the next room. This was another large *salon*, beautifully furnished, and standing by the window was a small boy in a white shirt and grey shorts. He was plump and not as tall as I, and had a flawless olive skin and large dark eyes. His black hair was thoroughly brushed and his clothes well pressed. Beside him was a tall, very thin elderly lady, in a dark blue dress, with a broad white belt which had a complicated metal buckle. She had a white cloth arrangement on her head, rather like a nurse I once saw. She was English, and the first to speak, in that language.

"You are Andrew," she said. This was a statement, rather than a question, and I was to find out that Miss Borland (for that was her name) did not understand about questions, but made only statements. She, of course, was the famous Nanny who had, alone, driven the King to safety during the uprising. Everyone in Baghdad (and perhaps the entire Middle East) called her Nanny and was afraid of her. "You will call me Nanny, and you will do as I tell you."

She turned to the boy at her side. "This is Andrew, Faisal. Andrew, this is His Majesty King Faisal II, but you may call him Faisal. Faisal, shake hands."

Faisal, who had his back to Nanny, pulled a funny long face at me and stuck his hand out. I shook it.

Nanny glared at Sergeant Abdullah, who stood by the door. "You may go," she said. The Sergeant winked at me and saluted, before turning on his heel and marching in an exaggerated sort of way out of the room. Nanny snorted.

"You two may go to play in the play-room for half an hour. After that we shall have tea. Remember to wash your hands before we have it."

Faisal headed for the door and I followed. We went down a short passage and ended up in a medium-sized room, with a bare floor and cupboards lining the walls. The doors of some of them were open and I could see more wonderful things than I had ever seen before. There were trains, cars, soldiers, building sets and every kind of game. There was a table and some chairs in a corner.

We played in a desultory sort of way with some toy cars, but mostly we talked. Faisal told me to call him 'Fizz' when no one was around; I could not think of anything special he could call me so I simply said: "Call me Andrew".

I told him about Poland, of which he had never heard, and of the Club, where I went swimming. He, in turn, told me that his life was the same every day, and very boring. He disliked his uncle, the Prince Regent, but loved his mother very much, and promised me that I would meet her. I did not explain my own mother's character to him, because I thought he was too young. But we agreed that Uncle Max was a splendid person, and also that we would have to be very careful what we said when Nanny was around. Fizz also said that Sergeant Abdullah was a fine soldier and a good friend of his.

"He is on my side," he said. He had this curious way of dividing people as being on his side or on the other side. His uncle, the Regent, was on the other side, while mine was on his side.

The difference in age was not much of a difficulty. Fizz had a natural dignity, a sort of distinction which gave him the demeanour of someone much older; I suppose it had been drummed into him at a very early age.

Then it was time for tea. Nanny appeared and made us wash our hands before returning to the playroom. The table had been covered in a white cloth, and as we sat down, two tall, black servants, dressed in white and with red sashes and hats, appeared with large silver trays bearing silver teapots and milk jugs and so on. There were plates of bread and butter and of very thinly cut cucumber and tomato sandwiches, with the crusts removed, as though we had no teeth. There was also a fairly plain cake, and delicate teacups with flowers on them. Not at all what I would have imagined a feast fit for a king and not serious food at all.

I sat quietly with my hands in my lap. Nanny turned her sharp blue eyes on me.

"Sit up straight and don't slouch, Andrew," she said. "You will never have a straight back if you loll about like that."

Fizz grinned, but Nanny saw him. I discovered later that she could see all round her head, like a lighthouse. I was certain that she could see through walls.

"Now, Faisal, behave," she instructed him. "You must set an example."

The meal proceeded. We had to have some bread and butter

before we were allowed to have a sandwich, and those had to be eaten before we were each rewarded with a slice of boring cake. In all, I was just as hungry when we were permitted to get down as I was when we first sat. Also, I had been cross-examined by Nanny who sniffed and snorted periodically when the strange and foreign behaviour of the Poles was described. I resisted telling her of Aunt's household. since I felt it would be a sort of betrayal. Nanny summed it all up at the end by stating that it all sounded very un-English.

Both Fizz and I thanked her for tea, and were told that we had another hour to play before the car arrived to take me home. Nanny disappeared and Fizz said urgently: "Come on. Don't make a noise."

We ran down another passage and into a room where Sergeant Abdullah and the two unimportant ones were having their tea. This was a proper tea: mounds of Arab bread and a large bowl of what looked like lamb stew. Much more substantial than silly little sandwiches.

The Sergeant rose to his feet, as did the two unimportant ones.

"Welcome to you, small King and small sergeant," he said. "Come and sit, and eat proper food for men and soldiers." He obviously knew the content of a Palace tea, and it was clear to me that Fizz came here whenever he could escape Nanny.

We sat on the floor in a circle and ate and ate. It was delicious. The three men looked fondly at Fizz, and I felt very special to be there with them all, as we chatted idly of this and that.

Suddenly we heard Nanny's voice in the distance. Fizz and I sprang to our feet and ran out of the room. By the time Nanny appeared we were strolling nonchalantly down the corridor; Fizz was trying to whistle.

"You have been with that Abdullah," stated Nanny. "How many times have I told you not to spend time with such ill-mannered. vulgar people. He is only your bodyguard, Faisal, so we must put up with him, I suppose, but that doesn't mean ..." Her voice trailed off as she noticed a lamb stew stain on Fizz's white shirt.

"Sayyid Ali," she called and, when the little man twinkled in said: "Take Master Andrew to the car. Faisal, shake hands and say goodbye."

I shook hands with Fizz, and politely thanked Nanny for a nice party. As I left, Fizz said: "Please come to visit me again." But Nanny had him by the arm and I could hear her say, as I followed Sayyid Ali to the big doors, "Now, Faisal, I see you have a stain on your shirt ..."

The journey home passed quickly. I had a lot to think about, but my main decision, which I communicated to Aunt and Mother when I was interrogated on my return, was that I was content to be me and had no wish to be a King. Another decision, which I did not communicate, was that I thought that Uncle Max and Entah were on my side; about Aunt and Mother I was not sure, except that often they seemed to be on the other side.

I visited Fizz about once a week during the holidays. Obviously, Nanny felt that I could be trusted with her charge and, while never really thawing out, she gradually unbent sufficiently to scold me every bit as much as Fizz. My friendship with Sergeant Abdullah deepened, and I began to appreciate his immense loyalty to, and love for his small King.

From time to time we were able to play outside, in the gardens. There were many paths and even a modest labyrinth. Our greatest pleasure was to drive two of several pedal cars which Fizz had, pedalling furiously along the paths and sometimes upsetting the cars on the sharper corners. As a *finale*, Fizz would get Sergeant Abdullah to push him fast along a straight bit. The sight of the huge Sergeant, bent double and red in the face, pushing Fizz along while Hamad and Hameed roared with laughter was unforgettable.

On one visit, Fizz took me to meet his mother. We walked for what seemed a long way into a part of the Palace which was unknown to me, and finally entered one of the most beautiful rooms I had ever seen. It was not very large, but everywhere there was silk: the chairs were covered with it, the curtains were made of it and even the Persian rugs on the floor and on the walls were silken. The colours were a pale blue and a sort of salmon pink. Not at all what I would like for my own room, but it seemed to fit the Queen Mother.

She was seated on one of the gilt chairs and with her were two ladies, both middle aged and dressed in what looked like great finery, with veils and feathers and lots of gold. Faisal's mother was a young woman and beautiful. She was slender and dressed modestly in a grey silk gown with a brocade shawl which covered her hair. Her oval face had the same flawless olive skin as her son, and she had huge dark eyes, which lit up when she saw Fizz.

"How lovely to see you, my son," she said in Arabic. "Do you bring your friend to see me?"

Fizz embraced her and said: "This is Andrew, my friend. He is of the House of Dr Max, who is his uncle."

I bowed deeply and the Queen laughed. "Welcome, oh Andrew, of the House of Dr Max our friend. I am pleased that you and my son have become good companions, as I have heard."

Nanny, who had accompanied us on the visit, said: "Andrew is quite reasonably polite and is not a bad example, so I have no objection to the boys being together, Your Majesty."

The Queen raised her eyebrows, and looked at me. "Hmm," she said. "If you can get such ringing approval from Nanny, you must truly be perfection."

I bowed deeply again. "Your Great Majesty, my uncle is a Pasha of the First Class and therefore I am worthy. But I am not perfect; nobody is, and besides, my mother and my aunt say that I am very far from it."

The Queen laughed. "Come here, oh nephew of the Pasha," she commanded. When I walked up to her, she hugged me warmly and said: "I am very pleased that you come to play with my son. Do not call me a Great Majesty; you are now our friend and you may call me *Umm Faisal*, or mother of Faisal, in our Arab way."

When I returned home that evening, and recounted my adventure, including my visit to *Umm Faisal*, as I called the Queen Mother in an off-hand sort of way, to Mother and Aunt, both were impressed. "You must have behaved well with such special and important people," said Aunt. "I am proud of you."

When I told Uncle Max the story later, he grinned and played his drum and said: " I thought you would get on with the Royal family. After all, they are just people."

Aunt was so pleased with my new relationship with Fizz that she decided to take me (and Mother) on a visit to the Three Princesses. These were sisters of the Queen and of the Prince Regent, and lived in the White Palace. They were all old friends of Aunt, who had for years performed the function of adviser on western manners, fashion and behaviour to all the Royal ladies. She had the official title of 'Lady-in-Waiting to the Princesses' and, as she told me on a number of occasions, had been invited to accompany the Royal Family to Cairo, when they were guests at the magnificent marriage of the Shah of Persia to the daughter of King Farouk of Egypt.

To hear Aunt tell it, the expedition was straight out of the Arabian Nights: perfumed rooms in the *harems* of the palaces, staffed by eunuchs, where the lady guests were lodged in great luxury; marvellous feasts, cooked by chefs imported from France and eaten off gold plates; jewels on display that could literally pay a king's ransom. Also more scandalous stories of, for example, King Farouk spying, through a hidden hole in the wall, on the assembled Royal ladies of the Middle East, who were, of course, in strict seclusion, and not to be looked at by any man. Aunt said he was a very unpleasant man and his whole court was full of horrible people.

Since the Royal Court of Egypt prided itself on its great sophistication and aped the manners of the French aristocracy, she had had to 'dress' the ladies and also explain to them the etiquette of formal dining, protocol and social graces. But she had a good time, and had all sorts of engraved, gilded menus, photographs and some splendid dresses and jewels (which were gifts to her from the Princesses as thanks for her help) as mementoes of her visit.

On the day, Mother and Aunt dressed carefully in some of their best finery, made sure I was encased in my formal outfit with hair slicked foully down, and embarked in the shining green Chrysler, driven on this special occasion by Ahmed, our driver. We drove across the bridge, following the road I usually went on when visiting Fizz, but turned off it half-way into a drive which was bounded by multicoloured flowerbeds. There was the White Palace, shining in the early afternoon sun, with palm trees and shrubs all around.

I was excited at the thought of meeting the Three Princesses. One of the fairy stories which Michasia had told me long ago in Poland was called 'The Three Princesses'. These were the wonderfully beautiful daughters of a King, who demanded impossible tasks from their suitors. But three brother Princes, together, and with the help of a cat, a dog and a raven did manage to fulfil the King's expectations and married the Princesses.

The entrance to the White Palace was not unlike the one in the Palace where Fizz lived and I noted that Aunt and Mother walked on the red carpet, not beside it as I always did. There was a tall, black servant, dressed all in white, to greet us and show us into an ornately decorated and furnished salon, easily as big as the swimming pool at the Club. At the far end, in a cluster of spindly-legged gilt chairs and sofas, were the Three Princesses, Bediyah, Abdiyah and Jelila, in order of age, height and beauty. None was as beautiful as *Umm Faisal* (I gloated over my authorisation to use the phrase, like a decoration) but they were pleasant, somewhat short and dressed rather plainly, given the setting. I was very disappointed.

They rose to greet us, embraced Aunt warmly, shook hands with Mother and advanced meaningfully on me. I hurriedly took some steps back and bowed deeply from the waist, thereby avoiding what I thought would be a protracted bout of patting, pinching and general man-handling.

But still, the three princesses were fascinating. As they chatted with Aunt and Mother, I had the opportunity to observe them as I sat quietly in a corner and tried not to attract attention. They always seemed to do the same thing, one after the other, in order of age. If Bediyah nodded and smiled, so did Abdiyah and Jelila, one after the other. If Bediyah said: "How interesting," then, after a short pause, Abdiyah echoed her, and after a further pause, so did Jelila. This meant that the only princess who ever said or did anything original was the eldest, Bediyah. Before very long, I was convinced that they had been enchanted.

Soon after we arrived, refreshments were brought in, on silver trays and with silver jugs. There was no bread and butter or sandwiches. Instead, there were heaped dishes of sweets, glutinous little cakes dripping with honey and difficult to eat, Turkish delight and various sorts of nuts and dried fruits. To drink there was a choice of sticky, warm pink lemonade or purple pomegranate juice. I chose the latter and was delighted by the strong, slightly astringent taste. I would happily have gone on eating almost indefinitely, but I saw that both Aunt and Mother were eyeing me rather coldly, so I stopped.

At that moment, a slight, very elegant gentleman wearing a beautiful pearl-gray suit came in. His hair, which was black, shone with the same lustre as his highly polished shoes, thus framing him neatly top and bottom. His eyes were also a sparkling black, though rather small, but his diminutive moustache was so perfectly proportioned and aligned, that every hair seemed to have had to pass some difficult test to be admitted to his upper lip.

Aunt and Mother sprang to their feet as the man came forward, smiling like a wolf with large, white teeth.

"Welcome, Madame Ina," he said to Aunt. "How very agreeable to see you. And this must be your charming and brave sister, about whom we have heard so much," he turned to Mother who was utterly entranced by this elegant person.

Aunt curtsied, and Mother followed suit. I lurked. The Princesses giggled.

"How kind of you, Your Highness," Aunt said. "May I present my sister Isabel, who has escaped from Poland and somehow managed to make her way here. Isa, this is His Royal Highness Prince Abdulilah, the Regent." Mother curtsied again and shook hands.

So this is Fizz's uncle, whom he does not much like, I thought. Well, he seems to be a bit slimy. Besides, I don't like his moustache.

Aunt suddenly remembered and turned towards me. "Andrew, come here. Your Highness, this is my nephew Andrew, who has also come from Poland."

"Yes, I have heard about him from Faisal and my sister," said the Regent. "Faisal has told me he enjoys your company," he went on, coming towards me with his hand extended.

I had no alternative but to shake his hand, although mine was liberally coated with honey from the cakes. He frowned and wiped his hand on a handkerchief. Aunt and Mother glared at me.

After some further desultory talking, we took our leave and I was made to go to a bathroom and thoroughly wash my face and hands before getting into the car. On the way home I was berated by both Aunt and Mother about how I had disgraced them, how I was badly behaved and how ashamed and embarrassed they had been. I tried to say that I had had no choice, but my small protest was drowned in the tidal wave of recrimination.

When I told Uncle Max about it that evening, he chuckled and chortled and beat his drum. I had the feeling that he, also, was not too fond of the Prince Regent, who was certainly on the other side.

The other part of my life went on much as before. The talking with my friends during the daily swims in the pool at the Club enabled me to improve my English, and my Arabic got better at school and in my conversations with the servants. With Aunt and Mother I still spoke Polish, though I was also trying to pick up a little French, from what I overheard of conversations at parties. With Uncle Max I continued to communicate in our special language mix.

A small thing I enjoyed was Aunt's and Hussein the butler's daily skirmish in the storeroom. This was a fair-sized room half way up the stairs, where Aunt kept her bulk stores of dry goods, and doled out rations according to each day's needs. After the decision on the daily menu, and on how many people would be at table, Aunt and Hussein (sometimes supported by Ali, the cook) would bargain and haggle on the amounts of supplies necessary. It was Hussein's aim to get as much as he could, for us as well as the staff, while Aunt was convinced that gross waste and misappropriation was taking place, and fought to keep the quantities to a minimum.

The room was stuffed full of sacks of rice, pistachio nuts, lentils, beans and other dried goods; there were large boxes of dried apricots, raisins, flour and salt; four-gallon tins of *ghee* (a smelly clarified butter) and olive oil; large cones of sugar, which had to be broken up with a small decorated axe; and smaller bags of coffee as well as many spices, peppers, and herbs. The mixture of smells was indescribable, and marvellous, and I sometimes could get away with taking, unseen, a large handful of pistachios or raisins, while the arguments washed back and forth over my head. When the battle ended with the inevitable compromise, Hussein and Entah would carry off the loot while Aunt double padlocked the door with a key which, I believe, never left her person.

On my tenth birthday I awoke to be told, by Entah, that there was something special for me downstairs. I rushed down to find I had been given, as a joint present from everybody, a beautiful crimson bicycle, with a pump, brakes, a small saddle-bag and a loud bell. I was delighted and immediately instructed Entah to teach me how to manage the machine. Of course, I thanked everyone profusely and tried hard, for some time, to cause no trouble and to be helpful.

It took me three weeks of intensive effort (and Entah's) to become proficient enough to wobble my way to the Club, to the envy and astonishment of my friends, whose parents did not permit them to ride around the streets. I took this for granted and no one seemed to notice, or worry over the fact that buses, cars, horse-drawn carriages, donkeys and pedestrians followed few rules of the road. I became nimble at avoiding collisions and even could pedal fast enough to get away from the bad-tempered dogs which abounded.

My bicycle gave me a new freedom, and I sometimes cycled out beyond the end of the road, past the Club and into the cultivated areas beside the river. Here were mud-walled gardens, criss-crossed by canals full of turgid, chocolate-coloured water. The gardens were full of date palms, orange and pomegranate trees, and the occasional mulberry. Growing on the ground there were melons, cucumbers, okra and many strange leaf vegetables. I got to know several of the farmers, and would sit with them on the mud bank of the Tigris, chatting and eating melons, cucumbers and pomegranates, as well as pumpkin seeds, spitting the husks into the muddy water and watching the fishermen and the boats. The river was about three hundred yards wide, but we could see, on the other side, the occasional passage of a tram, drawn by two horses and hugely overcrowded, with people on the roof and clinging to the sides. The farmers always laughed and pointed when the tram wobbled slowly by.

On one occasion, I got permission to go, for two days and a camp overnight, on a major excursion with Bendy and Barry, whose father invited me to accompany them on a visit to Babylon.

Early in the morning on the appointed day, equipped with two blankets, a thermos of lemonade and a pillow, according to instructions, I stood by the door awaiting the arrival of my friends. Punctually at six o'clock there was a shrill squeal from a horn and I went outside to see a decrepit van-like conveyance, dented and dusty, with a canvas back. In the front, I could see Bendy and a bright ginger-haired head. I walked up to the van and a small, chubby person bounced out, thrust out his hand and said: "Good morning to you, good morning to you; I am the father, but you must call me Ginger. Everybody does. You are Andrew. Put the things in the back and hop in. Barry is there. Off we go, off we go ..."

Before I could utter a word, he was back in the van and revving the engine. I climbed into the back, over canvas bags, jerry-cans, tins and packages and discovered Barry perched on one side. I sat down on the other as the van accelerated up the road in a cloud of dust.

Barry grinned and held out his hand, which I shook.

"You'll get used to him," he said loudly, "He is completely harmless and Bendy and I look after him to make sure he doesn't get into trouble. He only has two things he cares about: one is his engineering and one is the ancient history of Iraq, and he is pretty good at both. This thing ..." he gestured with his arm, "is not much to look at, but it will run forever and has never let us down. Its name is 'The Explorer' and he looks after it like a baby."

In the front, Mr Ginger (I could never bring myself to call him just plain Ginger, so I compromised by adding the Mr) was talking away, partly to Bendy and partly to himself. I could hear the occasional strange word like 'Ziggurat' and 'Nebuchad-something' and 'Babel'.

"Father is an engineer at the cotton factory in West Baghdad," explained Barry. "He spends every day working there and every night reading about ancient history. He drives The Explorer all over the country and comes home with bits of mud and stone."

We drove on and on, stopping after about an hour to stretch our legs and for a rest from the bouncing.

I took the opportunity to thank Mr Ginger for inviting me, but he hardly let me finish before starting another flood of talk, punctuated by his habit of running his fingers through his blazing mop of ginger hair, which stood on end all round his head like a halo.

"Delighted, my boy, delighted," he burbled. "Always a pleasure to take the lads out and any friend is welcome." He rubbed his hair with both hands. "You will find Babylon and the other ruins very exciting. You have to think of them as alive, with people there doing things like they used to, not just as broken-down bits of mud and brick."

We got back into the Explorer, and set off again. I noticed that Mr Ginger had another odd habit: before getting into the Explorer he always bowed slightly to it. I believe he treated it as a living thing and wished to show respect so that it would not let him down. I found myself doing the same.

We turned off the main road and bumped along a bad piece of track for some miles. It was mid-afternoon and I despaired of getting any lunch; it seemed that Mr Ginger and the boys paid lamentably little attention to food. But after an hour or so we stopped and Mr Ginger switched off the Explorer's panting engine. There was a great stillness in the bright sunshine and the browns and yellows of the desert, with some spindly trees and bits of scrub, shimmered in the heat. In the middle distance, some hundreds of yards away, there were brown ruins of walls stretching over a large area and a high mound of what looked like rubble. Further off was an even higher hill with a sort of ruined tower on top.

"There it is," exclaimed Mr Ginger happily, stretching his arms wide. "Great Babylon, wonderful Babylon and all the other bits." He gave a little pirouette. "But we must control ourselves; yes, indeed, we must. No rushing off and running about. Hungry. Thirsty. Eating. That's what we do now."

From the back of the Explorer, he produced a veritable feast of cold chicken and cucumbers and tomatoes (all in an icebox and deliciously chilled) with fresh Arab bread and lemonade. We sat in the sand beside the Explorer and ate. Mr Ginger opened up the Explorer's hood, muttering that the poor old thing deserved a breather.

"After lunch, we will have a look at Babylon proper, then tomorrow, before starting for home, rove about a bit and look at other things," said Mr Ginger. "But before looking, you have to be in the right frame of mind." He stood up and waved his arms around.

"You are now standing in the middle of the most important part of the ancient world," he said. "All over Iraq there are the sites of famous old places where civilisation began: Ur, Uruk, Nineveh, Ctesiphon and many others; but I think the best is Babylon, right here."

He marched about in an excited way. "There is very little sand and it all looks different." His sons and I looked at each other in a worried way. "No, I mean when Babylon was built, almost four thousand years ago," he paused. "It is one of the newer places, you see," he said apologetically. "Not really old like, say, Jarmo or Tell Uqair ..."

He pointed at the ruins. "The river has moved off now, the Euphrates I mean, which runs about two miles away. It was up to the walls then. And everything was green and there were lions and ostriches and many animals that have disappeared."

"Imagine riding up on your beautiful horse, with ornaments jingling. You have been riding for days, and at last you see an immense city, with high towers and walls, rising before you. On the river side, you see what looks like an enormous hanging forest ..." Mr Ginger was quite carried away with his description and stopped, so his sons and I picked up the lunch things and packed them away in the Explorer. We all got in and drove to the ruins.

Close up, the ruins were impressive: the walls were high and broad, the bricks, of which everything was made, were even and uniform and cemented with asphalt. We stood at the entrance to a broad avenue, paved with blocks of stone and pink marble. Here and there, in the walls, were the remains of blue enamelled lions and inscriptions.

Mr Ginger stopped. "Many of these walls are eighty feet thick," he said. "And the tops of the wall-towers were built so that a four-horse chariot could turn around on them." He didn't explain how they would have got up there.

"There were many famous Babylonians and Assyrians," said Mr Ginger. "*The Assyrian came down like the wolf on the fold...*" he paused, and then both he and his sons chanted together, with Mr Ginger conducting: "*and his cohorts were gleaming in purple and gold.*" Obviously not the first time the family had been regaled with the quotation. "*... And the sheen of their spears was like stars on the sea, when the blue wave rolls nightly on deep Galilee.*" Mr Ginger winked at me. "Lord Byron," he remarked. "I expect you have heard of him."

I did not admit that I did not know what he was talking about.

Mr Ginger continued, as we paced down the ruined avenue: "This is the main ceremonial road, and had to be built for wonderful religious processions of Marduk, and to allow forty armed men to march down it side by side. It leads to the Gate of the Goddess Ishtar and the Palace of Nebuchadnezzar. Also the banqueting hall of Belshazzar," he stood on tiptoe and spread out his arms like a huge bird, "*mene mene tekel upharsin!*" he declared. It sounded like gibberish. "And Hammurabi first codified law here. And over there is the ziggurat of Marduk (a pretty nasty god), and tomorrow we will go to the Tower of Babel and there is also ..."

I had stopped listening, since I could not follow Mr Ginger's enthusiastic commentary. I retreated instead into my imagination and there, sure enough, found the purple and gold chariots and uniforms, the braided beards and flashing spears, the short bows and temple incense and statues of lions and beasts unknown.

Later that night, as we sat round a little fire, under a clear sky bright with stars, drinking hot, sweet tea and eating big sandwiches, Mr Ginger told us stories about the place. He told us about the Greek theatre beside the rivercourse, and the capture of the town by Alexander the Great and the small hill where Alexander made a funeral pyre for the body of his great friend Hephaestus. He also told us that the tomb of the Prophet Ezekiel was nearby, near a Jewish village. "You see," he said, "everything meets here."

As we went to sleep in an untidy heap in the back of the Explorer, the vivid spirit of the place was bright in my mind.

The following morning we woke early and washed superficially in water out of a four gallon tin. Then, after some bread and cheese for breakfast, we explored the ziggurat (a large tower) and the Tower of Babel (an even larger tower, more of a hill). Mr Ginger explained that Babel was not built to reach heaven, as legends said, but was only a temple to the seven spheres of heaven and the sun god. The little extra tower on the very top had its bricks fused together by unimaginable heat and he said it must have been a huge lightning bolt. I preferred to think of it as the anger of a powerful god, disturbed by the activities of ant-like creatures daring to build large towers.

The last thing I remember about Babylon was the huge, now barren slope of earth leading up some two hundred feet to the southern, river wall. Mr Ginger, said that these were the ruins of the famous Hanging Gardens, one of the Seven Wonders of the World. He said that the Medean wife of one of the Kings was homesick for green hills and trees in the flat Babylonian plain, so her husband the King had vast quantities of river soil carried up by slaves to form enormous terraces beside the river wall. There he had planted large trees, flowers and bushes, so the Queen could stroll about with her ladies and not be homesick any more.

As we were walking back to the Explorer, we were suddenly accosted by a tall, ragged Arab with a rifle. This was something of a shock, since we had seen nobody during our entire time at Babylon, and the nearest human habitation had been a distant village on the bank of the Euphrates.

"Peace be upon you, oh Suleiman," said Mr Ginger with a grin, running his fingers through his mop of hair. "You smell like a goat," he added as the Arab walked up to shake his hand.

"And on you be peace, Father of these two young camels," said Suleiman. "*Shlawnak?* What is your colour this day?"

This was a common, exclusively Iraqi greeting, approximating "How are you?" Suleiman went on: "I know; *Ahmar, ya 'hmar.*" (A complicated Arab pun, meaning 'red, you donkey' – red signifying well), as he pointed at Mr Ginger's flaming hair.

Both men doubled up with laughter, slapping their thighs and hopping about. Bendy, Barry and I looked at each other and sighed.

"Now, oh rich and handsome one," said Suleiman when he could talk, "You will pay me half a dinar for looking at the treasures I guard, or I will shoot you and the young ones immediately with my rifle."

Mr Ginger handed over two half-dinar notes, one official and one 'for friendship', and we went on to the Explorer, accompanied by Suleiman, who chatted amiably with Mr Ginger and said he hoped to see him soon again and that he was sorry that unavoidable business interests had caused him to be absent on our arrival.

We bade him farewell, and after a small bow to the Explorer, started back for Baghdad, all three score miles and ten from Babylon.

We got home, tired, dirty and sweaty, in the late afternoon. I politely asked Mr Ginger and my friends to come into the house for refreshments, but Mr Ginger said that he ought really to be returning to his wife; this was the first time the boys' mother had been mentioned, but then, I did not talk about my mother either.

As the Explorer's engine clamoured, I bowed deeply to it and thanked Mr Ginger for the trip. He winked and said: "Not at all, not at all. It was a pleasure. You must come again. I am glad you like the Explorer." And with a roar and a cloud of dust, he was off. I could see Barry waving to me through the murk.

After a thorough wash, I told Aunt and Mother that I had enjoyed the trip and that I had learned a lot about Babylon.

"How nice," said Mother, "are you sure you have washed properly?"

Aunt was content to say that she was glad I had a good time. She said she did not know Mr Ginger or his wife, but had heard they were all right.

Uncle Max was pleased I had been to Babylon. "They were very clever people," he said. "Their medical skills were quite advanced and they could do trepanning (making holes in the skull to relieve pressure, you know) and also quite complicated surgery after battles too. If a doctor was successful, he would be rewarded, but if he made a mistake, they cut off his hand. It was hard being a doctor then ..." he played his drum for a bit, then added: "There is a lot to learn and a lot to know. Never turn down a chance to listen to people; you sometimes get good knowledge from unexpected places." I thought this was a fair summary of my excursion.

The only other expedition specially to see old places was a day trip to Ctesiphon, with Mother, Aunt and the Swedish attaché. This was different from Mr Ginger and the Explorer. We went in great comfort in Aunt's green Chrysler, so softly sprung that it made one feel sick. Ali, the cook, had prepared a splendid basket of delicacies for lunch, small things to nibble at (not proper food at all), and cold wine on ice. There was some orange juice for me.

When we arrived, and the huge umbrella had been raised, and cushions placed to sit on, we had our lunch. Both Mother and Aunt were dressed in floating flowery things and had large straw hats. The Swede wore a white suit and tie, and a straw hat as well, though his had only a narrow brim. I was made to wear my formal outfit of white shorts and bush-shirt. I could not see why we were all dressed up, since it made us hot and there was no one to see us, except some ragged Bedouin boys.

No one could tell me anything about Ctesiphon, or answer any of my questions. The ruin was a towering, soaring arch of mud and brick, about a hundred feet high; inside was a great emptiness. Attached to one flank was a three story façade of a building, made of bricks, which looked like the side of a house. It was a most impressive ruin, standing solitary in a flat desert plain. Apparently, as Bendy told me when I asked the following day, some people called Parthians had lived there. They were people, he said, who were expert bowmen on horseback, and would pretend to run away, then suddenly turn and fire a shower of arrows at you when you no longer expected it.

After lunch, Mother, Aunt and the Swede walked round the ruin, discussing the previous night's party at the British Embassy. They walked slowly, since the ground was covered in rubble and the ladies hobbled along in high-heeled sandals. I explored on my own, exchanging friendly insults with the Bedouin boys who had attached themselves to me, after finding that the adults would not give them any *bakhsheesh*, or handouts. It was clear that I had none to give.

We were home by teatime and, while glad to have seen the famous Arch, I regretted that I had not visited it with Mr Ginger and my friends, in the Explorer.

Among the luminaries invited by Aunt to her Tuesday luncheons were personalities of many nationalities and from many walks of life, who were passing through Baghdad. Normally, I had nothing to do with either the entertainment or the visitors. But there were one or two exceptions.

I happened to be in the house one Tuesday, making my way through the hall on the way to my room, when a very tall, thin person suddenly accosted me.

"I wonder if you would be kind enough to direct me to a place for washing the hands," he said in beautiful Arabic. I was astonished, since the person looked like a European.

"Certainly, welcome guest," I replied. "Through that door and turn right."

"My thanks to you, young fellow," said the person, but in Polish.

"You are welcome," I replied in the same language.

"Are you the son of the house?" enquired the person, in English.

"I am the nephew of Aunt Ina and Uncle Max," I rejoined, in the same language.

The person raised his eyebrows so high that they nearly vanished. He put his hand on my shoulder and said: "Come over here and sit down."

He then put out his hand to shake, and introduced himself: "I am Dr Mish, lately Professor of Languages at the University of Krakow and now sunk to the level of a Colonel in the Polish Army." He sighed. I noticed that he started his sentence quite loudly and then got quieter and quieter until at the end he was difficult to hear.

I introduced myself and said how interesting to meet a person from Poland who could speak Arabic.

He smiled. His almost bald head was very large, and appeared to be balanced somewhat precariously on narrow shoulders; in fact, he seemed to go down in a straight line from shoulders to feet. He was gaunt to the point of emaciation, though he looked strong. He had large, white hands and a pronounced twinkle in his eye. He was not in uniform, but wore a shapeless gray suit, which hung on him as on a scarecrow. This drab outfit was enlivened only by a bright blue bow tie.

"Actually," he said diffidently, "I know about twenty seven languages. It was my job, you see. That means all the European ones, and some dialects of Chinese and Indian, and bits of ancient Greek and Latin ..."

His habit of getting quieter and quieter was very pronounced and later I was amused to see him as the centre of a group of interested ladies, which pulsed inwards and outwards, like a well dressed sea anemone, as they tried to catch the last few words of each sentence.

I was extremely impressed and said so. I also told Dr Mish that I liked languages and was fascinated by them and wanted to learn many.

He nodded and said: "We must have a meeting and talk about this. I am most pleased to find someone of my own kind in this wilderness." I was immensely flattered.

He rose, and after nodding, went off to wash his hands and rejoin the party in the *salon*. I made my way upstairs, marvelling that someone could speak, and speak well, so many languages.

Within a week, he had arranged the promised meeting, the first of many.

Aunt and Mother were astonished when Dr Mish told them that he wished to talk to me. He came for morning coffee and I was permitted to sit with him in the *salon*, after many strictures and threats about behaviour.

It was remarkable. Dr Mish opened to me a whole world of speech and language and I began to have an inkling of what communication was about. Certainly, it was he who fired me with enthusiasm for language and languages.

He was a strange man, in many ways. His *diminuendo* in every sentence became unimportant, since what he had to say was always fascinating. His other main habit was uttering deep philosophical aphorisms which, on reflection, were not quite what they seemed. I could never decide whether he was being serious or facetious, though the sly sideways glance with which he punctuated his sayings perhaps gave a clue.

He would look down at me and say, for example: "Before you know what is different, you must know what is the same," or perhaps "to live a full life you must always leap before you look." Then the sideways glance.

The one thing he would never joke about was language.

This was as sacred to him as it became to me. He said that language was the telephone of the mind, and the more languages you knew, the more numbers you could call. He also said that it was courteous to address people, whenever possible, in their own language.

"Precision is most important," he declared. "Even people speaking the same language have to translate each other's words." He stood up and paced about. "How can you ever be sure that what is in your mind is exactly received by the mind of your listener."

"Listen," he would say, and then quote something in Mandarin, or Urdu or Hebrew. "I am speaking sense and you are hearing nonsense. And this often happens even when I am speaking a language you know. People hear what they want to hear, not what is said. A lot of trouble in the world could be avoided if people learned to speak and listen properly."

During our talks, I felt that he treated me as an equal and I never sensed that he was talking down to me. He was enthusiastic in his belief that communication between people, especially people of different language groups, was the most important aspect of living, and he also introduced me to the fascinating pursuit of word origins and meanings down the centuries.

I was sorry when, some two months after our first meeting, he left Baghdad for the Western Desert. But I was glad that, before leaving, he had the opportunity of meeting Uncle Max, whom I persuaded to come home one morning to meet my friend. As I fully expected, each was fascinated by the other, and there was no difficulty at all in the three of us, over cups of coffee, speaking and fully understanding the curious *argot* used by Uncle Max. I did not know of anyone else who could so perfectly communicate with my Uncle.

One Thursday afternoon, while the weekly quintet was enjoying the elegant tea provided during a break in the music, I was called into the *salon*. I was not particularly tidy or neat, but thought that, since I had been given no notice, nobody could blame me for this.

"Come here, my darlink," said Mother. "Come to me." Her English was improving almost as fast as mine, but I noticed that she was careful to preserve a Polish accent, which, she had been assured by numbers of bedazzled English gentlemen, was "perfectly charming and delightful".

I may say that Aunt, after more than fifteen years in Baghdad, and moving in mainly English-speaking circles, also had a "perfectly charming" accent. People avoided speaking of Uncle Max's special inflection.

Mother clasped me to her bosom and said to the cello, the piano and the viola: "Here is my little son. He is ferry musical and clever. I know. I feel it here," she placed her hand over where she imagined her heart to be. "He is now old enough to learn piano, do you not think so, Professor Hertz?"

I recoiled in horror. My friend Henry, at the Club, had told me that he had been forced to learn the piano from some Indian teacher, who made him practise the most boring things for at least an hour a day, and beat him on the head with a ruler if he made mistakes during his weekly lesson.

Jens, the Swedish attaché, tapped his viola and smirked. The Mayor, who played the cello, and seemed a nice man, asked: "But does he want to learn? One must be interested in order to learn."

Before I could seize on this, Mother and Aunt fixed me in a cross-fire of blue stares and Mother said: "I am sure that Jedrek longs to learn. Our whole family have music in the soul. He is MY SON," she added in capitals.

I could see that the battle was lost. Professor Hertz, sandwich in hand at the piano, said: "I happen for one more learner to have time and I to have Andrew as my pupil would be pleased." He turned to me, "We shall next week begin, little man."

I was speechless. Little man?! Why, he could not even speak properly; how could we communicate? I was trapped.

In the event, it was not as bad as I had feared. The Professor, who was an Austrian and Jewish, turned out to be a kind man. He spoke only German and English, the latter using the sentence structure of the former; thus all his verbs tended to be piled up in a heap at the end of his sentences. He was of average height, about sixty years old, and his two interests were the piano (which pre-war he had taught in Salzburg) and an inordinate appetite for cakes. This was shared by Frau Hertz, and, cake fed, they were both rosy, roly-poly people. She refused to have servants, and did all the housework as well as all the cooking; probably a unique arrangement among foreigners in Baghdad.

They lived in a little house not far from us, and within easy cycling distance. On the Saturday of my first lesson, dressed in white shorts and shirt, I presented myself at the Hertzhaus (as it was known) promptly on time.

The door was opened by Frau Hertz, rosy-cheeked and in a floury apron. "Ach, you must Andrew from Madame Ina be," she said, beaming. "Please to come in; the Professor for you is ready."

I went in and was shown to a small room, the greater part of which was occupied by a huge grand piano. There was a small chair and table beside the piano stool and nothing else. The Professor bustled in.

"On time, on time," he said loudly. "That is very good, *ja*." He sat down at the piano, and motioned me to the small chair.

"First, how to sit properly beside the piano we learn," he sat up straight and placed his hands ceremoniously on the keyboard. "Notice the back straight, always straight has to be and the front part of arms with the floor even to be held." I must have looked puzzled because he said: "Parallel, you say, *nichts*?"

He bounded up. "Now you do," he said. I sat on the piano stool, and held my arms level and my back straight. "Nein, nein," said the Professor. "You have to sit *mit* the right foot on the pedal and the left foot back."

"Excuse me, Professor," I said. "Why one foot back?"

"*Natürlich*, because if they vegetables and fruit at you when you play bad throw, then you can easily jump and away run," the Professor laughed loudly.

I also laughed loudly and after that we got on well together. Toward the end of the lesson, the Professor called out: "Anna, Anna, now the cake for my young friend bring."

Frau Hertz came puffing in with a tray. There were cups of sweet, hot chocolate to drink, and a splendid coffee cake, in layers, with lots of luscious, thick cream. With the encouragement of my mentor and the cook, I gorged myself. Frau Hertz was delighted: "How vonderful a young man to eat good it is to see. Now you know how a good cake cooking is." She turned to the Professor, who was also manfully demolishing a large second helping. "Aha, *liebling*, now competition you have."

The Professor also had a somewhat unusual teaching method, far removed from beating his pupils on the head with a ruler. When I had to play scales, he would balance a sweet on the back of each hand. If the sweet was still there after a scale, I could eat it; if it fell off, the Professor ate it.

This first lesson set the pattern for all my future ones and I looked forward to them. While my playing progressed only slowly, my appreciation for outstanding pastry cooking became expert. My initial fear of being unable to communicate with the Professor and his Frau was wholly unfounded, as was my dread of the lessons.

This summer of 1942 was an exceptionally hot one, with the thermometer registering a high 127° F. in the shade. We also had two bad dust-storms, when for a period of some hours visibility was limited to no more than five yards, and when the storm was over, everything had a thick and gritty coating of red sand, which got in everywhere.

My life was now a busy one. I continued to visit Fizz, go to swim at the Club, sit with my farmer friends on the banks of the Tigris, and learn the piano while stuffing myself with cakes. An additional bonus was a mysterious fire which wholly destroyed the school. It was not rebuilt until well after Christmas.

It was towards the end of summer that Mother became an officer. For some time, she had been helping Aunt and other society ladies in their twice weekly visits to the Indian Red Cross convalescent home for troops, mainly from the Indian sub-continent, who had been wounded in the Western Desert campaign, and were being repatriated, mainly by train through Baghdad. I heard that Tobruk had fallen and Cairo was about to be invaded.

Each lady would get her cook to bake cakes and biscuits, which she would then take to the convalescent home or a hospital train at the station, there to hand smilingly round, with cups of tea and packets of cigarettes, to the helplessly polite soldiers.

I was sometimes permitted to accompany the ladies and to assist. The soldiers were a great and exciting mixture: there were huge Sikhs, with enormous turbans and beards, who never cut their hair; slender, quick Punjabis, always smiling and looking fierce; small, wiry Gurkhas, with their amazing *kukris*, curved, razor-sharp knives with which they were deadly. Everyone was scared of them. I used to sit and talk with all these (in English) and they would tell me stories of battles and combat, especially in the desert.

The Indian Red Cross organisation in Baghdad was under the command of a grizzled English Brigadier, who had a soft spot for Aunt, and gradually an even softer spot for Mother, both of whom were dazzlingly beautiful, had a 'delightful, charming accent' and possessed one of the best, if not **the** best table in town. Mother, who was anxious to earn a little money and not be wholly dependent on Uncle Max's charity, had little difficulty in persuading the good Brigadier that he should commission her in the Red Cross as a full-time officer, responsible for 'Comforts for the Troops'.

So Mother (she was the only female European officer in the Baghdad organization), promptly designed and had made a stunning white uniform, with a pert white hat, which accentuated her natural gifts and caused heads to turn. She received a modest stipend, which was sufficient to enable her to buy some small necessaries.

She would stride about, chest out and chin high, smiling to left and right. She even evolved a specially feminine salute, more graceful than smart, but invariably well received by the Brigadier and any visiting colonel or general. In fact, I had the feeling that many of them would give quite a lot to have Mother on their staff. The troops were also self-consciously gratified when Mother was around.

On the occasions when I accompanied Mother to the officers' convalescent home (and here there were also English and Polish officers recovering from various diseases and wounds), I was much amused when men with legs in plaster tried to leap to their feet or those with arms in a sling tried to carry trays, all to help the beautiful blonde lieutenant in the white uniform.

Winter and Christmas came and went, and in the spring Fizz announced that he was going for two weeks to Rawanduz, in North Iraq, and wanted me to go along. Sergeant Abdullah encouraged him to insist, and even Nanny stated that I should come if I wished and Mother gave permission.

After discussions at home, it was agreed that I should go. Naturally, I was given a series of stern lectures on behaviour by both Aunt and Mother, and our Indian tailor rushed to make me additional khaki shorts and shirts for the trip which was for men only, so, as Fizz put it, we did not have to have any stupid frills and things. I was astonished that Nanny was willing to let him out of her sight, but then, I was sure she could see what we were doing even from some 600 miles away.

On the day agreed, the convoy drove north. It consisted of an armoured car in the lead, followed by some lorries full of soldiers. Then came the car in which Fizz and I travelled, as well as Sergeant Abdullah (who sat in the front seat). We were followed by two or three more cars, the first with the unimportant ones (Hamad and Hameed), then another lorry with soldiers.

"The servants and the cooks and the food have gone on ahead," said Fizz when I asked him what we would eat. "So have the tents and things."

Travelling with a king was a very different proposition from travelling with Mr Ginger. There was a good road from Baghdad to Kirkuk (set among the main oilfields), then the ancient city of Arbil and on to Rawanduz. As we made our slow and stately progress through little villages and towns, the whole population would come out to line the road and gape at the convoy, with its armed soldiers, royal pennant and armoured car. There was no cheering or waving, but a silence, whether of awe or antipathy I could not tell.

We stopped for lunch at a village, to be greeted and entertained by the headman. I suspect that the ingredients for the meal had been dropped off by the royal cooks on their way up before us, since there was fruit, cheese, cold meats and fine breads as well as fresh pomegranate juice and coffee – all of a quality much higher than one would expect.

Nevertheless, there were ceremonial speeches which were boring and to which neither Fizz nor I listened, although Sergeant Abdullah kept hissing at us to be polite and behave. So did the Colonel in charge of the convoy, although none of the royal party paid much attention to him.

But after lunch and the speeches, Fizz did say thank you in a royal sort of way and the local men cheered as we drove off.

The countryside was not at all as I expected. Instead of sandy scrub and desert the landscape was green and cultivated. There were small hills and grassy valleys with streams. Sergeant Abdullah told us the names of the villages and towns, which were a great mixture of Turkish, Persian, Arabic and ancient, from dead civilisations. He told us a bit about the history of the Turkish occupation and how the area through which we drove was immensely ancient and full of ghosts of the dead, not least those slain in the many battles over millenia.

"There are many *djinni* about," he said in his deep voice, frowning. "They are everywhere and come out at night." He spread out his arms, but the driver complained, so he sat straight again. "There are good *djinni* and bad *djinni* and you have to be careful not to annoy them. Sometimes they look just like ordinary people."

"How can you tell if they are good or bad?" I asked and Fizz added: "And how can you tell if they are people or *djinni*?"

Sergeant Abdullah stroked his moustache. "You can tell if they are *djinni* by their eyes," he said, opening his wide. "We have round pupils, the black bit in the middle," he pointed at his left eye, "but the eye of a *djinn* (may Allah protect and save us) is like a cat, straight up and down. They also have long faces," he added.

Fizz and I digested this information and stared into each other's eyes. "As for good or bad," continued the Sergeant, "you cannot tell, just as with people, until it is too late. Best to behave as though they were all bad and be careful."

"Have you ever seen one?" asked Fizz.

"Well ..." the Sergeant blinked rapidly, "not actually seen one, perhaps; but I am sure there must be some around when things go wrong."

The first night was spent in the house of the headman of a small town, who had given up his dwelling for the king's convenience. Fizz and I shared a smallish, mud-walled room and Sergeant Abdullah, reunited with the two unimportant ones, slept on the floor, wrapped in blankets, just outside the door. I was kept awake, for a time, by the howling of dogs and jackals, and then dreamed of long-faced *djinni* whose staring eyes had pupils that went straight up and down

We rose early, and after some superficial washing and a quick and simple breakfast of bread, yoghurt and hot, sweet tea, set off again. The Colonel tried to supplant the Sergeant in the front seat of the black Mercedes limousine in which we rode, but Fizz chased him out, announcing loftily that he felt insecure without his accustomed bodyguard. Sergeant Abdullah beamed at the Colonel, who departed in a rage.

I questioned the Sergeant further about the *djinni*. "What can you do to protect yourself from them?" I asked. "Are they not immortal?"

"Oh, small sergeant," said Abdullah, "you speak truth, by Allah. They cannot be killed or destroyed. But there are three secret ways to be safe from them." He looked slyly at us. "Because you are my life, small King, and the small sergeant is your friend, I shall tell you. But keep it secret."

He twisted round and faced us. "The three ways are that the *djinni* cannot abide iron, so if you have a piece, they will not come near you." He wiggled his hand into his pocket and produced a large iron nut. "You see," he said, "they stay away from me."

Fizz and I tried to remember if we had any iron about our persons; we did not.

"The second thing," continued Abdullah, "is to have something blue, like a bead or a piece of cloth." I remembered that donkeys often had blue beads woven into their bridles. Fizz and I had nothing blue.

"Finally, a little dab of *henna* on your skin or clothes will do the trick. But it must be visible." The donkeys often had a little orange splotch on their forehead. In all, they seemed much better protected than either Fizz or I.

We both felt uncomfortable until our next stop, where the Sergeant presented each of us with a small nail. "This will do for the moment," he said, "until you can get something better."

We continued our drive north. A night was spent in the large town of Kirkuk, which was the centre of the oil industry and full of English expatriates from the Oil Company. We were lodged at the Company guest house and had a good dinner. Unfortunately, the senior people from the Company crowded to be with Fizz, to talk to him and have photographs taken of him, which was a bore, especially the wives, all dressed up in their best frocks.

One particularly gushing lady, curious about me, asked who I was. I told her, in Arabic, that I was a *djinni*. She smiled uncertainly, and I overheard her saying to a crony that I was very young to ask for gin.

We managed to get away in the morning early enough to avoid most of the audience. We could now see, in the shimmering blue haze of the horizon, some quite high mountains. When we stopped at mid-morning for refreshments, we suddenly heard a commotion. The soldiers from the front lorries were pointing to a field on the right, and shouting. We both looked and saw two gazelles grazing peacefully about three hundred yards away.

There was a fusillade of shots, from twenty rifles and machine-guns. The gazelles were enveloped in a great cloud of dust where the bullets hit. When it blew away, I was relieved and pleased to see the gazelles bounding away unharmed.

Sergeant Abdullah roared scornful insults at the marksmen: "Oh blind and ancient cripples," he shouted. "May Allah have mercy on you in your feeble health and painful joints. Next time we will bring your little sisters to look after us. By Allah, never have I seen such pitiful donkeys dressed in uniform."

The Colonel, whose troops were the targets of the Sergeant's jibes, seemed to be occupied with a sudden inspection of the armoured car. The unimportant ones behind us were howling with laughter and pointing their fingers at the discomfited soldiers in front. Fizz and I joined in the laughter.

We passed through Arbil, an ancient, walled town, and the road began to climb into the mountains. These were quite high, and in the distance we could see snow-capped peaks on the border with Persia. The air was clear, clean and sharp, there were wild flowers everywhere, and little copses of trees leaning over ice-cold clear streams from which we occasionally stopped to drink. We began to see strangely dressed people trudging beside the road, sometimes with gaily decorated donkeys.

"These are Kurds," said Sergeant Abdullah respectfully. "They are not Arabs, but their own race; great fighters and they can walk in the mountains for days without getting tired. They have their own language."

The men mostly wore thick, felt coats, broad sashes and wide homespun trousers gathered at the ankle for easy riding. They wore large black turbans and were slung about with cartridge-belts; they carried a variety of guns and rifles.

When we stopped at a *chaikhana* or tea-house, we also saw Kurdish women, who were unveiled. They wore multicoloured robes, also gathered in at the waist and ankles. On their heads they had turbans decorated with chains of gold and silver coins, which were sometimes also looped under their chins. They looked fierce and every bit as tough as their men.

They offered us rosewater for washing and roast meat with a distinctive rough bread to eat. There was no special reverence for Fizz, but we were all treated with a cool reserve and respect, not least Sergeant Abdullah, who towered over them and was therefore accepted as a great fighter. Their language was incomprehensible, though one of the old men made a short speech in Arabic, bidding us welcome to their country and wishing us well. As we drove away, the Kurds fired their rifles into the air in farewell, and the women made a shrill noise.

Then Rawanduz. The village itself was not large or particularly memorable: a collection of undistinguished houses and shops, with a mosque and a sort of playing field. There were lots of Kurds about, who did not show much interest in our convoy, after establishing what it was all about. I could not see why everyone in Baghdad had seemed jealous when I told them I was going to Rawanduz.

We drove through and on into the mountains. After some time, we turned onto a small and dusty track and, coming round the side of a stony hill, stopped. I got out of the car and looked around me.

We were on the edge of a flat meadow, on which a number of tents had been erected. Some cars and lorries were neatly parked in a line, and there was a largish stream, almost a small river, running behind the tents. All around, the mountains reared their snowy tops and on their slopes we could see small forests, other meadows and valleys; the view was panoramic for tens of miles.

In front of one of the tents there was a fire going and the breeze wafted towards us an enticing smell of roasting meat and fresh bread. Sergeant Abdullah showed us where our tent was, and, having examined its modest comforts, we made our way to the fire, where most of the soldiers were already assembled.

The Colonel said to Fizz: "Your Royal Majesty, please go to your tent with your friend and the food will be brought to you. These common men should not eat with you. I will join you later."

Fizz glared at him and drew himself up to his modest full height. "I will eat with my friends," he said. "But if you wish, you have my permission to eat alone near my tent."

The circle of soldiers murmured, and Sergeant Abdullah beamed. The discomfited Colonel stalked away and the back of his neck was very red.

"Make room, make room, sons of camels, for my small king!" roared the sergeant. "Come and sit," he said to us, indicating a small rug which had been laid near the fire. "We will all eat like real warriors," he added, "not like picture soldiers."

And that is how we ate throughout our two weeks there. The food was good Arab fare, mainly meat, fish and soft, round bread, with vegetables and fruit and the occasional titbit of chocolate or biscuits as a special treat.

This period was my first experience of being away for a time from Aunt and Mother, exclusively among men, doing what I thought were manly things. We rode up and down the hills and valleys on little shaggy ponies, mostly led by a soldier but sometimes trotting free while we hung on for dear life. The countryside was wonderful: clear air, blue skies, not too hot or cold and everywhere trees and flowers. In particular there were whole fields of red, purple and white poppies which the soldiers called *abu el nawm*, or father of sleep. The sergeant told us that a good medicine could be made from these flowers which took away pain and made one sleep. We were careful not to touch them.

In the evenings, under clear skies, and wrapped in shaggy Kurdish cloaks, we sat around the fire and listened while soldiers took it in turns to tell stories of animals and *djinni*, and legends of ancient heroes, wizards and tragic lovers. The flickering firelight and the companionship were comfortable and pleasing. On several evenings we had *mazgouf*, river fish split and pegged round the fire, where the tangy smoke mixed with onion, garlic and oil to give the flaky white flesh an unforgettable taste.

On three or four afternoons we were allowed to shoot. This was a fairly ceremonial undertaking: all the soldiers were collected on one side of our meadow, while we faced the other way. A row of sticks was hammered into the ground some fifty yards away, and empty bottles impaled on them. The sergeant then gave us each a large revolver (I think it was a Webley .44)

117

and, having shown us how to hold it, told us to aim and shoot. The guns were so heavy we could barely lift them, but Fizz managed once to hit a bottle, to loud and prolonged cheers from the audience. I never did.

On one of these special shoots, we were, after much wheedling, permitted to shoot a whole magazine with a Thompson sub-machine gun. This was most exciting, with the bullets going all over the place as the gun bucked and jumped in our hands. The sergeant and the unimportant ones were close by us, with a hand steadying our arms, and there was little danger.

Nevertheless, thinking about it afterwards, Fizz and I decided not to mention the event on our return to Baghdad, since Nanny, Aunt and Mother, not to mention the Royal ladies, would probably have had a fit.

It was also on Machine-gun Day that the sergeant and the unimportant ones came into their own. After Fizz and I had had our fun, and the bottles on the sticks remained intact, as usual, the sergeant said that he would give a dinar to every soldier who hit a bottle.

"I, Abdullah, together with these two unimportant ones, will pay you such a magnificent sum for clever shooting with the Thompson – a full magazine each." He glared about him fiercely. "And you can do the same for us."

The soldiers gave a cheer and lined up. There were eight sticks and bottles in a line, and when they had finished shooting and the din had died down, two bottles were seen to be broken.

The sergeant grinned, and said that they had done well. He then told them that he and the unimportant ones would shoot, one after the other. The bottles were replaced, and Sergeant Abdullah stepped forward. Casually and almost without looking he fired a short burst, while sweeping the barrel of his Tommy-gun in an arc. When he stopped, all eight bottles were shattered. The two unimportant ones, consecutively, did exactly the same. Fizz and I cheered and after some resistance the soldiers paid up. The Colonel was nowhere to be seen.

We also tried to shoot some partridges with a couple of small shotguns, but while we frightened many, we did not actually bag a single one. We also tried fishing, but without success, unlike the cooks.

It was a happy time. The two weeks passed only too quickly, as did the journey back. I would have been glad to stay there for ever.

Two days after we returned to Baghdad, the Prince Regent came to dinner at Aunt's house.

The first I knew of it was when Entah told me that the plates were arriving that morning, together with the cooks and extra servants.

"What plates?" I asked. "What for? Aunt has those heavy silver ones."

Entah cast his eyes sky-wards. "The Prince is coming to eat, and always they send big gold plates and many cooks and waiters. They think that Ali, our cook and Hussein and I are not good enough."

I went to Aunt. "What are all these gold things and people?" I asked. "Go away," said Aunt in a fluster, "Don't bother me now."

"His Royal Highness, Prince Abdulilah, the Prince Regent has graciously been pleased to honour us with his presence," said Mother in a breathless voice. "He is a Royal person."

Both Fizz and I knew that he was on the other side, and I was surprised that Mother and, especially, Aunt made such a fuss about feeding him. Aunt said that I was not invited, but could watch from the roof if I kept completely quiet. The dinner was to be held in the garden.

Sure enough, at midmorning, three cooks and ten servants appeared from the Palace, with heavy boxes from which they unpacked large plates and serving dishes. I hung about the kitchen to watch, squatting in a corner out of the way.

The cooks made a few jokes with Ali, our cook, whom they knew quite well, and began to prepare the food. There were fish and partridges and pigeons and gazelle and lamb and kid; many different kinds of vegetables and fruit and spices; cases of wine cooling in blocks of ice which arrived at the same time in huge tin boxes; several ice-cream making machines (I was able to negotiate the turning of the handle on the mango one, my favourite, against the promise of getting the container to clean out later). To start with there were some fifteen pounds of the best Beluga caviar, with special bread made into toast. There were to be about fifty guests sitting at the tables.

Out in the garden, the servants, with Hussein and Entah, were busy putting together tables in a horseshoe shape, and covering them with long white table-cloths. Then there was the cutlery (also from the Palace), many glasses, plates, silver salt and pepper cruets, damask napkins and massive, decorative *épergnes*, with elaborate arrangements of fruit and flowers. Overhead, electricians were stringing coloured lights from tree to tree and a small dais was placed in a corner for a chamber trio from the Semiramis Hotel. Finally, the shining, engraved gold plates were ceremonially set in front of each place. The elegant chairs, with red velvet, came from the hotel.

I managed to hang about, staying out of the way, until the guests began to arrive. They were all dressed up, the men in tailcoats with medals, and the ladies in long dresses, with bare necks and arms covered in jewels. The whole of Baghdad society was there, and I recognised quite a few of them, not least Nuri Pasha al-Saïd (the Prime Minister and crony of Uncle Max) as well as the whole Cabinet, various Ambassadors, senior officers and many foreigners. I watched from the kitchen as they all arrived and was particularly pleased with myself since I had persuaded Ali to cut the crusts off the toast **after** spreading the caviar, not before, and thus stuffed myself privately on the best Beluga.

The cooks had also prepared a dessert which was simply magnificent. It was a three foot wide confection of birds and animals in spun sugar, which stood in a collection of multicoloured *gateaux*, puddings and jellies arranged to look like a jungle. The whole was to be brought in on a six foot table-top.

Aunt suddenly appeared in the kitchen for an unannounced check-up and told me to go upstairs immediately. Just then, Hussein appeared in a flurry, saying urgently: "Memsahib, memsahib; His Highness has arrived."

I followed Aunt onto the front terrace, and there he was, in a splendid uniform covered in medals and gold braid. He advanced upon Aunt, holding out his hand. She gave him hers, which he kissed elegantly. I was standing beside her and he turned to me, also extending his hand.

"Ah, it's you," he said, putting his hands quickly behind his back, and turning back to Aunt, who was swelling with rage, "how kind of you to invite me," he said, and they made their way to the garden, where Uncle Max and the Premier were waiting.

I scuttled upstairs to the roof, and spent the following three hours sitting dangerously on the parapet, watching the goings on. The display of puddings, carried by four servants, made a triumphant entry to general applause. Entah smuggled up to me a huge tray with some of everything and I was content.

It was at this party that I noticed a particularly elegant English-looking gentleman, who was hanging around Mother, on whom I was keeping an eye. I also noticed that she was not displeased with him for doing this. When I asked her the following day who it was, she went somewhat pink and said: "Oh, nobody special, darlink. Just a nice Englishman from the oil company."

The party was judged a great success, and a long and fulsome article appeared in the English newspaper about it. When I spoke to Uncle Max and told him I had watched it all from the roof he said: "Ach, all nonsense. It makes your Aunt happy and all the people like to eat and drink, and the gold plates and everything. But there are too many poor people here."

I did wonder why such a party was necessary at all.

Life was uncomplicated and undemanding and I enjoyed my days. Time passed almost imperceptibly and obviously it was all too good to last.

The blow fell one summer afternoon in 1943. I had returned from the Club early, since there was to be a dinner party and I wished to investigate the contents of Ali's pots and pans. Mother saw me and told me to wash my face and come to the sitting room. There I found Mother and Aunt, together with the nice English gentleman from the oil company and another, a friend of his. I was introduced to them and they were named Mr Arnold and Mr Grafton. Everybody shook hands.

"MY SON," began Mother. I knew this was serious since it always was when she spoke in capitals. "We have decided that you have to get a proper education. You cannot run wild here for ever. You are now eleven and must go to a proper school."

"But I am going to a proper school," I protested. "It has been rebuilt and it is holidays now. I can't go there during holidays."

Aunt said: "No, you don't understand. By proper school we mean an English school."

"I can't go to an English school if there isn't one," I said reasonably. "And there is a war so I can't go anywhere else. Anyway, you are all here."

Mr Arnold smiled at me and said: "The school we are thinking of is in Egypt, and Egypt is quite safe now. The Germans have all been chased away. It is a very good school, called Victoria College, and I have friends in Cairo who have arranged everything."

"But we are all living here," I said to Mother. "You are working in the Red Cross, and Aunt has to give parties and Uncle Max ..."

"No, my darlink," interrupted Mother. "I have decided that for your sake, my son, I have to make a great sacrifice, although my heart will be broken." She gave a great sigh and covered her eyes with her hand. Aunt put an arm around her and the gentlemen looked solemn.

"You will go alone and leave me here," said Mother dramatically.

"But you can come back for nice summer holidays," said Aunt. "And you will see us all once a year, so it won't be so bad."

Mother gave a muffled shriek. "How can I live without my son?" she whimpered, "he is everything I have. Am I strong enough?" Mr Arnold took her hand and patted it. "There, there," he said. "It will all be all right, you will see." Mr Grafton and Aunt were discussing Egypt.

Everyone seemed busy, so I excused myself and went up to my room to think about it. On the face of it, there were some silver linings. I would miss my friends, and Entah and especially Uncle Max, but I would be on my own, like in Rawanduz, and free to do what I wanted. And in the summer I would be coming back to the Club and there would be a lot to tell my friends. It sounded like an adventure, though I was sorry for Mother.

When Uncle Max appeared shortly thereafter for his usual late lunch, I went and told him about it, but he already knew.

"Na, it will not be a bad thing, you know. Here you are wasting your life, there you will learn all the things which you will need when you grow up. English schools are different from others, but they have their good points."

He paused and munched some rice. "What is more," he said, "it is better you go to the school in Egypt than to an English school in India. I know about Victoria College for many years and it is good. Also, we have arranged that you can fly to Egypt in an airplane."

"What?" I jumped to my feet. "Me? Fly in an airplane, really?" This added a whole new dimension to the adventure and totally reconciled me to going.

Uncle Max smiled. "Yes, very exciting, I am sure. But I prefer my feet on the ground."

It appeared that all had been arranged, and I was the last to know. There was a time of preparation, of outfitting me with suitable clothes, such as grey shorts, white shirts, black shoes and socks, underwear and so on. The blazer, cap and ties which were obligatory, would have to be purchased at school, after I got there. A splendid brown leather suitcase was bought for me and my name was written into everything. This seemed unnecessary, since I had always managed to recognise my own things until then.

The day of departure arrived. I had a letter to give to the school and a letter to give to the friend of Mr Arnold, a Squadron-Leader Hart, who was to meet me off the plane at Cairo Airport. Uncle Max had surreptitiously given me a wonderful pen and pencil set from his magic cupboard, and I had succeeded in concealing it from Aunt and Mother. I also had a E£5 note, pinned inside my pocket, for emergencies. Finally, there was my new suitcase and a large and humiliating label tied to my lapel, with my name and Squadron-Leader Hart's on it, as well as UNACCOMPANIED CHILD in large red letters. I hid it as soon as I could, since I had promised not to tear it off.

The airport was a busy place, with exciting airplanes standing about and one landing with a great noise. The one I was due to go in was, I think, called a DC-3; it had two engines and when you went into it you had to walk uphill to your seat.

Fizz had told me that flying was fun. He suffered from something called asthma, and if it got very bad, he was driven to a private airfield and taken up to, he said, about 10,000 feet in an open two-seater. This made him feel better and he enjoyed it, because he made the pilot fly low over the palace and Sergeant Abdullah and the unimportant ones would wave.

But he was sad to see me go and said: "Well, we can see each other when you come back in the summer, but I will miss your visits." I also said the same and was unhappy when making my farewells to *Umm Faisal* and Nanny (who surprisingly gave me a little purse to keep things in, which she had made for me). Sergeant Abdullah said gruffly: "Well, small sergeant, good luck to you. We soldiers must go where we are sent, and I am sure we will meet again." We shook hands and he embraced me. The unimportant ones also shook hands for a long time.

One of the saddest partings was with Entah, who cried (I also did, a bit). He promised me that he would be there when I returned and gave me a sandwich, wrapped in newspaper, to eat on the journey, but Aunt took it away at the airport.

Everyone was there to see me off: the whole family and also Mr Arnold. Mother was in tears, but bearing up bravely. Uncle Max gave me a huge hug, and I later found another five pound note in my pocket. Mother gave me a number of lipsticky kisses, as did aunt, and Mr Arnold shook hands and said: "Give my regards to old Hart, won't you?"

I was put into the airplane, and a lady in uniform showed me how to wear a sort of belt round me. I was sitting near a window and I could see everybody quite well. Uncle Max was waving and the others were clustered round Mother. The engines started and there was so much dust that they all disappeared from view. The floor levelled off and with much roaring and trembling, we were off.

CHAPTER FOUR

Egypt – Cairo

It was too exciting to be frightening. As the plane laboriously climbed away from Baghdad, I could see the edge of the town, with toy houses and tiny people moving away beneath us. It occurred to me that it must have been difficult for the Germans to drop bombs on particular things from so high up and I concluded that they probably didn't care what they hit. It also became clear why the Stukas came screaming down to dive-bomb and machine-gun people; it was much easier from low down and close to the target. They must have enjoyed themselves.

Anyway, here I was, in the belly of a roaring mechanical bird, being carried away on an adventure into an unknown country. The lady in uniform told me that I could unfasten my belt and brought me some cool orange squash. She said we would have something to eat later.

I looked around. It seemed I was the only young person on board. The others were mostly men in uniform and two gentlemen in suits, who looked like important Arabs. They were all talking quietly or reading. I wanted something exciting to happen, but nothing did.

After some sandwiches and more orange squash, I fell asleep. When I woke, it was because of a big bump; we were landing.

The plane bounced and vibrated as we coasted to a stop and then there was a great stillness and quiet. It was dark but I could see figures moving about in the pools of light cast by the lamps of a shabby-looking building close by. The lady in uniform told me that we had stopped for some fuel, that we were in Haifa and that I could get down and walk about to stretch my legs.

I climbed down the steps from the aircraft and went to look at some men in overalls who were standing on the wings with hosepipes. There was the sweet smell of petrol about. I then followed the other passengers into the building, which was rather bare and had a bar at one end. There were many soldiers standing about, armed and in khaki uniform. I thought they looked a bit nervous.

Soon, the airplane lady called out that we should go back to the plane, and with no ceremony we were off again. I went to sleep almost as soon as we were airborne, and woke to a sunny morning, as we began our descent into Cairo. My heart gave a jump as I realised suddenly that we were flying over the Pyramids. Before I had time to look for the Sphinx, there was a final bump and I was in Egypt.

We all lined up to leave the plane and the lady in uniform told me to wait at the bottom of the steps. The others all filed out and I waited until she came down and told me to follow her. We walked to the big airport building; there were planes everywhere, mostly military-looking and large numbers of jeeps roaring about with soldiers in them. There was still a feeling of war and fighting.

In the building, the lady took my paper-passport and gave it to a man in a glass box.

This paper-passport was something Mother had arranged to have issued for me by the Polish Legation in Baghdad. I had no documents at all, and the only proof of my existence was a small note on Mother's Polish passport. The paper-passport was just a piece of paper with my name and photograph and a few particulars, signed by a Polish official. There was a rather nice red seal on it.

The military-looking person in the glass box frowned at my paper and glared at me. I felt uncomfortable and remembered how important it had been in Poland to have the right papers; perhaps mine were wrong and he would call the men in leather coats and have me taken away. I remembered Mother saying that one should avoid eye contact, so I looked away.

I heard a loud thump and the lady gave me back my paper, with a large Egyptian stamp on it; we were free to go and I was much relieved. It seemed I had got away with it again and my luck still held.

We collected my suitcase and stood at a counter while a villainous-looking Customs official in a fancy uniform pawed his way through my belongings. He reluctantly nodded, made a chalk mark on the suitcase, and waved us irritably away, all without saying a word.

"Well, that's it," said the lady, looking around. "Now to find your friend, the Squadron-Leader."

"He is not my friend," I remarked. "I've never seen him before, though I hope he will be my friend, because I don't know anyone else in Egypt."

We noticed an RAF officer, small and round and with a bright red face and large brown moustache, bearing down on us. He was in uniform and I could see some medal ribbons on his chest. He wore leather gloves and carried a little leather stick.

"Can it be Andrew?" he boomed as he approached. It was a very large voice for such a short body. "Of course it is, of course it is. I'm Hart. Jolly good show. I say, good flight, what?"

The lady took a step back. Squadron-Leader Hart seemed to occupy more space than his physical body actually took up; there was a sort of aura which formed a defensive sphere round him.

"Good morning, Squadron-Leader," said the lady. "This is Andrew, and this is his suitcase. We have been through Immigration and Customs, and he is free to go. Here are his papers. I would be grateful if you would please sign this receipt for him, which says you now assume responsibility." She produced a piece of paper, which the Squadron-Leader signed, saying jovially: "I accept delivery of two parcels, one leather and one human, har, har, har ..."

The lady sighed, kissed me on the cheek and whispered: "Good luck," before nodding at my companion and walking away. I was rather sad to see her go, since the Squadron-Leader seemed a bit peculiar.

"Har, har," he boomed. "Welcome to old Gippo-land. Call me Johnny," he added, "everyone does. Not the natives, of course, but normal people, you know."

"Porter wallah, porter wallah!" he called, and a big man in a *djellabiyeh*, or white native smock and a red *tarboosh* hat came up. "Here, you take this and follow us to the car, d'ye hear," Johnny pointed to my suitcase with his stick. "Now come along, what," he said to me and marched off, swinging his arms. I followed and so did the man with my suitcase.

We wound our way among crowds of people, mostly military or Egyptian, heading for the big doors. Some soldiers saluted Johnny, who casually touched his hat with his stick in reply. There was a lot of noise.

Outside, we made our way to a blue-grey car. A young RAF airman saluted and opened the boot. Johnny told the porter to put my suitcase in, and thrust some small coins at him. "*Imshi, imshi*, buzz off," he said. "No need to hang around."

"Thank you, my uncle," I said to the man in Arabic. He gave a surprised grin and touched his hat. "Allah guard you, young master," he replied.

"Ah, you know the lingo, do you?" said Johnny. "I never bother. If they want to understand me they better learn English," he added. I thought of Dr Mish.

We got into the car, and Johnny said to the driver: "Groppi. Take us to Groppi and after that to the school." He sat back in the seat. "I'll brief you on the situation," he took of his hat and wiped his shining red face. "You must be hot, so I'll take you to Groppi, which is the best ice-cream place in the Middle East, and we will have a bite. I am a bit hot myself; it's this bloody country."

We drove through streets teeming with people, buses, trams, many military cars, taxis and even horse-drawn carts. There were tall and elegant buildings, occasional trees and gardens, but a lot of noise and dust. The feeling was of a huge multicoloured swirl of random jigsaw pieces, with nobody to put them together and make the picture.

"Now then, listen, young feller," Johnny tapped me on the arm with his stick. "Pay attention. I have been posted to Cyprus urgently, and I will be leaving tomorrow, so I can't look after you. But I will take you to the school, and they can take you on, so you will be all right and tight. The headmaster is English, you know, so you will be quite safe. Sorry, and all that, but there is a war on, you know ..."

I did not completely understand what he was saying, but it sounded as though I would not have to put up with him for much longer. He spoke very fast, very loud and in a gruff sort of voice, like a dog's bark, so I mentally gave him the name of *sawt el kelb*, or Dogvoice.

We arrived at a *café*, with ornate doors and a large porter to keep away the beggars who clustered round the entrance.

"We'll be about an hour, Jones," said Dogvoice to the driver. "Go and get your rations and report back here at twelve hundred. Now come along, come along," he said to me, shouldering his way across the pavement and through the doors. "Don't dawdle, get on, get on."

We were shown to a small, marble table in a corner. Dogvoice took off his hat and put it, with his stick, on a spare chair. He turned to me: "Don't you speak English?" he demanded, frowning, "**Do you understand what I say?**" he asked slowly and clearly.

I suddenly realised that I had not opened my mouth, except to thank the porter, in Arabic, the whole time we had been together. Of course it was impolite, but I felt I had not really had a chance.

"Oh yes, I do, thank you, Squadron-Leader," I said. "I just had nothing special to say and I was listening to you. Also, I have this letter for you." I gave him one of my envelopes.

"Good, good, first rate," said Dogvoice in a relieved way. "I was a bit worried there, har har har ... Arnold did mention you were a foreigner." He opened the letter and perused the contents rapidly. "Everything is fine," he said. "Just confirmation of what Arnold already wrote, what ..."

A waiter came, and Dogvoice ordered large slabs of chocolate cake, iced coffee and a portion of chocolate ice cream for each of us. "I know you young fellers," he said jovially, "Can't get enough ice cream and chocolate, what. We may not be together for long, but you'll remember me, har har har …" He was right.

We ate the food and it was truly delicious. The ice cream was the best I had ever had and the chocolate cake was every bit as good as that of Frau Hertz.

During the meal, Dogvoice asked after Arnold (who, I worked out, was Mother's friend, Mr Arnold). They had been to school together at Brighton College, in England, although they had not seen each other for years. It was only owing to a chance meeting with a mutual acquaintance that Mr Arnold had discovered that Dogvoice was in Cairo. "Wizard chap, Arnold," said Dogvoice. "Splendid cricketer; you know, keeps wicket, what." He was hard to understand.

After our chocolaty breakfast-lunch, Dogvoice suddenly went even more red than usual and said to me gruffly: "Do you want to…you know…har har…wash or anything?" I assured him I did not, much to his relief. He paid and we went out to the waiting car. It must have been twelve hundred of whatever they were.

I thanked Dogvoice politely for my meal and said I had enjoyed it. I also offered him the E£5 note, which I had surreptitiously unpinned from my pocket.

Dogvoice was embarrassed. "No, no, old boy, har har …" he protested. "Have this one on me, for old times sake. Yes, jolly good show, what. And don't flash that money around," he added. "They're all thieves here and will skin you for fourpence." I nodded, as though I understood.

We drove and drove, through masses of traffic and down big streets, boulevards and avenues. It was quite hot and very dusty and I was getting tired. The large cargo of chocolate I had taken aboard was beginning to make its presence felt.

We drove beside iron railings, which stretched on and on, enclosing what looked like playing fields, and came to a fairly ornate set of gates, through which we drove. There was a large, brick building with steps, and that is where we finally stopped. The place was deserted.

"Well, here we are, here we are, what," barked Dogvoice. "You wait here and I'll see where we go now. This is your school. Victoria College, what."

He got out and marched up the steps. Jones turned in his seat and asked: "Are you stayin' 'ere, then?"

"I think so," I answered. "I have been sent here from Baghdad, where there are no good schools. They said this one is English, and therefore good."

Jones grinned. "That's the ticket," he said. "You'll be fine 'ere. Anyway, better than wot you would be wiv 'im," he remarked, jabbing his thumb over his shoulder in the direction of the steps. "Proper terror 'e can be, and no mistake. Yus!" he said reflectively, and sucked his teeth. "But drivin' is a cushy number, so I don't mind."

I could see that my English was not as good as I had thought.

Dogvoice suddenly appeared at the top of the steps and beckoned violently with his arm. "Come up, come up," he shouted. "I've found him. Come on. On the double."

I climbed out of the car and trotted up the stairs. Dogvoice turned and I followed him into the building.

There was a large, empty, echoing hall with a marble floor and corridors leading off it in various directions. There was a strange mixed smell of polish and cooking. Dogvoice marched into one of the corridors and I followed. We came to an open wooden door which we entered, then through a small room with a desk and filing cabinets, into a pleasant study, comfortably furnished with a shining desk, armchairs and tables, and with large windows looking out onto an enclosed garden. There were pictures on the walls of solemn-looking gentlemen in square hats and robes and on the floor a large rug (not nearly as nice as Uncle Max's).

Behind the desk was seated an imposing personage. The predominant impression he gave was one of greyness: grey suit, grey tie, grey hair, grey face and hands. His shirt was white, but when he stood up and came towards us I could see that his shoes and socks were grey too. It was as though he had strayed from a black-and-white film into a coloured world.

"This is the Headmaster," said Dogvoice. "We're lucky to find him."

"Welcome to Victoria College, Andrew," said the Headmaster. "The Squadron-Leader has told us about you. Naturally, we already know quite a lot from the letters we have had from Baghdad." His voice was grey. He put out his hand and I shook it; it was cool and dry, like a lizard.

"You realise, of course, that we don't actually start until tomorrow, so you have us at a disadvantage. But the Squadron-Leader has explained the situation, and we must all pull together in these difficult times, so we have undertaken to accept you today."

Dogvoice was standing uncomfortably to one side, with a fixed grin on his face. "Well, Headmaster, I must be going. Must keep on kicking old Jerry, what, har har ..." He turned to me. "You're in good hands here. I'll tell Jones to leave your suitcase in the hall. Right-oh. Off I go, Headmaster. Mission accomplished, what. Cheerio, old chap. Give my best to old Arnold when you see him, har har ..."

Before I could thank him, he turned on his heel and marched out. I could hear his steps grow more and more faint until there was silence.

The Headmaster and I stared at each other. "Hmmm," he said finally. "We have decided to put you in the Wildernesse."

I was puzzled. Wilderness? A jungle? Outdoors?

"No, no," said the Headmaster, who could see that I did not understand. "No, the Wildernesse (it has an 'e' on the end and is a name, not a description) ..." he gave a small, stifled laugh, "is a separate house where we put young, new boys of European extraction for the first year. You will like it there with your new friends. We are quite sure of that. They will not be arriving until tomorrow, of course."

I noticed that he never said 'I' or 'me'. It was always 'we' or 'us' and he also had the nervous habit of glancing over his shoulder as he said it, as though he was surrounded always by a ghostly group of companions on whose behalf he spoke. It was a bit creepy, and that was the name I gave him, there and then.

Creepy went back to his desk and picked up the telephone. He dialled and waited, then said: "Ah, Morton, there you are. Sorry to call on you today, but we have a small emergency. Young Andrew (from Baghdad, you know), has been dumped here just now, and we have agreed to take him in a day early. We realise it is a nuisance, but would you mind terribly coming over from the Wildernesse and taking him off our hands? We'll send his case later."

There were high-pitched protestations from the phone, but Creepy was ruthless; he interrupted with: "Yes, yes, we know, but there it is, sorry," and put the phone down.

He turned to me: "Mr Morton looks after the Wildernesse and will be coming over to show you where it is and explain things. Go and wait for him in the hall; we are busy." He picked up a piece of paper and began to read.

"Thank you, sir," I said and went out to the hall. There was nowhere to sit, so I walked around and read the notices on the boards fixed to the walls. There was also a large wooden board, high up, with a list of names. These were the Heads of School, whatever that was, and many of the names were most peculiar and hard to read: a mixture of many nationalities.

Some of the notices were incomprehensible, and dealt with people being awarded colours, or elected to be secretary of debating, or doing hall duty. Others, which I could understand, were teams in various sports, many reminders to do this and not to do that, and allocations to dormitories in the main house for the new term. There was a short list, in one corner, which gave the names of the 'Wildernesse Boys'. Apart from my name, there were four others: Chantry, Perrault, Woomey and Kristopolous. I wondered what they would be like, since they seemed to have been allocated as my friends.

There was a shrill buzzing, like an angry bee, and a little man came bouncing through the door and towards me. He was making the noise by vibrating air through his clenched teeth. As he walked, he raised himself to his toes with every step, so that he bounced, like a large ball.

"I'm Mr Morton," he said. "I am the Wildernesse. I rule there and you all obey. You are Andrew and you will obey. I will not have any disobedience from anyone." Dzzzzz dzzzz …"You are most inconvenient, arriving early …"

"Please, sir, it was not my fault," I said. "The Squadron-Leader had to …"

"I will not be interrupted," he interrupted. "Excuses, excuses;

it's all I hear. Nonsense. Dzzzzz. You are inconvenient, and I will be obeyed."

I thought it best to remain silent. Mr Morton looked at me irritably and buzzed. "You will come with me," he said and turned on his heel, walking out through the door and down the steps. We marched down the drive and out of the gates, and turned down the street. We were immediately followed by a band of young Arab boys, obviously habitual adversaries of Mr Morton, who took no notice of their jeers. I was surprised, since they were hurling quite serious insults at him.

Getting no response, they turned their attention to me.

"Aha aha," they cried. "Is it a new little girl come to the big house? Is it a precious little doll to be protected from nasty street boys? Oh pretty English puppy, will you lick the feet of the little fat man? See how he minces along, see the little gentleman ..." and so on.

I lost patience and stopped. "Oh mongrel dogs fathered by scabrous jackals," I yelled. "Foul-smelling brood of dirty goats; may your mothers be cursed with boils and your fathers lose their noses ..."

The boys checked, and stood there silently, as though struck by a thunderbolt. Mr Morton also stopped and looked at me in astonishment. "Good Heavens, boy," he said. "Where on earth did you learn to speak like that and what on earth did you say?"

"Oh, I just told them to stop being a nuisance," I said modestly. "We had to know a few phrases like that in Baghdad."

"Well, I never, dzzz dzzz," said Mr Morton, bouncing up and down on his toes. "You will have to teach me some of the phrases."

The boys still stood and looked. The biggest said: "We did not know you were one of us, oh one with the tongue of a loud snake. Welcome. What are you doing with the fat fool?"

"I will tell you another time," I replied. "Go in peace."

Mr Morton had begun buzzing, and we continued down the road. Some hundreds of yards later, we went into a villa, in a small garden full of trees. We were in the Wildernesse.

The villa looked just like somebody's house; there was a sitting room, a dining room and Mr Morton had a study. Also downstairs, there was a big room at the back, which had five iron bedsteads in it, some wardrobes and a small bedside table beside each bed. There was a small toilet off it. The room was our dormitory. We were not permitted to go upstairs, which was private Morton territory.

"You will have breakfast and all the other meals at Big School," he said. "In the evenings, after activities, dzzzz, you will come back here to sleep."

A lady walked into the room. She also was small and plump, but there was a hardness in her face which made me wary. "This is Mrs. Morton," said her husband. "She must be obeyed just as I am obeyed."

Mrs. Morton nodded. "It is inconvenient of you to arrive early," she said in a rather harsh voice. "Still, we must accept the rough with the smooth."

Mr Morton said: "Right. Give me all your money. We do not permit boys to have money. You shall have ten piasters a week pocket money but no more. I will be obeyed. Dzzz."

I obediently handed over the E£5 note given to me by Mother and, after some thought, also the purse made by Nanny with the other note, from Uncle Max, in it. This seemed a sensible thing to do, since there was nowhere to hide it. I also gave Mr Morton the second envelope, but he just put it on the table. Mrs. Morton opened it and glanced through it. "Hrrmph," she muttered. "Just as I thought."

"Well now," she added, as she took charge of the notes. "Aren't we rich! This is far too much for a boy like you to have, but we will keep it safe." She wrote in a little book and put everything into a tin box. "When your case comes, you may unpack. Since you are the first, you may also choose your bed. Then you will pick a book from this bookshelf and sit quietly until dinnertime. Tonight, as a special treat, you may eat with us, if you behave."

And so it was. I found a book called "The Last of the Mohicans" and read until a miserable dinner of nondescript and tasteless meat and boiled vegetables. I wondered how the Mortons could be so round and rosy on such a diet.

The unpacking took only a short time, under Mrs. Morton's supervision. "You are lacking a number of items of uniform," she said accusingly. "The letter asks me to get them for you. You need a blazer, a cap, some football boots and games kit and two school ties. Well, I presume they will go on the bill."

At eight o'clock I was told to go to bed. I washed superficially in the hand basin in one corner of the dormitory and climbed onto a hard little mattress. I had chosen the bed near the window. The lights were put out by Mr Morton, with a gruff "Good night. Getting up at seven o'clock, dzzz ..."

It took a little while to get to sleep. There was a lot to think about and arrange in my mind, and I lay there watching the shadows of the curtains swing, in the breeze, across the white ceiling. It had been an eventful two days since I had left Baghdad, Uncle Max and Entah. I missed them.

I woke in the morning to the loud twittering of birds in the trees outside my window. It took me a moment to realise where I was, but before I could get out of bed, there was a loud ringing noise and Mr Morton came in, swinging a large, brass handbell.

"Time to get up, time to get up. Rise and shine, dzzz ..." He stopped ringing. "Up you get, young fellow. Be ready in ten minutes and then we will go to Big School. Hurry up or you will miss breakfast, dzzz dzzz."

I washed and got dressed, and sat on the bed until he returned. We went back to the school building. I noticed the Arab boys behind us, but keeping well away. I surreptitiously waved a hand at them, which they acknowledged; Mr Morton did not notice, and bounced along happily, buzzing.

Breakfast, which I ate alone in a large hall full of long tables, was not bad. There were fried eggs, and bread and butter and tea. There were people walking about, and one of them approached me. "I am Winter," he said. "You will be in my class, Upper Third, and I will be teaching you English and History. I am also your year-master and if you have any questions, don't bother anyone else but come to me."

He was a tall, extremely emaciated man, with long arms and legs. The general impression was that of a crane-fly and you could almost see the articulation in his joints as he moved his attenuated limbs about. He had black, piercing eyes which looked through you rather than at you. I don't think he saw the surface of things at all, but only the inner workings. However, he spoke kindly and was not frightening.

He led me to a classroom on the first floor and we sat down, he on a chair behind a table on a platform, facing the room, and I at a desk in the front row. The desks were for two people each, with a bit of a squeeze. They were wooden and had interesting things carved on the top which would repay study later.

"Now, then, young fellow," he said. "There are many rules here, but they are all for your own good. We get boys from all over the place, and the war has meant that many of them ..." he frowned, "probably like you, have no idea of discipline or proper behaviour."

I thought it best to say nothing, so I put on my polite attentive face, and waited. I found that this system usually worked to keep me out of trouble.

"I will be saying this to all the new bugs," he added. New Bugs?

He read my mind. "Yes, new bugs, new boys, you know. But since I have you here, you may as well get some advance knowledge. I am a firm believer in old-fashioned, gentlemanly behaviour." He stood up and marched up and down the front of the classroom. I had noticed that men always seemed to do this when they were talking about something they felt confident about. "Now I don't suppose you know what a gentleman is really like, do you? No, you're a foreigner; how can you know."

Mr Winter perched on his desk, and sat there swinging his immensely long legs, which even there almost touched the ground. "The main things to remember about a gentleman are One ..." he held up one finger, "he is unfailingly courteous and polite. This oils the wheels of society. Two ..." he held up a second finger, "he remains unobtrusive, with quiet good taste, good modest clothes and he never boasts or shows off. And Three ..." he predictably held up the third finger, "he supports the weak (especially the ladies), never sneaks and is an honest faithful friend."

There was something to think about in this, because if these were the things to do to stay out of trouble in this school, I had to remember them.

"Now cut along, young fellow," said Mr Winter. "The day is free for you. We start properly tomorrow when everyone has arrived. Remember lunch is at twelve-thirty, in the Dining Hall."

I stood up, inclined my head politely, and went out to see if any of the boys had come.

They began to arrive at about midday, in all shapes and sizes, with and without parents, in cars and taxis. Soon, throughout the school building, there was a muted roar as the boys (who mostly could not wait to get away from their parents) sought out their cronies and began to exchange news of their holidays and plans for the new term.

Since I did not know anyone, I went alone into lunch and discovered a small table, in the corner, with a paper notice which said "Wildernesse." I sat down only to spring to my feet as Mr Winter appeared.

"You will not normally have a special table, but I thought it would be a good thing to have today so that you can all meet each other; you are all new, of course." He smiled and looked through me. "You were wondering how you would know the others, eh?" He just knew what one was thinking. Weird.

He departed, to be replaced by an olive-skinned, tallish boy of my age. He had glistening, curly black hair and large black eyes, with long eyelashes. His thick, black eyebrows met above his nose.

"I told to sit here," he growled in a deepish voice. "I am for Wildernesse. Are you same?"

"Yes," I admitted. "Have you just arrived?"

"I come from far," he said. "I am Nicos Kristopolous and my father is bigshot. I am very strong," he added.

I could see he had some way to go towards being a gentleman, but he was, of course, foreign. I told him my name, and added that I had come from Baghdad. He was unimpressed. "I come from more far," he said. "Where is Baghdad?"

Just then, we were joined by another boy. He was as unlike Nicos as it was possible to be, and he was crying. Nicos sneered. I asked if he was for the Wildernesse and the boy nodded.

"I a-a-a-m," he gave a sob. "My Mummy just left me and went away. I w-a-a-a-nt to go (sob) home." He was an angelic child, as blond as Nicos was dark, with a pink and white peachy complexion and bright blue eyes, rather red-rimmed. I asked his name and he said: "B-b-b-obby (sob)."

"B-b-b-obby what?" asked Nicos. I kicked him under the table.

"Bobby Chantry," said the blond child, wiping his eyes. "Don't make fun of me."

"Huh," said Nicos. "I do what I want. If we are Wildernesse we have to be all strong and together; not crying for Mamma."

"I agree," I said. "We are all new and we have to stand together."

"Is Wildernesse?" said a thin, fluting voice. We looked round and there was yet another boy, with bright green eyes and brown hair. He was wearing a small, striped bow tie on which we all fixed our eyes.

Before Nicos could say anything, I told the new boy that this was, indeed, the Wildernesse table and introduced us all. The boy, who spoke with a strong French accent and rolled his r's said that his name was Pierre Perrault and that he was an orphan whose uncle hated him and wanted to get rid of him. We were a bit embarrassed by this sudden confidence and Nicos (of course) said gruffly: "What is funny thing on your neck?"

Pierre raised his eyebrows. "Why, it is *papillon*," he said. "How you call in English?"

"Bow tie," said Bobby, who had stopped crying. "Looks silly," he added. There was a chorus of agreement and Pierre pulled it off.

By then, some food had arrived, brought by white-clad servants who circulated round the hall bringing food and removing the dirty dishes. It was quite good: a sort of stew with vegetables and then some fruit. There was bread on the table and water to drink in a jug.

Mr Winter came by. "Ah, so you are almost all here," he said. "There is one more to come, and he should be here shortly. His name is Graham Woomey and I am sure you will all be great friends."

"Huh," muttered Nicos, but did not say anything more.

Sure enough, just before we finished, a boy with bright red hair and a green suit with long trousers (we were all in shorts) appeared. He seemed quite at ease and said breezily: "Hullo, I'm Graham Woomey. I'm also a member of the Wildernesse."

I had been so preoccupied with my companions that I had not bothered to notice what went on in the Dining Hall. When I looked, I saw a great number of boys, sitting at the long tables and all talking loudly as they ate. They were all ages, from my own up to about seventeen, and all, except some new boys like me, were wearing school blazers and grey shorts.

During the afternoon I wandered round, and explored outside the school building. On two sides, there were playing fields set out for football. There were some tennis courts in a corner, with a row of thick bushes dividing them from the railings on the street. I noted this for future reference. There were also all sorts of little sheds for a multitude of activities, and also Creepy's house, a little way from the main building. Altogether, a terrain of much potential.

I also met a couple of new bugs who were not in the Wildernesse, but had been allocated dormitories in Big School. This was, I found out, because although they were boarders like me, their parents actually lived in Cairo and just felt that the boys would do better living in the school with other boys, rather than at home. One was a Jewish boy called Henry from Heliopolis, and the other was George, whose father (an RAF Group Captain) and family, lived in the garden suburb of Ma'adi. Both became good friends of mine.

The day passed quickly, and after supper in the big hall, we heard a loud call of "Wildernesse, Wildernesse, dzzzz. Come to me, Wildernesse ..." It was Mr Morton gathering his flock to escort to the villa. We met in the main hall, where he was bouncing on his toes and buzzing, and went with him.

As we trotted behind him down the dark street, I felt a tug at my sleeve and slowed down. A voice breathed in my ear: "Go slowly, serpent tongue. I wish to talk with you."

It was the leader of the street boys. I slowed down and tried to blend into the shadows. "I hear you," I whispered. "What do you desire?"

"When the moon is half up, come to the gate of your house," he said. "I will wait."

"I do not know if I can, but I will try. Now go, or we will be seen."

"The buzzing man is a great fool," said my new acquaintance. "But I will do as you wish." He disappeared in the gloom and I hurried to catch the party up.

We went into the villa, and Mr Morton took us through to the dormitory, where he and his wife gave again the lecture I had heard the previous day, and where the new bugs were divested of their cash. Bobby had none and Nicos had almost fifty pounds; we were amazed and even Mrs Morton was too stunned to say anything.

Before long, we were in pyjamas. Three of us had normal stripy ones, but Bobby had white ones and Nicos black ones. Somehow it seemed to fit. We all brushed our teeth at the basin in the corner and went to our beds. Mr Morton turned out the lights and, for a short time, there was silence. Then there was a stifled sobbing from Bobby's bed and Nicos' gruff: "Shut up, baby, or I come shut you up good." It worked and there was silence. No one seemed interested in talking.

I lay awake. After a half hour or so, Mr Morton peered in at the door, and satisfied that all was well, went upstairs.

It was a clear, moonlit night. Through the window, I could see the trees swaying in the breeze. The window was open and it would be easy to climb out, but I debated for some time if this would be a good thing to do on only my second night. The moon was half up and it was time, if I was going to go. Well, it would be a harmless adventure.

I slid silently out of bed and cautiously put on my clothes. There was silence in the room, except for a small, grumbling snore from the bed next to mine where Nicos was sprawled on his back. The dormitory was at ground level, so it was easy to slither through the window and out.

I paused; there was still silence. Gradually I became aware of the small night noises in the garden, but they were not alarming. I made my way quietly to the gate and looked back. The house was dark.

"Pssst," came a sibilant noise. "Welcome to the night." I could see the dim outline of my street friend. "Come with me," he continued, "and have no fear. I am called Ra'is, or the boss, because I am the leader of our band. I am the master of these streets." He was not much older than I was in years, though seemed much wiser and more experienced in the ways of the world.

Ra'is wore a rather grubby white smock, with a sort of dark waistcoat over it, and a small embroidered cap. On his dirty feet were worn sandals.

"My name is Andrew," I said to him. "I have only just arrived in Cairo to go to the big school."

"That is no sort of a proper name," said Ra'is. "You shall be known as Abu Lisaan, or Serpent-tongue, among us. You curse well," he added. "It was a big surprise when you showed us."

"Thank you," I said. Somehow it seemed appropriate to do so, since he had just complimented me on an admirable accomplishment. "Abu Lisaan is acceptable."

"Yes," he said. "Names are important."

While talking, he was leading me away from the Wildernesse. I was not afraid, but wondered where we were going, as we threaded our way through narrowing, deserted streets, with smaller houses and gradually more broken pavements.

"We have a special place to be," said my guide. "I am taking you there, but you will have to swear on blood that you will never tell where it is."

We had been walking for perhaps half an hour, when my guide suddenly ducked into a hole in the wall beside the pavement. I followed, and found myself in a derelict building, mostly open to the sky and with crumbling walls. A little deeper in and we came to a large room; the band was there.

There was the light of a small kerosene lamp, by which I could see a huddle of several boys, dressed like Ra'is, sprawled on the dirty floor. He gave a sharp whistle, and his band woke and got up, complaining.

"I bring you Abu Lisaan, the cursing one, from the school," he said. He has escaped from the sleeping house and comes as a guest. He is welcome."

"Welcome!", the voices came. "Peace on you."

"And on you be peace," I replied. This was turning into a

splendid adventure. "Is this your house?" I turned to Ra'is. "Is this where you live? Where is your family?"

"We live here and we are the family," he replied. "I have an uncle and aunt who live among the tombs in the City of the Dead. The rich people build big tombs for their dead, but the dead do no need them, and the tombs are dry and keep out the wind, so people live in them. They just stack up the bodies in the corner and then there is room. But my uncle has a big family so I do not live there. Anyway, my family is here."

He made a space beside the box on which the lamp stood. "Sit and drink tea," he said. "Hasan, make tea for the guest."

A boy a little younger than the others obediently went into a dark corner and lit a small Primus stove on which he placed a kettle, into which he sprinkled some tea and sugar. Soon I was holding a tin mug full of a hot, sweet liquid from which I took a sip before passing it on. Everyone took a sip.

"We will go now," said Ra'is. "It is not good to make the first time long. You will come again, and we will talk and you will swear on blood to be one of us and not tell." He rose and the others also stood to say farewell.

We hurried back, by a different route and it did not take so long. At the gate of the Wildernesse, Ra'is clapped me on the shoulder and said: "Let us meet here after three days. We will see if it was all well tonight. Peace with you." He vanished into the darkness before I could reply.

I carefully made my way back through the window, and began to undress. There was no sound other than breathing. As I slipped into bed, there came a growl from the bed beside me: "Where were you? I woke and your bed has nobody." It was Nicos.

"Oh, my stomach was much awake, so I spent time in the toilet," I hastily improvised. "I am not used to such food."

"Huh," he said. "I, also, do not like such food. In the house of my father there is much better food. And more," he added.

I was lucky; it seemed I had got away with it. I went to sleep with my head whirling with thoughts of my adventure, and coming adventures. The future, on the whole, presented an exciting prospect. Cairo was going to be fun.

In the morning, Mr Morton's enthusiastic bell clanged us out of bed. We washed and got dressed into yesterday's clothes; we did not yet have our proper school uniforms. Suddenly, we noticed a perfumed smell spreading throughout the room. Mr Morton, who had just entered, also wrinkled his nose and exclaimed: "Heavens above; what on earth is the smell, dzzz dzzz?"

Nicos appeared from the direction of the bathroom, with a bottle in one hand and the other scrubbing vigorously at his glistening black curls.

"Is it you who is responsible for the dzzz smell?" asked Mr Morton.

"I am said by my father to put special oil on the head every day," said Nicos. "He say it make me strong and women will run with me ..."

"You will give me the bottle at once, dzzz dzzz, boy," shouted Mr Morton loudly. "I will be obeyed. You will not use this frightful stuff in this house and you will go and wash your hair now. What you do in your dzzz dzzz home is your affair, but here you will obey me." He was quite red in the face. "And you will not speak dzzz dzzz of women."

Nicos looked sulky, but gave up the bottle with bad grace and slouched to the bathroom, to emerge, after a few minutes, with wet hair still smelling of his hair oil. It was our first sight of an angry Mr Morton and it caused me to wonder if my plans for nocturnal escapades were worth the risk.

The day was Saturday, and we were told to go to Assembly. The whole school gathered in the Big Hall and we sat on the floor facing a sort of stage, with the masters sitting on folding chairs on it, Creepy in the middle. When we were all there, he stood up and made a speech, surrounded, as always, by his invisible grey companions, at whom he continually glanced out of the corners of his eyes. I was glad I had a small blue stone in my pocket.

Creepy stood up and came forward. "We welcome you back to school and we extend a special welcome to the new boys. On this day, we want to remind you why you are here, and why your parents, in their wisdom, have sent you to us, both as boarders and day-boys." Creepy glanced round his band of ghostly supporters. "You are a great mixture of boys, but here we try to give you all the distinctive and enviable manner of English gentlemen."

I remembered Mr Winter's lecture and tried to recall what the three fingers represented.

Creepy was talking on. "The ones who need an explanation are only the new boys, and we are sure that Mr Winter will tell them what it's all about. You boys who return to us are already on the way though ..." he smiled without humour "... few are yet what we would call complete gentlemen. Then, of course, there is the question of academic excellence. Do your lessons, obey your masters, follow our rules and you will leave the school proud to be like us."

I did not want to be like Creepy, or like Mr Morton, but if it was necessary to be an English gentleman to escape the wrath of the authorities, then I would try to be one. It seemed to me that the rules of Mr Winter would work well if everyone followed them, but I wondered how they would work if some people did not.

Creepy went on for a bit, naming things called prefects, and captains of teams, and introducing a new master, a red faced person who looked nervous and ill at ease. Finally we all stood up, as the staff filed out, and then pushed our way out of the hall and to our classrooms. Mr Winter was there and told us to sit where we liked. I managed to sit next to Henry.

Thus began my first term at the school. The lessons were better managed and more interesting than in Baghdad, the masters, on the whole, somewhat kinder. But the really big difference was that I found some close friends, with whom I spent all my time. Especially the boy called Henry, who liked the same things that I did, who was a splendid supporter in trouble and who was quite without fear.

Friends, as well as a reasonably strong body, were the necessary attributes of anyone who did not wish to become a 'slave'. 'Slaves' were those among the younger boys who either could not stand up for themselves, or who had not formed mutually supportive groups. Older boys terrorised them and made them perform disagreeable tasks like running errands, cleaning shoes, cleaning lockers and so on. The British system of 'fagging' was not part of the official school culture, so the boys established their own.

Our group, made up of Henry, George and me, with the occasional addition of Nicos (when necessary), managed to remain independent; but the natural victims, like Bobby, were immediately enslaved.

I had been looking forward to the third night, when I had my appointment with Ra'is. Unhappily, the Mortons had chosen that particular night to have a party, and people were going in and out and laughing and talking late. I assumed that Ra'is would understand, and stayed in bed. It was just as well: Mr Morton looked in on us three times, presumably to make sure we were not taking advantage of what was happening.

Going to school the following day, and coming back in the evening, I kept my eyes skinned for Ra'is, but there was no sign of him. He was like a wild animal, easily frightened off, and I worried that I may have scared him off for good.

But two nights later, as I lay in bed watching the shadows half an hour after Mr Morton had put out the lights, I heard a gentle scratching at the open window. I looked towards Nicos, but he was snoring softly, as usual. I got out of bed and moved to the window.

It was Ra'is. "Where have you been, Serpent-tongue?" he whispered. "Come now." There was a rustle and he vanished.

I quickly got dressed and slid out into the garden, and towards the gate. He beckoned and we walked quickly away in the direction of the gang's living place. As we walked, I explained what had prevented me from keeping our appointment.

"It is well," he muttered. "I thought you had become frightened, and we could not let you go on, without the oath and knowing what you know." This was a chilling thought, which had not occurred to me.

When we got to the gang hideout, the others greeted me in silence and there was a strong air of suspicion. But Ra'is explained, ordered Hasan to make tea, and the others relaxed.

There was one boy in particular, whom I watched very carefully. He was named *El Kebir*, or The Big One. He was the largest of the gang, black and at least twice as heavy as me. I gathered that when anything physical had to be done, The Big One was the enforcer. He seldom smiled or showed any emotion.

After we had all sipped from the tea mug, Ra'is said: "Let's do it."

The gang made a circle, and sat on the floor. Ra'is pulled me into the middle and stood facing me.

"This is the hour of blood," he said. "We now make you the brother of us all. Take out your knife."

"I haven't got a knife," I said.

Ra'is and the others looked at me aghast. "No knife? … He has no knife … How can he … No knife!" They all muttered and looked at me with new suspicion. "You are not a girl-boy?" Ra'is demanded with disgust. "Why do you not have a knife?"

I pondered a reply. I felt in a state of acute danger, since the gang would be convinced that I had, at best, made fools of them and at worst that I was a spy. I decided to play safe, and lie.

"It was taken from me by a teacher at school, yesterday; I tried to make him frightened (the son of a sick pig), when he said my work was not good."

Everyone looked at me doubtfully. I pressed my advantage. "Perhaps I can get a knife from you, if you have a spare one." Ra'is decided to believe me. "Hasan," he said, "bring the bending one." Hasan disappeared into the gloom, to return with a clasp-knife. It was well worn, with a four-inch blade and as sharp as a razor. "How will you pay?" asked Ra'is.

This had not occurred to me; I racked my brains. "I will give you a special golden pencil, part of a treasure given to me by my uncle, a Pasha."

Ra'is recoiled. "A Pasha?" he shouted. "Your uncle is a Pasha? A curse upon you and your uncle. The Pashas walk on the faces of the people and eat their hearts. All the Pashas should be killed, as well as the Fat King. So say the men of religion and the people …"

"Wait, wait," I said. The situation was ugly. "The Pashas in Baghdad are not the same. My uncle is a doctor and a big friend of the people. He cures them for nothing and only takes money from the rich ones to pay for the poor ones." I went on the offensive. "How can you think that I, Serpent-tongue, would be on the side of those who walk on the faces of the people!" I snarled, holding out my new knife. "My uncle is a great man and on our side. You are fools."

There was a longish pause and, for a bit, nobody moved. Then Ra'is spread his arms wide.

"I believe him for now ... we will see in the future. A mistake is quick to correct." He turned to me. "Now, about the payment for the knife. I will decide about the golden pencil when I see it. In the meantime, let us make the oath of blood. You will stand here with your knife and I will stand opposite, with mine."

He pulled out, so quickly that I could not even see where he kept it, a wicked-looking knife with a thin, long blade.

"I will say the words and you will say after me. When I shout BLOOD, you will cut your arm here," he pointed to the outside of my forearm, "and join it to mine."

"I swear on death and blood and Allah ..."

I repeated his words.

"... that these my brothers are brothers to death and beyond death ..." I repeated. The circle was muttering the words in a low rumble. The light from the little lamp flickered and the shadows danced.

"... and when we exchange blood, there will no power part us or divide us or know our secrets and we are one brotherhood of men. We swear this forever on BLOOD!"

Ra'is and the others yelled the word and the circle sprang to their feet. Ra'is cut his arm with his knife and there was a trickle of blood. I clenched my teeth, shut my eyes, and made a tentative cut at my own arm. Fortunately, the knife was so sharp that some blood oozed out.

Ra'is grabbed my arm and pressed his own against it. He grinned fiercely at me, his face inches away. "Welcome, Brother," he said. "It is done. Bring more tea, Hasan."

The others crowded round me, shaking my hand and slapping me on the back. The Big One gave me a bear hug which made my ribs creak.

"Now we will eat," ordered Ra'is. Hasan brought a large tin tray on which there was a great mixture of different foods: some rice, bits of cooked meat, vegetables, fruits (rather bruised), half a roast pigeon, part of a chicken and some anonymous items. "This is from the eating house of the cousin of Shafiq, in the town," explained Ra'is. "He gives us what is left at the end of the night." I looked at Shafiq, who was a tall, thin boy dressed in a torn shirt and shorts. He grinned at me and I saw that his teeth were brown. "Of course," continued Ra'is, "we also steal food from the market stalls."

The gang and I fell upon the food, which was soon gone. When we had finished, Hasan brought more tea in the mug. Somebody belched.

"Why do you live like this, with the stealing and the hiding?" I asked.

"Well," Ra'is said, "what else can we do? We have somehow to pass the time between being children and being men. None of us has a home. The Big One, for example: his father was killed by a bus in the street and his mother brought men to the room where they lived and the men beat the Big One until one day he put his knife into the throat of one and had to hide." I glanced at the Big One, but his face was impassive.

Meanwhile, Ra'is was continuing. "My own brothers and sister are dead from sickness. My mother and father are also dead, I think. I came home one night and they were gone. The neighbours said that some men had taken them away. I looked and looked, but could not find them. This was some years ago." He took a sip from the mug, and passed it to me. I remembered that in Poland men came and took people away too.

"Anyway," Ra'is looked fondly round at his gang, "this is my family. We live well and we are content. When we are men we will do much bigger things."

We sat and talked for some time. Then Ra'is said: "You must go now. There is danger for you, my brother, if you stay too long away from the villa." I was thrilled to be called brother. "Come, we will all go."

So I was ceremoniously escorted back to the villa by the whole gang. There was a moment of danger when we saw two policemen walking ahead of us, patrolling the street. We fell to the pavement; I could smell the damp earth and hear the sharp breathing of the gang around me. The policemen turned a corner and disappeared. We went on, keeping to the shadows.

When we reached our destination, there was a sibilant whisper of *salaam*, and my brothers silently melted into the darkness. I returned to bed and, although I had been away a considerable time, no one appeared to have noticed. I lay awake until the sky began to lighten, thinking over the many new things I had experienced. My new knife lay under my pillow.

The only notable thing to happen the following day was that I fell asleep in class in the afternoon. I was wakened at my desk by Mr Winter (whom the second year boys called 'Snowy' behind his back). He shook my shoulder while the others sniggered.

"Well then," he said. "Am I so very boring? Or is your social life so hectic that you have to catch up during the day ..."

I gulped. Surely he could not truly see inside me. "No, Sir," I replied. "It must be due to all the hard work you make us do."

Snowy grinned. "Hmmph," he grunted. "You have a smooth tongue." It was eerie. "Stay awake, and write me a hundred times 'Mr Winter's lessons are interesting'. I want the lines tomorrow morning."

School life progressed in a gentle stream, sometimes disturbed by unusual events, such as poor Bobby Chantry fainting during lunch (we all said it was the food, but the authorities did not say anything). He was taken off to the villa, where we saw him, pale and wan, in the evening, feeling sorry for himself. We reminded him that English gentlemen did not whine, but it did no good. Nicos, as usual, had the last word: "Bobby should have been a girl."

I got my first letter, in Polish of course, from Mother; I did not, after the first week or two, think often of Baghdad, so it was a shock. She addressed me as 'My beloved far-away darling son' and assured me that she was bearing up under our forced separation. Mr Arnold had convinced her that boarding schools were very good for boys, and she said that even so, it was hard on loving mothers. Everyone was fine, but Uncle Max was not behaving very well and absenting himself from parties. She ended by saying that summer was not so far away, only nine months, and she would be so glad to see me again. There were lots of capital letters and underlinings.

We had to write home every Sunday afternoon. My letters simply reported, without detail or opinion, the week's activities. I felt no one was particularly interested, provided I was not ill or desperately unhappy. I was neither.

Time passed. I still saw Ra'is and the brothers about once a week; he had accepted the golden pencil as payment for the knife.

I also learned the rudiments of football, and played for my class at full back. This entailed preventing the opposition from approaching my goal, using whatever means were available. I developed a system of hiding a sharp stick in my stocking and poking opposing forwards with it on the side away from the referee (Mr Winter). He suspected something, but I was never caught. The opposition tended to keep away from me.

My friendship with Henry and George grew. They were very different, but we all got on well together. Henry came from a Jewish family living in Heliopolis. His father worked in a bank and he lived in a large flat with his parents, his younger sister and his old, widowed grandfather. He was a kind, generous person, always willing to share his good events and my bad ones. He was slight and not too tall, but strong and wiry all the same.

George was really the opposite. His father, a Group Captain in the RAF (higher up than Dogvoice), his mother Margaret, sister Polly and small brother Tim all lived in the garden suburb of Ma'adi, near the Club. George was big, rosy-cheeked and jolly, with bright, straw-coloured hair. He was very English, in the best sort of way, hearty, honest and lacking guile. But open and soft hearted as well.

I was surprised one day when he announced importantly that he had news for me.

"It's all fixed up," he said in his loud voice while we sat in the corner of the courtyard during break. "I did it. Everyone has agreed."

"What are you talking about," I enquired.

"It's a surprise." He stood up and twirled round in a circle, before bowing to me. "You are spending the Christmas holidays with us in Ma'adi."

I was astounded. It had not occurred to me that I should spend the holidays, now nearly upon us, anywhere but in school.

"But what ..."

"I tell you it's all fixed up. Snowy wrote to your mother, and spoke to Dad and Creepy knows and everything is arranged." His face suddenly dropped. "You do want to come, don't you?" he asked anxiously. "Perhaps I should have asked you first, but I wanted to make it a surprise ..."

I reassured him that I was both surprised and delighted. His normal sunny smile returned. Henry, who was sitting with us announced: "Fine. I will fix up that you spend Easter holidays with us. Would you like that?"

"Oh, yes. Thanks." I was overwhelmed and could not think what to say. It would certainly be much more fun than staying alone at school.

I now began to look forward to the holidays. I had never stayed with anybody before and I was not too sure how it would be. Fortunately, I got a letter from Uncle Max, sent without Aunt's knowledge, enclosing a E£5 note and an almost indecipherable scrawl which wished me a good Christmas and told me that Entah was well, and that Fizz sent his regards. This made me feel more secure.

Just as things appeared to be going well, and a couple of days before the holidays started, Mr Morton came into our room in the morning, and sat on a bed, something he had never done before.

"Dzzz ..." he buzzed, rather unhappily. "I have something sad to say to you and I wanted you to know before anyone else, because dzzz ... we are a family here."

We looked at each other in a worried way.

"You know that Bobby went home early, two weeks ago, because he was not very well." He blinked and gave a small buzz. "I am very sorry to tell you that he died yesterday. It was more serious than anyone thought."

We did not know what to say, or where to look. We went to school silently and felt bad for the whole day. That evening, Nicos pronounced Bobby's epitaph: "He was soft, but inside he was all right." We never found out what had happened.

The last day of term arrived and all was bustle and movement. There were farewells and packing and a stream of cars collecting boys all day.

I packed a small suitcase, bought for me by Mrs Morton for the occasion with my remaining pocket-money. There was not a lot to pack. I had also obtained, through a secret arrangement with one of the school servants who had a brother who worked in an office, a large box of Groppi chocolates, as a Christmas gift for George's family. I gave him my E£5 note from Uncle Max, but he assured me there was no change. Still, Uncle Max had told me that one should, as a guest, always arrive with a gift. I wrapped it in a newspaper purloined from the Morton sitting room and tied it around with string.

Mr Morton also presented me with a large English dictionary, which he said was from Mother and Aunt, who had sent him some money so that he could buy me a suitable Christmas present. I thanked him and put it away in my locker. There was also a letter from Mother saying how sad it would be at Christmas for everyone in Baghdad that I was not there and wishing me a happy holiday with George.

There was also the problem of my knife. I could not very well take it with me to a harmless family like George's, and I could not leave it at the Wildernesse, where it would undoubtedly be found. So I persuaded Nicos to give me some of his smelly hair-oil (he had a second bottle, of which Mr Morton was unaware), which I rubbed all over the blade to stop it rusting. I then put the knife in a cardboard box, and buried it in the corner of the villa garden, one night before the end of term.

In the afternoon of the last day, George burst into the villa, where I was waiting with my suitcase, and shouted: "Come on, come on. Dad's here. Let's go."

After saying goodbye to the Mortons, who were hovering round the door, I went out. George's father was standing beside a large, impressive car. He was an exact replica of George, though much bigger; as though George had been pumped up with air to twice his normal size. There was the same bright straw-coloured hair, the same broad stocky body, bright blue eyes, big grin and sun-reddened face.

"Ah, there you are, Andrew," he boomed. "Splendid. In you get, in you get. Is that all you've got?" he asked, pointing at my suitcase.

"Yes, Sir," I answered. "This is all."

"Jolly good. In you get. George, throw the case in the boot, old boy. Oh, by the way," he paused. "Don't call me Sir. Call me 'Group', like the rest." I noticed he used short words and seldom tried anything complicated.

We got into the car, and drove off, with Group tooting his horn. The holidays had started.

We drove a long way; all through the streets of Cairo, which were, of course, strange to me; on through the suburbs and into the fringe of cultivated fields. There were occasional glimpses of the Nile: a huge, mud-coloured river slowly flowing along, with many boats and quite large *fellucas*, or sailing boats with drab, triangular sails. There were palm-trees, oleanders and a feeling which reminded me of Baghdad.

During our trip. Group seemed happy and cheerful, and talked quite a lot about what fun Christmas was, about how it was a shame there was no snow and about how it did not feel the same in a non-Christian country. We also sang a song called 'She'll be coming round the mountain when she comes', which George knew and which I quickly learned. The tune was good but the words made no sense.

We arrived in Ma'adi, which was known as the Garden Suburb. There were quiet streets full of trees in bloom, and houses, set well back from the road, each in a good-sized garden full of flowers. Group's house was a villa, not unlike the Wildernesse, white, square and on two floors. We drove in through the open gates, tooting the horn. A servant in a white *djellabiya* or robe appeared, closely followed by Mrs. Group and the family.

Mrs Group was a short, roundish lady, with a permanent smile; she radiated motherliness and good nature. She immediately hugged me and said I was welcome. Her daughter Polly, who was George's twin, was a girl version of him and of her father: the same bright hair, rosy cheeks and blue eyes. She shook hands with me in a rather circumspect way. The youngest, Tim, was seven years old and obviously a brat. He looked quite different, with his dark hair, dark eyes and slim build. Mrs Group always joked that he was a changeling and that she wished the Gipsies would bring the real Tim back. I don't know if Tim also thought this was a joke. But at our first meeting, when we shook hands, he left a piece of well-chewed gum in mine.

I thoroughly enjoyed being with Group's family. I shared George's room and was treated entirely like a Group. The food was delicious and plentiful, Tim's occasional pranks were bearable and Polly seemed to like sitting next to me in the car and when playing games in the house. There was one game in particular which I learned, called Monopoly, in which there was buying of houses and charging rent. The names of the streets and the colours on the title-deeds were exciting, because they were in London, and Group would describe them to me when I asked. All the Groups were particularly kind, since my English, though much improved, was still far from perfect, and they were the sort of English people who felt both pity for and an obligation to those unfortunates who could not speak their language.

Group had taken some leave, so as to be with us during the holiday.

He piled us all into the car and took us to see the Pyramids, where we all (except Mrs Group) crawled about in the passages and rode camels. I remember thinking that the Sphinx was smaller than I had imagined. We also went to the fancy Gezira Club, which was a much grander sort of affair than the Club in Baghdad, but had quite a respectable swimming pool.

"Now that Jerry is on the run," declared Group, "it is only a matter of time. The pressure is off, and we can relax a bit." He took us to Groppi where we ate a lot of chocolate. I remembered my visit there with Dogvoice.

But most of all, we prepared for Christmas, now upon us.

It was quite different from the Christmases I knew. In Poland, the important time was Christmas Eve, or *Wigilia*, with its fish, horseradish and a poppy-seed cake; presents given out after supper and songs round the Tree.

The English Christmas happened on Christmas Day itself. There were presents under the tree, but no one was allowed to touch them, or even look, until after breakfast. I had put my gift, in its newspaper wrapping, with the others, where it looked a bit drab.

When I woke on Christmas morning, I found a stocking on my bed, bulging with things: there was an apple, there were sweets, little toys, nuts and so on. I woke George, who was not surprised, and said it happened every Christmas. I thought it was a marvellous gift, but he said that the real gifts happened later.

Everyone rushed down to breakfast, which Abdul, the servant, had laid in the dining room. Tim was jumping up and down and urging us all to hurry. Finally Group opened the sitting room door and we all went in.

The tree was all lit up with electric bulbs and decorated with shiny baubles and chains; it looked wonderful and almost reached the ceiling. Under it was the pile of coloured parcels. The gramophone was playing religious songs in a scratchy way, and Mrs Group constantly wound it up and changed the record.

Everyone had presents. I was given a book of stories about animals, a pencil-box shaped like a car, and a pair of sunglasses. I was quite overwhelmed.

When Mrs Group unwrapped my gift, she remarked that it was very sensible to wrap presents in newspaper and began to cry. She also gave me another large hug and thanked me very much, as did Group, in a rather gruff voice.

Suddenly Polly called me. She was standing in the doorway, and beckoned me to go to her. When I did so, and much to my astonishment, she threw her arms round me and gave me a long, lingering kiss on the lips. It was not unpleasant, but after a while I began to struggle, and heard the Groups laughing loudly. When I had freed myself, Polly pointed to a wizened twig pinned to the door frame.

"Mistletoe, mistletoe," she chanted, as the family continued to laugh. "You can kiss people under the mistletoe."

I looked at George, and he nodded, grinning. Later on, after tea, I ambushed Polly in the doorway and kissed her soundly. Though she squealed a bit, I had the impression she did not mind.

Lunch was an experience. Polish Christmas meals, though tasty, were not especially plentiful. But here there were mounds and heaps and mountains of food. There was soup, then a vast turkey with different stuffings and cabbage and potatoes and sauces and other vegetables. Lots of helpings of this. Then a strange pudding actually on fire and things called mince pies and more sauces. Then fruits and sweets and nuts and drinks of different sorts. We all ate until we could eat no more and then staggered into the sitting room where everyone had to tell a joke and then we played games and sang until tea. There appeared cakes, and buns and other things. I could not believe my eyes; this indeed was Christmas, such as I had not previously known. Before falling asleep that night I wondered what Ra'is would have made of it all. I also felt sad that Ryszard had died before he could see and taste all these wonders which I was lucky to have.

The holidays drew to a close, and it was time to return to school. When we were all ready to go and our suitcases were loaded into the car, I thanked Mrs Group who clasped me in her arms and said I was a very good boy and that I was always welcome to stay with them. Tim shook hands but Polly embraced me and said in a breathy voice that she would never forget me. I told her that I also would remember her for ever.

The drive passed all too quickly, and we were back at school before I had a chance to adjust. The holidays had been wonderful; it was a revelation to me that adults could be fun and actually spend time playing games. I had had a thoroughly good time. Group tooted and waved as he drove away.

One of the first things I did, after greeting Nicos and the others, was to retrieve my knife. It was fine, but smelt of Nicos' hair-oil. In fact, Mr Morton gave a suspicious sniff when he passed me in the corridor; Nicos glared at me and said: "He find out and I kill you!" Fortunately, the smell wore off in a week or so.

The second term was much easier: I knew my way about, I had friends and I knew the rules. Our lessons went on much as before and I tried to stay out of trouble.

The big difference was Ra'is. There was no sign of him or of the brothers. After about a week, I sneaked out of the dormitory one night and made my way to the hideout. It was abandoned, and it seemed that the building was being knocked down. Certainly there was no sign of the gang and no clue as to where they might have gone. The only indications I had was the restaurant where they got food, but I did not know where it was and also the tomb in which the uncle of Ra'is lived, but I did not know how to find it. So that was that and I never saw any of the brothers again.

It was ironic that on this, my last excursion, I should be caught. But as I turned in through the gate of Wildernesse, I could see the lights were on and there were signs of activity. I peered through the window and saw Mr Morton, buzzing loudly, and surrounded by my colleagues, all talking at once.

I walked up to the window and climbed in. Mr Morton stared at me, speechless, and the others also became silent.

"It wasn't anybody," I said loudly. "I looked all round the garden and a bit down the street, but I didn't see anyone."

"What ... what ... dzzz ..." Mr Morton gobbled. "What nobody? What garden, dzzz? What are you talking about, boy? Where have you been?"

I tried to look innocent and brave. "I was in bed and I heard someone moving about just outside, and a sort of scratching and a sort of mumbling and I thought it must be a thief getting in. I thought that an English gentleman would protect his friends, so I got dressed quickly and went to see ..."

I could see that Nicos had a smirk on his face; Mr Morton looked at me in astonishment, but rather suspiciously.

"You mean, dzzz ... that you went out to look for a thief? What nonsense is this?" Mr Morton got red in the face. "You will go to bed, all of you, dzzz ... and you will not talk. You!" he pointed a finger at me. "You will come with me tomorrow morning to see the Headmaster."

He stamped to the door. "Into bed. Into bed, dzzz ... all of you," he said loudly. "No talking." He turned off the light and marched out.

"Hah," said Nicos, "now you'll catch it. Thieves! Hah!" The others all added their comments; no one believed me, but no one knew what I had been doing. I said nothing, being bound by my oath.

In the morning, after breakfast, I was marched to Creepy's study, escorted by an angry Mr Morton. I waited outside, while he went in to explain the situation, and then was marched in.

Creepy was glancing round at his ghosts and had a cold smile on his face. "Now then, young sir," he said, "what is this we hear?"

I told my story again. Creepy looked round at his friends and said: "We don't believe you. What were you really doing?"

I stuck to my explanation. It took time, but eventually Creepy gave up. "Very well," he said. "We know you are not telling the truth, whatever the truth may be." He then launched into a long tirade about 'letting the side down' and 'these are not the standards we expect' and 'gentlemen don't lie' and so on. It went on and on. Finally he stopped and looked at me coldly.

"We do not like doing this and we always hope it will not be necessary. We shall beat you, boy, and we shall write to your parents about this. We hope it will be a lesson to you." He glanced at Mr Morton. "We are sure you agree." Mr Morton made an indistinct noise.

Creepy went to the umbrella stand by the door, and produced a thin, four foot cane. "Now, sir, you will bend over this chair. We shall give you four."

I bent over, and there was a swish and a lot of pain; four times. I gritted my teeth, determined not to let Creepy win. "Stand up, boy," said Creepy. "You must thank us for correcting you."

"Thank you, sir," I muttered. It was still very painful. Mr Morton took me by the shoulder and led me out. "Stay out of trouble," he said. "I do not like my boys being dzzz … beaten."

On returning to class, I found that the grapevine had worked, and everyone knew what had happened. I was something of a hero. But Snowy paused by my desk and said softly: "You fool!" It still hurt.

That evening, at the Wildernesse, my colleagues demanded to see proof that I had had the 'swishing'. I protested, but Nicos and the others adopted threatening attitudes, so I duly displayed my marks of martyrdom.

There was a sharp, collective intake of breath, so I assumed there were visible signs. But it was not until Pierre produced a small mirror that I saw, in a series of contortions, the neatly defined bruise lines across my behind. The pain had almost gone and the admiration and respect these honourable wounds aroused made the whole episode almost worth it.

The letter from Mother which referred to Creepy's report did not make much of the incident. As usual, there was plentiful underlining and many capitals, but the gist was that she was sure she need not be ashamed of what I did, since I was her darling son, and that Mr Arnold had assured her that a beating now and then did no harm to boys and, on the contrary, helped to build character and discipline. In fact, he had said that the boy, in transgressing and the master, in correcting, both showed the right spirit.

The Spring term passed quickly, and without any notable events. I missed my forays with Ra'is, which had added a welcome spice to the rather monotonous passage of time. My twelfth birthday came and went, unmarked except for good wishes from Mother, and another secret banknote from Uncle Max. My English continued to improve and Snowy, noticing my interest in language, went out of his way to help and correct. This was in stark contrast to Nicos, whose opinion it was that English was 'stupid, sissy language. It has not the Greek manly ways and is speech of servants, not of war'. In fact, he spoke badly on purpose and, when Snowy finally lost patience, got a 'swishing' of three strokes; we admired the proof in the evening, but since I had had four, I remained still the bigger hero. Nicos said it was nothing.

When the holidays finally came, it was Henry's mother who picked us up in a little, rickety car. It might have been the small son of Mr Ginger's Explorer: loud, uncomfortable but utterly reliable. Henry said that it was part of the family, and older than he was.

Henry's mother was a small, dark and very intense lady. She was always in motion, with quick, short movements which gave the impression of great restlessness. She was pretty, with black hair and eyes, and spoke good English. She said I was welcome, that she hoped I would not find the flat too small and cramped, and that I should tell her at once if something was not to my liking. I thanked her, and assured her that I was happy and grateful for the invitation.

We drove out to Heliopolis, the new suburb. It was some way out of town, but as we approached, we could see the gleaming, white multi-story blocks, all looking new, and rising among trees and green areas like cubes of sugar on a billiard table.

Henry and his family lived on the fourth floor of one of the blocks. We parked, and went up in the lift, carrying our suitcases. There was a corridor, which smelt faintly of food, and then, at the end, the door to the flat. Henry's mother unlocked the door, and he ran into the flat.

His father was not yet home, but his grandfather, an ancient person dressed all in rusty black, with a small cap on and a huge white beard and whiskers, embraced him and said something in a foreign language. Henry introduced me, and the old gentleman, whom Henry called *Zaydehle*, said "Shalom". I answered "Salaam", since obviously it was a greeting, and the old man smiled. Then we just stood and stared at each other for a bit.

I suddenly noticed a big, dark eye, peering round the edge of an open doorway. Henry also saw it and, going to the door, pulled in a girl, who had been lurking there.

"This is my sister, Minna," he said. "Welcome my friend Andrew, Minna," he said, turning to her, and she obediently kissed me on the cheek. I dutifully returned the kiss.

Minna was my age, twelve, but was already filling out and losing the straight up-and-down girl figure. Her face was heart-shaped, framed by black hair over her shoulders and her skin was very white. But the most arresting feature was her eyes: they were huge and completely black, so that you could see no division between the pupil and the iris. Also, she hardly blinked and moved her eyes slowly and deliberately, not glancing here and there like most people. The result was that I felt I was looking down the barrels of two cannon, aimed squarely at me. I fancied that inside her head there were little men loading the cannon with appropriate ammunition before shooting me dead. Minna was the most beautiful and exciting girl I had ever seen.

On the second day, I presented Henry's mother with my box of Groppi chocolates, which I had obtained as before, but had asked to be wrapped as a present. This was done at no extra cost and the family were delighted with a gaily wrapped gift; a great improvement on newspaper and string.

Although the household, with the exception of the grandfather, could speak English, among themselves they spoke something which I could not really understand. There were occasional words which sounded like Arabic, and some Spanishy ones, but mostly it was strange. Grandfather could speak Arabic, so I could communicate with him. He would think for a while before saying anything, and stroke his beard. I rather felt that he was expected to be very wise, so he had to be careful not to say anything foolish.

The atmosphere was quite different from that of the Groups. Although Henry's family was every bit as loving and close as George's, they took this much more for granted, and seemed so confident of their relationships that they could do things separately, while still being together. So Henry, Minna and I spent most of our time out and about, in the small parks and gardens of the neighbourhood, with others of our age from the surrounding buildings, doing this and that. Gradually, Minna and I tended to go off on our own, to sit close together for long periods of time, and talk. I told her about Poland, and Baghdad, and Ryszard, and Fizz and Uncle Max and Entah, while she spoke of her parents, and her school; she had never been out of Cairo.

The days passed quickly. There were interesting meals of dishes I had never had and curious divisions between meat and dairy products; wonderful cakes and pastries and strange breads. Henry's mother did all the cooking and cleaning of the house, and Minna sometimes helped. Henry's father was hardly ever there, leaving early and returning late; he mostly read papers and magazines when he was home. Grandfather sat and stroked his beard and tried to think of wise things to say.

As the holiday drew to its close, both Minna and I became more and more tense and on edge. Neither of us realised how fond we had become of each other and the thought of parting was hard to bear. This was all quite different from Polly, who was a jolly, happy interlude. Here was something different: I felt stirrings and emotions strange to me, unexplained, worrying and potentially hurtful.

On the day we went back to school, I bid farewell to Henry's father, and thanked him for a wonderful time and to the *Zaydehle*, who stroked his beard and said, in Arabic: "The wounds of youth heal quickly, but the scars remain." He nodded wisely, and I looked impressed and thanked him.

Minna asked her mother if she could come with us to the school, since there was room in the little car. Henry sat in front with his mother, and Minna and I sat in the back, with our arms round each other. The trip went by in a flash, and we were there. I thanked Henry's mother and said I had had a marvellous time; she gave me a hug and said I was always welcome. Henry went into the school and his mother tactfully climbed back into the car.

Minna and I looked at each other.

We both had tears in our eyes. She gave me a quick embrace and whispered: "Write!" I kissed her on the cheek and she ran to the car and got in without looking back. I stood and watched the little car disappear, with its attendant aura of blue smoke. There was a pain in my chest; it was a new pain, one which I had not experienced before.

The summer term was nothing special. We learned the rudiments of cricket; a game I though rather silly, since it usually ended in a draw. But we were told it was part of an English gentleman's armoury of accomplishments and therefore we put up with it. Of course, we also put up with it because we had to.

The Wildernesse remained unchanged, although we noticed that the window had been fixed so that it would only open some six inches. No one mentioned this, except, of course, Nicos.

"We are prisoners now, because you are foolish," he said to me. "Next they make torture and maybe killing. We will be dead English gentlemen."

Lessons continued reasonably interesting. In History, we learned about English kings, and we were told that the British Empire was the reason why the world was civilised. In Geography, we were told that the British Empire went all the way round the world, so that the sun was always shining on some part of it.

There was also Arithmetic, and English Language, and Science, where a merry teacher called Mr Stanford liked to startle us by making bangs and horrible smells. There was also Gym, where a tough and wiry person we knew as Gym-Jim made us climb ropes and jump over boxes and generally risk life and limb in the pursuit of what he called "The great god fitness".

Towards the end of term, Mr Morton called me to the sitting room in the Wildernesse and said: "You will be dzzz ... flying to Baghdad at the end of term. Your Mother has asked that you are taken to the airport, and Mr Winter has kindly agreed to do that. You must pack everything in your trunk, which will stay here, for next term, and only dzzz ... take a small case."

It was a wrench to think I would be going, although I was also looking forward to seeing Uncle Max, and Entah and Fizz again. I had received a letter from Minna, which circumspectly told me what she was doing at school and how the family were. It was just as well that she wrote about these things, since the letter was given to me opened and, presumably, scanned for unsuitable sentiments by Mr Morton. I also wrote, recounting my activities and expressing innocuous opinions. No one noticed that there were discreet X's dotted about the text, here and there. Curiously, it was possible for Minna and me to read love, affection and that we missed each other desperately into the most innocent phrases. Henry had already promised that I would be invited to his house for the next Christmas holiday. "We don't have a Christmas feast," he said earnestly. "I'm sorry about that. But you will be with Minna."

So at the end of term, Mr Winter came to pick me up in his marvellous red, open two-seater, and we went whizzing off to the airport. There was so much wind and noise that we could not talk. But when he handed me over to the airline stewardess, he solemnly shook hands and said: "Good luck to you, old chap, wherever you end up. Sorry I will not see you next year."

This was a rather mysterious statement, but he went before I could ask him what he meant. Was he leaving? Why? We all liked him and thought he was our best teacher. Well, we would see.

The flight back was uneventful. Although I thought of myself as a seasoned traveller, it was still a thrill to feel the pressure on my back as the plane rose into the air, and the sight of the earth crawling past underneath the wing.

We landed safely at the airport in Baghdad, and there were Mother and Aunt waiting for me. Mother rushed forward and clasped me to her bosom. "Ach, my darlink SON," she exclaimed loudly, to the amusement of my fellow passengers and my great embarrassment. "You have come back to me! How I have suffered all these months. Come and I will tell you what we have all been doink." Her accent was charming and polished. She spoke in English.

In the car, alone with Aunt and me, she reverted to Polish and said that there was really not a lot to tell, that Baghdad society was much as before, and that Mr Arnold had been a great support. Aunt chimed in to say that it was nice to have me back and that Uncle Max was sorry he could not come to the airport.

They then began to speak of the party which was due to happen the following day, specifically whether fish or meat should form the main course. Ahmed, the chauffeur, had winked at me as we got into the car and had a big grin on his face all the way to the house.

At the house, Aunt and Mother disappeared into Aunt's bedroom to continue their discussion, and I rushed to the kitchen to find Entah and the others.

We were all pleased to see each other, and sat together, eating an illegal cake which Ali, the cook, had baked in my honour, while they plied me with questions about Cairo. I told them everything (except about Ra'is, because of the oath) and they nudged each other and winked when I spoke of Polly and Minna.

"He is growing up," said Hussein. "He is finding out what is important."

They laughed gleefully when I told them about the 'swishing' and asked lots of questions about the food, the manners of the people and the way they lived.

Entah just sat quietly and smiled and smiled.

The best part was when Uncle Max came for lunch. We sat together, as always, while I told him all about my time in Cairo. He asked some questions, but mostly was content to let me run on. At the end, he patted my hand and said: "Na, it all sounds all right so far. English values are good values, but remember you are a Pole, and Polish values are sometimes a little different. Best thing is to learn everything and then choose what you want." He beat his drum for a moment and sniffed. "But I am very happy to see you back. It is good to talk. We will talk more."

I settled back into my normal Baghdad routine: the Club, the bicycle, swimming with my friends. We still were comfortable together, though their year had been spent at an English school in India and although we exchanged stories, we no longer felt quite so close.

I also visited Fizz. Sergeant Abdullah was delighted to see the small sergeant, and even the two unimportant ones shook me warmly by the hand. But Nanny had moved rather into the background and there was an English governess, a youngish woman who drove one of the late King Ghazi's cars (an open Bentley Eight) round the town. I heard her described as fast, although one could not drive very fast in the town, and she disapproved of everyone who was not English. Fizz's mother, *Umm Faisal* , was ill all the time, so I only saw Fizz twice during the whole holiday. He told me that more and more of the people round him were on the other side. I was sorry for him.

Mr Arnold was often at the house, and was very helpful to Mother. He was kind to me and always polite, although I could see that he could also be tough when he wished. It was during one of his visits that the bombshell fell.

We were all in the sitting room. I had been called in to shake hands with Mr Arnold when he suddenly said: "Well, Andrew, I hope you like Alexandria next year as much as you liked Cairo."

"Alexandria, Sir?" I asked. "My school is in Cairo and that is where all my friends are."

"Well," he answered. "There will only be day-boys in Cairo next year. So you have to go to the seaside, ha ha. I am sure you will like it even better."

I excused myself and rushed up to my room. I could not quite absorb the news. All I understood was that I would never see Minna again or George or Henry. I would never see Minna again. How could I live with this? Now I understood Snowy's remark at the airport.

Never see Minna again. I lay on my bed and wept a bit, but then sat up again. I had started a new life in so many places that this was just another time. I remembered *Zaydehle* saying that the wounds of youth heal quickly. I hoped that he was right.

CHAPTER FIVE

Egypt – Alexandria

The holiday in Baghdad drew smoothly to its close. There was the swimming in the Club, the odd visit to see Fizz and bicycle rides to my farmer friends on the banks of the Tigris. In the back of my mind was a bruised feeling of yet again having made friends only to lose them, and especially the different emotion I had felt with Minna.

I continued to have my meals with Uncle Max. He was interested in my stories of Cairo and in the customs and habits of the school. He also told me that the war was going much better for us and that in the end Hitler would be defeated and the world would be at peace again. "But there will never be peace everywhere," he added, "because there will always be men who can only obtain what they want by force. You must always resist such men."

When the time came to leave, my thoughts were overlaid with the excitement of the new school near a beach. My experience of beaches was limited to hearsay and I wanted to explore the sea; after all, swimming held no terrors for me and I was completely at home in the water.

During the flight to Cairo, I was proud of the fact that I knew what was going on, and felt sorry for two of the passengers who were nervous and frightened. However, we flew through a storm, and when the rain lashed the windows and the plane behaved as though there were pot-holes in the sky-road, I became as worried as the others and was glad when we finally arrived.

In Cairo, I was met by an Egyptian clerk, sent by the school, whose duty was to escort me to the railway station and see me safely onto the train for Alexandria. He was delighted that I spoke Arabic, but insisted we used English "for honour of the school", he said.

The railway station was exciting. There was much noise as crowds of Egyptians in white *djellabiyas* and red *tarbooshes* or white turbans milled around, all talking at the tops of their voices. The trains were standing at their platforms, hissing and grunting, steam spurting and leaking from the locomotives. People were getting on, some carrying suitcases, others with bunches of live chickens trussed by the legs, or with big baskets of fruit and green vegetables. Small boys, also with baskets, were selling pumpkin and melon seeds, and peanuts, in little twists of newspaper as well as bottles of drinks all the colours of the rainbow. There were also men who sold skewers of roast meat and flat, round Arab breads. Permeating everything was a damp smell of steam, oil, grilled meat and assorted rotting fruit.

The clerk led me to a second-class carriage and we mounted the steep steps to get in. It was quite big, and there were seats upholstered in some sort of material, rather shabby and with holes. We found a seat by a window and he handed over a packet of sandwiches and a bottle of lemonade, introduced me to the conductor and told me that my trunk had already been sent to Alexandria and that I would be met there by someone from school. It was all over very quickly and he left. A few minutes later we steamed out of Cairo, north towards the sea.

I had been expecting desert; after all, Egypt was supposed to be mostly desert. But I was astonished to see that we were puffing and clanking through lush green fields and groves of palms and other trees. It was hard to make the connection with the last time I had been in a train, during the escape from the Germans; the sights, smells and atmosphere were so different.

We passed through Tanta, about half-way on our journey, and the landscape continued green, with fields criss-crossed by rivulets and ditches, and white-clad *fellaheen*, Egyptian farmers, usually raking and digging, or driving oxen and donkeys about. I suddenly realised that this was the famous Nile Delta.

I ate my sandwiches, of a pungent cheese, and drank my warm lemonade. There were several other passengers in the carriage: an old man, who slept all the way, grumbling restlessly under his breath, was in the seat opposite; further up there was a family, with several shrill-voiced young children. One of them, a little boy of about four, came and stood in front of me for quite a long time, not saying anything, but staring at me unblinkingly with huge, black eyes. I offered him a drink of my lemonade, but he ran back to his mother.

We finally arrived in Alexandria and puffed and sighed our way into the station, which was almost as crowded as the one in Cairo. Many people were milling about and when I had climbed down the steep steps, I stood for a moment wondering what to do next.

Somebody grabbed my arm, and I saw a busy little man, with a tiny, wizened face, like a small monkey. He efficiently gathered me and my small bag, thrusting us into a taxi. He said his name was Taha, and that it was unnecessary to speak or thank him; so I did not. I simply assumed he was from school, and so it proved.

We drove for some time, partly along the coast. It was late afternoon and the sea looked exciting and mysterious and dark blue. It had a special smell, sort of weedy and sharp. The water was calm, and broke in lacy frills of white foam on the yellow beaches; there were not many people there. I was impatient to explore and swim.

After some time, we turned inland into a suburb, full of trees and villas behind high walls. We drove on until we came to a wide gate, set in high railings stretching in both directions. Through the gate we went and along a straight drive, flanked by playing fields, to a large building.

This was of honey-coloured stone, three stories high, in the shape of a huge U. We stopped at the open end and I could see that at the far, closed end, there was a five story square tower. In the middle was grass, with boys walking and running about.

But I had no time to look properly. Taha took my case and hurried me to a door in the building and into a room with some chairs and a desk.

"Wait here, boy," he said, and rushed out. I sat and waited.

After some time a man came in. He was of wiry build and of medium height, with a freckled face and thinning, carroty hair. His skin had the paleness of red-haired people; he wore an open-necked shirt with sleeves rolled up to reveal sinewy forearms with muscles which writhed and rippled as he closed and opened his fists in a nervous sort of way.

"You're Andrew Kronman," he said in a deep voice and a strong Scottish accent. "At least you have a good name, if nothing else." I looked blank. "St. Andrew, boy, patron saint of Scotland." I felt confused; who or where was Scotland?

"Yes, Sir," I answered. "I have just arrived from Baghdad and Cairo."

"Aye, I know that. I am Mr Brighouse, your Housemaster. You will be in my House, and obedience and loyalty are to the House and to me." He looked at my small bag. "Now pick that up and follow me." He turned and marched out, without looking to see if I followed. I followed. He gave me the strong impression that he always got what he wanted and was a dangerous man to cross. I resolved to wait and see.

We marched deeper into the U, and suddenly turned in through a door and up a staircase. On the second floor we entered a long room, with a row of beds on each side (I counted twelve in each row). These were lined up with great precision, and each had a blue blanket, taut and unwrinkled, a white sheet precisely folded over the top, and pristine pillows. Beside each bed was a low locker, with nothing on it. The floor was of highly polished wooden planks.

"This is your dormitory," said MrBrighouse. "Your bed is the third one along here. Put your bag under it and follow me." Again he turned and marched out without looking.

We went down the stairs and out of the building. The grass space inside the U, which I was later told was called the Quad, had two huge trees on one side: a gigantic black mulberry and an immense rubber tree. The road ran round beside the building. There were boys of all sizes everywhere. Mr Brighouse let out a sudden loud roar: "Chakli, Chakli, here, on the double."

A boy, of about my age, came running over from the Quad. He

was stocky, with black, curly hair and a pale, curiously impassive face. He was dressed in white shorts and a white shirt. He ran up to us and stood waiting.

Mr Brighouse looked at him: "Your shoes are dirty," he said. "Clean them before I see you next." Chakli said nothing.

"This is Kronman," said Mr Brighouse. "He is new and I've put him in the Second Dormitory, with you. Show him the ropes." He turned on his heel and marched away, without looking back, confident that his orders would be obeyed.

Chakli and I stared at each other. I felt already that there was a subtle difference from the school in Cairo, if only in the fact that surnames were used, even, as I later found, between friends – one of the curious English public school customs.

Chakli put his hand out. "My name is Sadi Chakli," he said brusquely. "Do what I say and there will be no trouble." It was unclear to me if the trouble thus avoided would be with the school or with him. I decided to be circumspect and to lie low.

We walked slowly along one side of the Quad. "Be careful of Brighouse," said Chakli. "He is known as Whipper, because he likes beating. Sometimes he has to invent reasons for beating, so it is good to stay away from him. This is hard to do in the dormitory."

"What is this House thing?" I asked. "We did not have it in Cairo."

"You were in Cairo?" asked Chakli. "We heard that the boarders were coming, but I think you are the only one."

"There is no one called Woomey or Kristopolous who has come?" I asked. Were none of my friends here?

"No, I haven't seen any like that," said Chakli. "A House is something everybody belongs to, like a big family. There are two Houses for the boarders: Brighouse, who are Blues (that's us), and Keiths, who are Reds (that's them). Brighouse is our Housemaster, and Keith, who is called Sloop, because he has a boat, is theirs. Then there are two day-boy Houses, but we don't care about them."

Chakli showed me round the school. The classrooms were in the right arm of the U and the dormitories were in the left. The large dining hall was on the ground floor of the end tower, and that is where we ended up, in time for supper.

The food was plentiful and good, just like in Cairo. There was the usual rice, meat, *moloukhiya* and Arab bread. There was also always some *leben*, or yoghurt, to pour over the rice if one wished. For pudding, there was sometimes semolina, fruit, or a sticky cake. We sat at long tables, eight to a side, strictly by age; there was a senior boy at the head of each, who was supposed to keep us in order, but all ours was interested in was getting the best titbits from the serving dishes. I sat next to Chakli, who continued to tell me about the school. There was an enormous amount of noise.

"Are you strong?" asked Chakli suddenly.

"Pretty strong. And I have a knife and I can fight with it."

He seemed unimpressed. "Good. It is necessary here," he said. "We sometimes have to fight, occasionally with other people here in the school, and now and then with people outside, from another school, who hate us. You should never go out of school grounds alone or they will jump on you. Last term one of the Keiths was badly cut, but he didn't die, so it was all right." I thought this all sounded ominous, and I was glad I had Ra'is's knife.

Chakli told me his father was a big and important politician in Damascus and that he was also going to be one when he grew up. He said that I would meet Ridha, his friend, after supper. Ridha, he said, was from Lebanon, and came from an extremely wealthy family; he also had an elder brother at the school, which was useful. In return, I told him a certain amount about myself.

After supper, Chakli introduced me to Teddy Ridha. Rid, as Chakli called him, was the most beautiful person I had ever seen: shining black hair, an oval face glowing light brown, big black eyes and a fine nose. He looked like an angel from a religious picture.

Chakli said to me: "If you can prove yourself, you can be our friend. We would make a good three: I am a Syrian and very strong, Rid is Lebanese and knows how to make people do what he wants, and you are a Pole who has travelled a lot. That makes a good three. But you must show us you are worth it."

"What do I have to do to prove myself?" I asked. Was this going to be the blood brother thing all over again?

"Nothing special," said Chakli and Rid grinned. "We will watch you for a bit, and tell you when we are ready."

By the time we went up to the dormitory to sleep, I had met several other boys, but I liked none as much as Chakli and Ridha; I was determined to pass their test, whatever it was.

When we had washed and changed into pyjamas, Chakli, who had the bed next to me, said: "Did you wash your feet very much?"

"Not specially," I replied. "Why?"

"You'll see. It is best you find out for yourself." Chakli's face was its usual impassive mask.

Just then, a tension became apparent in the dormitory; boys stopped chatting and sat quietly and warily, every one on his own bed. I had not heard anything, but in a minute or so Mr Brighouse entered the room.

He stopped at the door and looked around. His fists clenched and unclenched, and the muscles on his forearms writhed. He had a mirthless smile on his face.

"Time for games," he said loudly. "Are you all here?"

There was a chorus of: "Yes, Mr Brighouse." I noticed that neither Chakli nor Ridha said anything.

Mr Brighouse looked at me. "You, Kronman, isn't it? You're new so I can start with you. Aye, that's it," He walked to my bed. "Now then, sit here and show me your feet." Chakli, on the next bed, had a faint smile on his face. "Right, now wet your finger and rub your foot here, just under the ankle". I felt the rest of the dormitory watching. "Rub hard, rub hard …"

I rubbed and found there were little rolls of skin under my finger. "Ha," said Mr Brighouse loudly. "Stop. Take your finger away. See," he said pointing at my ankle. "You're a dirty boy, Kronman. You don't wash."

He stood up. "Bend over the bed," he ordered. I looked at Chakli and Ridha, but their faces showed nothing. Mr Brighouse took off his slipper and hit me, hard, three times with the sole. It hurt a lot, but I tried not to show anything.

"Next time wash properly," said Mr Brighouse. "I shall be

watching you." He then smiled broadly and produced a lighter and a tennis ball from his pocket. "Now, Kronman, put this lighter on the floor at the far end. You can have first go. Roll the ball to knock over the lighter."

I tried and failed. The boys took it in turn until one succeeded. He was rewarded with a sweet from the Brighouse pocket. It was then time for 'Lights Out' and Mr Brighouse marched away.

"This happens every night," came a soft whisper from Chakli's bed. "It is impossible to be so clean that you don't get any crumbles. Whipper will anyway go from one to another until he can beat somebody. The ball thing is stupid as well. Nobody likes him."

"It hurts a lot," I whispered back. "Why didn't you warn me?"

"We wanted to see how tough you were," he replied. "Usually new boys cry," he added. "Anyway, you can call me Chak and call Ridha, Rid. We will call you Krow. Now be quiet; Whipper sometimes creeps back to catch us talking and then there is serious beating. Good night."

"Good night, Chak," I whispered. My behind was tingling, but I soon fell asleep, amidst snores, grumbles and sniffs from the twenty three boys around me.

The next few days passed quickly. Chak and Rid showed me the school, both the official and the unofficial places (like the paved area behind the kitchens where formal, or 'honour', fights took place). Matron, who was a forbidding person of indeterminate age and nationality, unpacked my trunk with me in attendance. She said my allocated number was 154, and that everything I owned had to be numbered. I asked if that included my body, but she just snarled and told me to go away.

I stayed out of Whipper's way and scrubbed my ankles every night.

The classrooms were ordinary, the teachers unremarkable. It was obvious to me that as long as I behaved reasonably and did not get caught doing anything, I could manage as well as in Cairo.

Chak and Rid had an emergency ally, upon whom they called only in times of great need, since he was wild and uncontrollable. I met him quite by accident, but was very glad to make his acquaintance.

We three were walking peaceably behind the main building when abruptly five rather bigger boys surrounded us; they were day-boys and Egyptians.

The leader, who was both tall and heavy, blocked our way. "Hah," he sneered. "Three foreigners and boarders, too. And pretty boy Ridha." He looked at his gang. "Time for a ransom. Give us your money or suffer and kiss my shoes."

We immediately went into defensive posture; Chak and Rid had taught it to me. We stood back to back, facing outwards. Our knives came out.

"Go and love your sister who looks like a camel, oh Ali," hissed Chak. He put two fingers in his mouth and whistled shrilly twice.

"So the sheep want to play." The leader took a step forward. He and his friends also had knives out. They moved them up and down, and from hand to hand; they obviously were not novices.

The gang slowly circled round us, and we turned with them, so that Chak was always facing Ali, the leader. Rid was humming under his breath.

Suddenly, there was a confused noise and a large body smashed into the gang leader and flattened him. "Now!" shouted Chak, and we darted our knives at the gang and closed with them. I was grappling with one of the day-boys, and had his right wrist in my left hand while jabbing at his side with my knife. Out of the corner of my eye, I suddenly saw Ali, the leader, fly through the air and land on his front on the gravel. My opponent turned and ran, as did two others. Chak was holding one off the ground with both hands and butting his face with his forehead. Ali was motionless on the ground.

Chak let his antagonist go and he ran away as fast as his legs would carry him; his face was covered in blood.

I looked round: we had been joined by a huge, black boy, who was grinning a wide, white grin and rolling his eyes in a ferocious sort of way. He had one foot on the fallen leader's neck and was pressing down quite hard, in the attitude of a hunter posing for a photograph with his prey.

"Let's fix him," he said in Arabic. I got nervous; I did not want to be a party to murder.

Chak looked at me and laughed. "Don't worry, Krow," he said. "There is no permanent damage."

Our huge friend sat the leader up. He was rather groggy and his face was scratched, bloody and had bits of gravel in it. Chak took a large handful of his hair and sawed it off close to the scalp with his knife, leaving a short, ragged patch in the middle. He then cut the leader's belt in half, cut his shoe-laces and slit his left sleeve open. It seemed to be a ritual.

"Now go, illegitimate dog turd," he kicked him upright. "Never try this again or you will be really sorry." The leader hobbled away; it seemed his leg was injured. We appeared to be unhurt, except for some bruises.

"This is Mahmoud," said Chak, slapping the huge boy on the back. "He is our friend, and we can ask him for help when we need to. It is lucky he was close by this time. We call him Beast, because he enjoys fighting ..."

"... and it is very hard to make him stop," added Rid.

Beast grinned and shook my hand. "I've heard about you, Krow," he said in a deep voice. "You hold a knife well. But you don't have to worry if I am around; just whistle."

He turned to Chak. "Thanks, Chak," he said. "I enjoyed that." He walked away, whistling under his breath.

"We are lucky he likes us," Chak remarked. "He refuses to be in any band, or to have any special friends. He is Sudanese, and hates the Egyptians, so he helps us when they attack. But always be nice to him, your life may depend on it."

Another person I met that day was the Countess. I had been told to report to the piano room, on the first floor of the tower, at four o'clock. I knocked at the door and a gruff voice told me to enter.

It was a large, gloomy room. The only light came from a high window in one wall and a single, bright lamp which cast its light onto an enormous piano. Seated beside the piano in a high-backed chair was an ancient crone, dressed all in black. A small, white, poodly dog stood up and yapped at me.

"Come and sit down, boy," she had a voice like tearing calico. "You will address me as 'Countess'. I am of noble blood and a true Russian, not the trash which now lives in our country and calls itself by our holy name. Who are you?"

The Countess spoke with a strong Russian accent, rolling her r's and pronouncing English as though it was a Slav language.

"*Ya paniemaje gavaritch pa Ruski,*" I said out of politeness, "I can speak Russian."

The gaunt, black figure rose slowly from her chair. She raised both arms above her head, as though about to pronounce a malediction on me. I took a step back and the little dog nipped me on the leg.

"You will speak English," she screeched. "You will not desecrate our beautiful language here. Never, never again must you speak anything to me except English." Her voice rose to a climax. "You understand? Now sit down. Who are you?"

"I am Kronman," I said, much subdued. "I was told to come." The nasty little dog lay down beside my foot, growling faintly.

"They tell me you wish to learn from me the piano," said the Countess. "You are very fortunate for me to teach you. I have not yet decided, of course. You will play and I will judge. I am excellent judge and I play most beautifully. Sit and play."

She leaned back in her chair and closed her eyes. I sat down at the huge piano and began to play an elementary piece I remembered from Professor Hertz. I made many mistakes and forgot the end. After a short time, the Countess roused herself and announced: "Enough. I have decided."

She stood up and paced slowly round the room in a rather dramatic way, not unlike the way Mother sometimes did, except she was old and ugly. Her face was seamed and lined and she had heavy make-up, especially a smeary scarlet mouth. Her hands were veined and freckled, her fingernails were bright red .

"I have decided to teach you. You cannot play and are ignorant, but you have a touch and the rest can be taught. Ach, that I have come to this. You will come on Mondays and Thursdays at 5 o'clock. Now go."

I stood up and hurried out. I could hear her voice saying: "Now, Ninotchka, we are alone again; I will play for you ..." The sound of the piano being played indeed beautifully faded as I ran down the stairs. I was not looking forward to sessions with the Countess.

On the Saturday, after a game of football in the early afternoon, we went to the beach. It was wonderful.

The beachfront of Alexandria was divided into neat patches by waist-high fences running down to the water. These patches, which were numbered, catered to different social classes and it was important for those who worried about such things to be seen at the right numbered beach. We went to beach number 5 and were told to behave, not to make a noise or annoy other people and to come when called. Naturally, as soon as the teacher who was supervising us (a weak and soft man called Babbitt and whom we called Rabbit) released us, we took no further notice of him.

We ran and swam and shouted and threw a tennis ball about, much to the disgust of the adults on the beach, who were sitting about in deck chairs and inside little huts, which could be rented for the season. There was a great mixture of people, although on Beach number 5 there was a majority of what looked like Europeans. I noticed that next door, on Beach number 4, there were a great many servicemen with attractive young ladies.

The water was clear and warm, the sand was yellow and everything was just as I hoped it would be, if not better. Chak, Rid and I swam along the shore to other beaches, which were crowded. On one, we found a whole girls' school swimming and caused havoc by splashing them, grabbing their ankles underwater and causing mayhem. We were chased by a fat lady teacher who had no hope of catching us, though we had to be careful to lose her so as not to be traced back to our proper beach. It was an exhilarating afternoon.

The first letter from Mother came. As usual, there was not much real news; mostly there were comments on her continuing sacrifice at having her 'darlink' son so far away. But I noted that there were increasingly frequent mentions of Mr Arnold, and I sensed a curious background coyness. Uncle Max was well, as was Aunt and also the household. There were big plans for a fancy-dress party for Christmas, which everyone was anticipating with great excitement; Mother said that she and Aunt would wear their usual Polish peasant dresses.

The days passed. I managed to avoid trouble, except for one 'honour' fight, which was forced on me. An 'honour' fight was distinguished from an ordinary one in its cause. If there was an insult, verbal or physical, or a simple challenge for a favoured seat in class, or private lounging area in the Quad, an 'honour' fight ensued.

This entailed a formal ritual, with seconds, a referee and choice of weapons – a wholly civilised procedure. The challenged could choose between knives (limited in size), cricket stumps, bare knuckles or kicking only. There was a time limit and a vow of silence where the masters were concerned.

A particularly obnoxious day-boy in our class, Wilhelm by name and with suspected German antecedents (he refused to disclose details of his parentage), spilt some ink on my desktop. I thought he had done so on purpose and demanded an apology. He, egged on by his day-boy friends, made a false and impertinent assertion about Mother and the circumstances of my birth. The ring of boys around us started chanting: "Challenge, challenge …" I had no choice, and smacked Wilhelm across the face. "I challenge you to an 'honour' fight. Chakli will speak to your second."

We had to sit down then, since Whipper, whose class it was, suddenly appeared in the doorway and barked: "Sit down, all of you. What do you think you are doing?"

After the lesson, Chak, Rid and I had a council of war. Rid suggested that we set the date for the fight a good while ahead, so that I could have time to practise with whatever weapon Wilhelm chose. Chak was all for getting it over as soon as possible.

"Wilhelm is nothing without his friends," he said. "he wasn't expecting a challenge from you and I bet he is as scared as anything now. Before we make up our minds, I will find out what he chooses."

Later that afternoon, Chak found me and told me that Wilhelm had chosen knives, because he thought that I, as a new boy, would be scared and take the dishonourable option of running out on my challenge.

"The fight will be two days from now. This gives us time for a bit of coaching. I have already spoken to Beast, and he will help."

A knife fight was usually until the first drawing of blood, normally a small scratch somewhere. But there was always the possibility of something more serious. I did some training with Beast, who was not very good since he usually fought with his hands, being enormous and strong. But Chak was quick and showed me certain feints and how to use the left arm, around which a combatant wrapped his jacket. The mistake was to wrap it too tightly, since a useful trick was to get the opponent's knife entangled in the cloth, thus opening the way for a telling thrust or slash. It was also a good idea to leave one sleeve dangling, because then one could perhaps flick it into the opponent's eyes.

Fighting time came all too soon. Chak, Rid and Beast escorted me to the paved area behind the kitchens. Wilhelm was already there, with a gang of day-boy supporters. I was glad to see that I also had a handful of partisans, both Blues and Reds united against the day-boys.

The referee, a senior boy unknown to me, but approved by Chak, inspected our knives and pronounced them acceptable.

The audience formed a ring. Wilhelm and I took off our blazers and wrapped them round our left arms; I noticed that his was done up tight and presented no danger. The referee called us into the middle.

"When I say 'go', you can start. When I say 'stop', you must stop at once. If you don't, you forfeit the fight and I declare the other the winner. Now, do you wish to shake hands and forget any insult or hurt?"

The circle of boys began to chant: "Fight, fight, fight ..." I shook my head and Wilhelm said: "No," loudly.

"Very well," the referee stood between us and put his hands on our shoulders. He took a pace back and said: "Go!"

Wilhelm tried a quick stab, which I parried with my jacket. I then swung the loose sleeve at his face, and he backed up a step, blinking his eyes. This was good. The chant of "Fight, fight ..." went on in the background. We feinted and danced round each other, knives to the fore. Wilhelm suddenly charged me with his shoulder, giving a yell. I jumped backwards, and stumbled on a small hole in the asphalt. I was down on one knee when he rushed forward again. I heard Chak and Rid shout: "Sleeve!"

Wilhelm had his arm stretched out with the knife in low position. I flicked my sleeve at him, and it wound itself round his arm. I pulled, and he came towards me. I slashed my knife at his arm and drew blood.

"Stop!" yelled the referee. I stood back, but Wilhelm, furious, tried to charge me. The referee grabbed him by the neck, and his seconds came to hold him.

The referee examined the bleeding cut on Wilhelm's forearm. "Kronman wins. It's all over. Everybody disperse."

Chak and Rid were hugging me and dancing. Beast had his enormous arms round the three of us and danced as well. The Blues and Reds were cheering as the group of day-boys walked away in silence.

This was the only 'honour fight' I had during my time in Alexandria. I was glad it was over. I felt that Ra'is would have been proud of me.

The piano lessons with the Countess were a great burden. Twice a week I had to go to her and suffer for an hour. I also had to practise every day for half an hour; she always knew when I cheated, I do not know how.

"You waste my time," she would say. "Why I bother for a lazy child like you when I have such brilliance? Tell me, Ninotchka, is not this boy a stupid and worthless creature?" I thought it odd that she called the dog Ninotchka, a girl's name, when it was male.

She had the unpleasant habit of rapping my knuckles with a long, round wooden ruler, whenever I made a mistake or if my posture at the piano did not meet with her approval. I was painfully learning, for the Easter Concert, Mozart's Turkish March, with a difficult middle bit. On one occasion, Ninotchka surreptitiously and copiously peed on my foot, under the piano. I kicked him under the chin and fortunately the Countess did not notice.

I longed to give up these piano lessons, and wrote imploringly to Mother, who eventually agreed. She said, however, that I must first perform in the Concert.

Another matter which preoccupied me at the time was how I would be spending the three weeks of Christmas holidays. Chak and Rid were going home, to Syria and Lebanon, and Beast was going to spend his time with a much hated aunt in Cairo. I asked Mother, in one of my letters and she replied that she was sure the School would arrange something.

I finally plucked up courage and asked to see Whipper. He saw me in his study, one afternoon after school. It was a small room, lined with books. By the door there was a hollowed-out elephant's leg full of canes; I tried not to look at it, but there was an awful fascination about it, like a gallows or a dungeon, and my eyes kept going back to it.

"What is the matter, Kronman?" asked Whipper. "Anything special?"

I was staring at the elephant's leg.

"Well, well ...," Whipper began to clench and unclench his fists on the desk top; the muscles writhed. "What do you want? You seem to have settled down reasonably well so far. At least, I haven't caught you yet. But I will, I will ..."

I stood before the desk. "I wanted to ask you, Sir, what is happening to me at Christmas, because I am not going home, Sir." Whipper liked lots of 'Sirs'.

"Aye, that's right." Whipper nodded his head. "You can stay here at school and amuse yourself. I am away to Cairo, but the Headmaster has kindly invited you to Christmas lunch, so you better behave. You should have a good time; no lessons or anything."

"Sir, is anyone else staying, Sir?", I asked.

"Not as far as I know, not this time. But you will be fine. The servants will feed you as usual, and you will have the run of the school. If you like, I will arrange for Matron (she will be here) to open the library for you when you ask, and there are plenty of books there for you to read."

"Sir, yes please. Thank you, Sir."

"Very well, boy. You can go now." Whipper picked up some papers and gazed at them. I turned, and looked closely at the elephant's leg as I went out. There must have been fifteen canes in there, all of different thickness.

I asked Chak about this and he grinned and said: "Ah yes, when Whipper beats, you get the choice of canes. I recommend the thickest you can find; it hurts more at the time, but the pain doesn't last so long." He paused. "Of course," he added judiciously, "that's only my opinion and it is a very personal matter. You will find that people have different feelings about it; some prefer the very thin ones. You will have to make up your own mind when you have some experience." He grinned again and slapped me on the back. Rid smiled and said: "I like the thick one best as well."

The end of term arrived all too quickly and I stood in the Quad watching everyone leave. The sight of the empty Quad and a complete and unaccustomed silence were a bit disconcerting; I had never experienced silence in these surroundings.

After a while, I went to find Matron. She grumbled but agreed to open the library for me to choose a book. I selected a book of Sherlock Holmes stories.

"Now don't come bothering me every day, Kronman," she complained. "It has been a long term and I have earned my holiday without being constantly bothered by you. I really don't know why you have to hang around here and not go home like everyone else ..."

"I don't know either," I said.

I read the book very slowly. My meals were in the dining hall, at the usual times. It felt odd to be there all alone, surrounded by empty tables. The servant who brought the food was polite but refused all attempts at conversation.

The time passed slowly. I had a tennis ball, which I kicked about the Quad. I sat just inside the railings of the football pitches and stared at the passers-by. I went upstairs and lay on my bed and tried to sleep. I practised the piano. All in all, I looked forward to my meals as the high points of each day.

After a week, I went to Matron again, to change my book. She was in a better mood.

"Tomorrow is Christmas Eve," she remarked. "Come and see me at teatime, and I will make sure you have the right clothes to wear for your lunch with the Headmaster." She gave me a biscuit and a piece of chocolate, as Christmas presents and a propelling pencil which Mother had sent from Baghdad.

"There is also a sum of money from your Uncle, but we will add that to your pocket-money fund," she said.

The Headmaster was almost completely unknown to me. He was an Olympian figure, visible on the platform at school meetings, and sometimes marching along in the Quad, reputed to be strict but kindly and more interested in the running of the school than in the boys. He was tall and big, with a balding head, crinkled up eyes and a large, brown moustache.

Dressed in my best clothes, which consisted of blazer, well-pressed shorts, white shirt with school tie and long school socks, as well as highly polished black shoes, I presented myself at the door of Headmaster's House, in a corner of the school grounds, at precisely 12 o'clock on Christmas Day. I knocked on the door.

The door opened and I was faced by a black person, robed in white and with a red tarboosh on his head.

He looked down at me. "Yes?" he enquired, somewhat haughtily.

"I am Kronman," I said. He stared at me.

"I am having lunch with the Headmaster," I added in a casual manner, "so you better let me in."

The person opened the door and bowed, in a somewhat exaggerated manner. "Please to come in, your Excellency," he said. "We are honoured." I do not think he was being serious. "Your grandmother was a crocodile," I said under my breath; I don't think he heard.

I marched into a large hall, and was greeted by the Headmaster, who was coming out of a room at the end.

"You must be Kronman," he announced in a high-pitched voice. "Merry Christmas and all that. Come in, come in ..." He ushered me into the room at the end.

This was a big sitting room, crammed with furniture. There were fat armchairs covered in flowery cloth, leather sofas, wooden stools, tables and bookcases; so many that one had to weave one's way round and between them to get anywhere. In one corner there was a big Christmas tree, all lit up and decorated with sparkly, coloured ornaments: baubles, chains, silvered fruit, lights and small crackers.

I was gazing at this, enchanted, when I suddenly noticed a thin lady, obviously Mrs Headmaster, sitting in one of the chairs. She was wearing a flowery frock, and one could hardly see her against the chair. In the next chair was a girl of roughly my age, with a pretty face but a nasty sneering expression on it.

"This is Kronman, my dear," said the Headmaster. "Kronman, this is my wife and that is Julie, my daughter."

Mrs Headmaster smiled, and held out her hand, which I shook. "I am glad you could come to us," she said, as though she was flattered that I could squeeze the visit into my busy social programme. "Come and sit by Julie, and we will have a drink before lunch." She had a nice smile and her hand was warm. But there seemed to be a formal atmosphere; no one was relaxed. I remembered Group's and Henry's warmly affectionate households in Cairo.

I sat down on the chair next to the girl, who went on sneering and said nothing.

There was desultory conversation during which I was interrogated about my history and family; I answered the questions warily.

"Oh, you are from Poland, are you," Mrs Headmaster remarked. "How interesting. They are some of our gallant allies, you know. Mr Churchill has said that the war is going well and that we will win. We got quite a fright here, when that beastly man Rommel almost came to Cairo. The Headmaster was quite worried, weren't you, dear?"

The Headmaster nodded. A servant brought a tray of drinks: what looked like sherry for the adults (just like in Baghdad) and orange squash for Julie and me. She still had said nothing.

Finally we were told that 'Lunch is served, Madam'. We all trooped into the room next door, where a table was set with crackers, paper holly and coloured napkins. I had kept an eye out for mistletoe, but did not see any.

The meal was a good one: soup, a thin very long-legged turkey with carrots, potatoes and cabbage, and a Christmas pudding which the servant kept trying to light but which kept going out. There were also mince pies and fruit and nuts. We pulled the crackers (I pulled mine with Julie, who looked even more sour when the major part remained in my hand), and we all put on paper hats.

The Headmaster and his wife were kind to me, and tried to make the conversation interesting, but it was too formal and didn't work. I ate an enormous amount.

After lunch we returned to the room with the furniture and played   Monopoly. I remembered playing it with Group and his family. The Headmaster was lucky in his dice rolling and rapidly built lots of houses and hotels. I landed on his hotel in Park Lane and was the first out.

"Never mind, Kronman," said Mrs Headmaster sympathetically. "That was unlucky and unfair."

"Nonsense, my dear," said the Headmaster. "Don't give the boy wrong ideas. It may have been unlucky, but it was not unfair. Life is like that and he has to get used to it." I thought he was right.

Before leaving, Mrs Headmaster gave me a completely unexpected present, a rectangular parcel wrapped in red paper. When I had thanked her and opened it, I found to my surprise that it was a book of Sherlock Holmes stories, the twin of the one I had just returned to the library.

I bowed and shook hands with everybody, while thanking the family for being so kind and giving me a marvellous meal. As I left the room, I overheard Mrs Headmaster saying: "Such quaint, charming manners, these Europeans ..."

I went straight up to the dormitory and lay on my bed, trying to digest the rich meal, and pondering on the different sorts of families there were. I thought it was strange that I could have spent more than four hours with the Headmaster's family without hearing a single word from his daughter.

The kindness of the Headmaster's wife continued, however, and I was surprised, some three days after Christmas, to be called by Matron who announced that Ali, one of the Headmaster's servants, had been instructed to take me to the cinema in town the following day.

When Ali duly appeared, he turned out to be the one who had opened the door on my visit on Christmas day. He was amiable and we chatted in Arabic, all the way into town on a bus. The chosen film was an American musical with Deanna Durbin (with whom I immediately fell hopelessly in love) although the story was rather boring. Ali bought me a delicious choc-ice, and on the way out, a little paper twist of pumpkin seeds, which I ate on the bus.

When we got back to school, it was quite dark and I was just in time for supper. I thanked Ali very much and he smiled and said: "You know, my grandmother is nothing like a crocodile." I felt very bad, and apologised and we parted friends.

The following day I wrote a careful note of thanks to the Headmaster's wife and delivered it to her house. I saw Julie, who was looking out of the window and who put her tongue out at me. I still had not heard her speak.

The interminable holiday finally came to an end and Chak and Rid were back. So was Beast, who said he had an awful time with his aunt.

School life resumed its normal flow and the Easter concert inexorably approached. My 'Turkish March' made slow progress, the Countess grew more and more irritable as her annual showpiece came closer. This irritation manifested itself in a hair-trigger reaction with her wooden ruler.

"You do not have the feel," she would complain. "How you can miss such large key on the piano; how you forget to leave go of pedal; how you have no SOUL ..." This was the ultimate shortcoming in a pupil.

The concert itself took place, towards the end of term, in the school hall, a large, empty place now arranged with rows of wooden chairs. Attendance was compulsory for the school, and there were many parents who had come to hear their offspring perform. The staff, with the Headmaster's family in the centre, sat in the front two rows. The stage was bare, but for a grand piano, the piano stool and a couple of wooden chairs for cello players.

The Countess, clad for the occasion in a dark purple gown, and with a matching hat, was Mistress of Ceremonies. The teachers of other instruments had been relegated to the third row in the audience. Ninotchka had been tied up in the wings and a servant was deputized to stop him yapping; no easy task.

The Countess stood in the middle of the stage and clapped her hands loudly. "Attention, attention," she shouted. "We are now begin the concert." Her English always deteriorated in moments of excitement. The hall grew quiet.

"Now all my little pupils will pleasure you with their art," she said. One of the 'little pupils' was seventeen years old and had a moustache. "We have all worked hard for such music and I have done the best with such material as comes to me."

Performance was in the order of from youngest to oldest; I was number four.

The first two performed elementary pieces of no merit or interest. The audience applauded, led by the Countess. The third, to my astonishment was Julie, the Headmaster's daughter, and the only girl among several hundred boys. There was ironical applause from the school when she appeared and sat at the piano. She still had an unpleasant expression on her face, but when she began to play a difficult Chopin waltz she played brilliantly, without a mistake or hesitation; and her face, transformed in a sort of ecstasy, became radiant.

The hall was silent. We were all astonished, transfixed by Julie's skill and the effortless flow of the music. From the wings, I could see the Headmaster and his wife: they looked smug.

When Julie finished, there was a roar of applause, and several whistles. She made a small curtsy, and marched off the stage with her face assuming its habitual sour expression.

I was next.

"Go on, go on," said the Countess, pushing me. I resisted. I was terrified. My playing was not good enough for a concert; I had to follow Julie's virtuoso performance; and I needed to go to the bathroom – desperately.

"You **will** go now," the Countess hissed in my ear and gave me a hard push on to the platform.

I sat down at the piano and began to play. The first bit was not too bad, but the harder second bit was my downfall. I got very mixed up and my shoe got caught under the pedal. I remembered Professor Hertz joking about how one leg had to be tucked under the stool ready for you to jump up and run away when the audience started to throw things. Any time now, I thought. I was panic stricken, I was drenched in sweat ... No ... Unspeakable horror! For the first time since my babyhood, I had wet myself.

I sprang to my feet and rushed off the stage. I stumbled over Ninotchka and fell flat on my face. As I looked up I saw the Countess, her face as purple as her gown, glaring at me and almost speechless with fury: "Go, go, and never again to me come for nothing, you ... you ... you ... **BOY!**"

I ran. I would be the laughing stock of the school, but this would pass. The glorious silver lining was that I could now give up piano lessons for ever.

Summer term was the best of the three. I learned the rudiments of cricket, which reminded me of Mr Winter and his rules for English gentlemen, though these were not nearly as much in evidence as in Cairo.

I enjoyed cricket. There was never any problem about the weather and it was the sort of leisurely game I could appreciate. I became the wicket-keeper of the House team and crouched behind the stumps, quietly calling the batsman rude and insulting names. For official matches we wore white and in one match, against a day-boy House, I had the great pleasure of running out our old enemy Ali, by tripping him, accidentally of course.

Rid, Chak and I had a couple more fights with day-boys, at which we acquitted ourselves well, even though Beast was not in the vicinity, and did not come in spite of some rather desperate whistling. In one of these fights, Chak got a cut on the forehead, which gave him a splendid scar, of which Rid and I were jealous.

We also managed to obtain permission to attend Life Saving classes, which were run at a swimming pool not far from the school. We were escorted there once a week, but succeeded, after a time, in lulling Whipper into trusting us, so that we were able to go there alone, though we had to be back unfailingly by a certain time. We missed alternate classes, and instead wandered about the town, sometimes pausing at coffee shops. There we ate *basbousa*, a sticky sweetmeat made of oil, nuts, sugar and dough and drank small cups of bitter, black coffee. We even tried to smoke a *nargileh*, or water pipe, but this made us all feel rather sick. Nevertheless, we felt wholly adult, sitting at little round tables among men (there were no women in coffee shops) and being addressed as *khawaja*, or 'master', since we were obviously not Egyptians with our pale complexions and European dress.

We also began to ogle the girls, and made rude remarks such as: *"Ha, ha, shoof; and'ha toom, ya Beg!"* which translated as, "Wow, look, she's got garlic (she's sexy), mister!"

On one such truancy, Chak said: "Listen. Rid is in the infirmary with something, so there is only us two. I have had a plan for some time, and I have arranged with a day-boy to borrow his father's sailing dinghy. We could sail round the harbour and look around. Are you game?"

I stopped and looked at him. We were on the way to the pool. "Sure," I said, "if you think we can be back in time."

"Oh yes, there's plenty of time and nobody will know."

We caught a bus to the harbour and Chak led me to a jetty where there were many little boats tied up; he had obviously scouted out the situation before, although I did not know when or how.

"Here we are," he said, climbing into a little dinghy with a white sail all wrapped round the horizontal boom, moored about half-way down the jetty. "Get in, and I'll tell you what to do."

I got in and he showed me how to hoist the sail and let the centre-board down. We cast off and he took the tiller. I sat amidships and leaned one way and the other, according to his instructions.

We sailed off into the middle of Alexandria harbour. The sky was bright blue, as was the water, there were exciting ships everywhere and just enough of a breeze to enable us to bowl along at a good rate. The harbour was huge, and had two sides lined with jetties and towering cranes. Although there were many grimy cargo vessels of all sizes, there was a definite military air about the scene, and numerous gray warships, of many nationalities, tied up as well. We tried to tell what they were by the flags, but there were some we did not know. Ships were coming and going all the time, and there were motor boats and launches whizzing to and fro, which we had to be careful to avoid.

I was enjoying it enormously and we were both laughing all the time with sheer joy, as we tacked to and fro, causing irate sailors to shout at us from their boats as they passed.

We sailed quite near a marvellously painted and gilded ship, which Chak said was the yacht of King Farouk; I remembered Aunt talking of him as an unpleasant man who peeked at ladies through holes in the wall.

We then headed for a sinister looking warship, painted gray like the others, which Chak said was American. She was long and narrow, and looked very fast. There were large guns, in front and at the back, and we could see white-clad sailors moving about on her deck. A Stars and Stripes flag fluttered at the stern and a wisp of smoke curled out of one of her two funnels.

Chak said: "Hey, I've got an idea. I've always heard that Americans are kind and very generous. Let's upset the dinghy and pretend we can't swim. Maybe they will give us something ..."

I was a bit doubtful about this plan, but before I could argue, Chak swung the dinghy round, close to the American warship, and managed to capsize us. We both splashed about and, although we were perfectly happy in the water, made a lot of noise and shouted for help.

We saw some faces look over the side, and two lifebelts came sailing down from the deck. We grabbed them, and were hoisted up.

We stood dripping on the deck and looked around us. We were ringed by about ten sailors, who stared at us. One of them, a huge man with hairy, tattooed forearms and many stripes on his sleeves said, speaking very slowly: "You dumb kids; you could've drowned. And I guess you can't even understand what I'm saying to you ..."

Chak and I looked at each other, and Chak replied: "Excuse me, Captain, but I understand you perfectly. It was our misfortune to capsize near your vessel and we are both grateful that you saved our lives." With that, he rolled his eyes up in his head and dramatically collapsed onto the deck. I knelt down beside him.

The huge sailor, whose jaw had dropped during Chak's speech, stooped and picked him up. He shouldered his way through the others and walked through a door and into the ship. I followed close behind.

We went into what looked like an infirmary, where there was an officer wearing a peaked cap. "What's cooking, Bosun?" he asked the huge sailor.

"Just some kids we fished out of the water, Sir. One of them keeled over on the deck." He put Chak down on a bunk and did not see him wink at me.

The officer examined Chak, who pretended to wake up, and said that he would be OK.

We spent an hour on the ship. We were shown all over it by the Bosun, who took us in his charge and who gave us thick towels to wrap ourselves in. He also gave us each a large bag full of marvellous chewing gum, sweets and fruit as well as 'cookies'. When we visited the galley we ate the most wonderful ice-cream we had ever tasted. The Bosun tried to find out who we were and where we came from, but we ducked his questions and gave out almost no information.

When we finally returned to the deck, we found that our dinghy had been righted. So we sailed off, after thanking the Bosun effusively, with the sailors cheering and waving. We felt rather guilty but consoled ourselves by munching on our loot all the way back to school.

Whipper was waiting for us.

Chak had left his watch at school, and neither of us had realised that mine had stopped after our immersion; we were two hours late and Whipper was furious.

He clenched and unclenched his fists. "Where have you been, hey?" he grated. "You're two hours late and I know you were not at the Life Saving class. I knew you were not to be trusted."

We had no story prepared. I kept silent and Chak started to explain: "On our way to the pool there was a terrible car accident and we were helping and then at the hospital ..." his voice gradually stopped. Whipper glared.

"You are making it worse. You will have six right now, and

you will not go to these classes again. Come!" He turned on his heel and marched off toward his study. We followed, clutching our almost empty bags.

"You first," said Whipper to Chak. "You wait outside," he pointed at me.

So here it comes, I thought to myself. Now I will find out. I think I will choose a thick one; after all, both Chak and Rid say it is better. Rid will laugh his head off ... My thoughts were interrupted by a swish and a thud from behind the closed door. I could hear it quite clearly. There was no other sound. Then five other swish-thuds followed at intervals.

After a short time, Chak came out. He was rather pale and was biting his lip hard. He jerked his head at me to go in. "Say nothing," he muttered.

I went in. Whipper was standing by the desk, holding a cane. He pushed it at me and said: "Will this do?"

I looked at it; it was reasonably thick, and, after all, Chak had chosen it so I may as well follow. I nodded.

"Trousers down and bend over, boy," Whipper flexed the cane in his two hands. I undid my shorts, which fell to my ankles, and bent over the chair in my underpants.

Swish ... thud. The pain was excruciating. The caning by Creepy in Cairo and even the slippering by Whipper in the dormitory were nothing compared with this. Swish ... thud. In exactly the same spot. And then four more.

"Now go, boy," said Whipper. "Stay out of my sight for the rest of the day."

"Thank you, Sir," I said through gritted teeth, as I had been instructed, pulling my shorts up. I then painfully made my way out to the Quad, where Chak was recounting our adventures to Rid and Beast, both of whom were in fits of laughter and thoroughly unsympathetic, as they ate the remains of our loot.

"Why do we have to take our trousers down?" I enquired. "Surely it makes little difference to the pain."

"Ah," said Rid. "There are boys who try to pad themselves before going in to be swished. They mainly try to use damp blotting paper to make a good sound. Whipper found one out and now he makes us drop our shorts so that he can see there is nothing there."

"It really hurts," I said. "And it was only six."

"Yes," Beast growled. "There was a boy two terms ago who was given twenty-four, all on one day. He had to go to hospital, he was bleeding so badly. After that, if it is more than six, Whipper gives them six a day for two or three days." I could not imagine what crime would merit twenty-four!

That evening, in the dormitory, I managed to look in the mirror and saw six clearly defined purple lines, very close together, on my behind. Two had broken the skin and bled a little, but it was not serious. Whipper picked on Chak and me to examine our ankles for crumbles and, although we had scrubbed and scrubbed, inevitably there were one or two. He then slippered us on exactly the beating spot; it was very painful and we both slept on our fronts that night.

The remarkable thing was that Whipper made no further attempt to find out where we had been and we anyway got our Life Saving Certificates through the mail. Also, we were heroes among the boys for some weeks when the full story got about. But when Chak suggested we try the adventure again, with a different ship, I refused. I thought that a second time carried the risk of expulsion and there would have been nowhere else for me to go.

A letter came from Mother with a bombshell: I was not to go back to Baghdad for the summer holidays but Mother and Aunt were coming to Egypt and we were to go to Cyprus for a month. Cyprus? Why? And what about Uncle Max?

I wrote back immediately and Mother answered that she and Aunt were fed up with Baghdad in the summer, and that the war had removed itself from the Mediterranean, and that Cyprus was very nice and that I would enjoy it. They were arriving in Cairo on the last day of term and I was to meet them there, at the Continental-Savoy Hotel, the following afternoon.

This was duly arranged. I caught the train and, on arrival at Cairo railway station, got myself and my bag into a taxi, and went to the Hotel, as instructed. I enquired for Mother's room and went there, up the plush stairs, to be swept into perfumed embraces by both Mother and Aunt, and incoherent squeals of:

"My DARLINK SON ... how wonderful to see you ... I have been so suffering and impatient ..." and so on. Aunt, also, seemed pleased to see me and remarked that I had grown. She also said that Uncle Max sent his love and was sorry he could not come. Oddly, we had begun, without noticing, to speak to each other in a mixture of Polish and English; a habit that was to persist from then on.

It was strange to eat in a luxurious restaurant and sleep, in a soft bed, alone in a room. I had not, in fact, slept or eaten outside the school for some nine months and was used to dormitory and dining hall smells and noises.

We visited Groppi, where I remembered Dogvoice with affection and also the enormous, dusty confines of the Cairo Museum, full of badly arranged mummies, statues and all forms of ancient Egyptian bits and pieces. Mother kept saying: "Ach! How wonderful ... how ancient ... what a culture ..." and so on.

After a couple of days, we went to the airport and got into a smallish airplane, called a de Havilland something, Dragon or Rapide, which had double wings fastened together with a cat's-cradle of wires. I thought it looked rather unsafe, but no one else seemed to mind. It belonged to Misr Airways.

We took off with a great roar and climbed slowly north. Both Mother and Aunt had stuffed their ears with cotton wool and so were incommunicado. But as we followed the Nile, and were not very high, I sat with my nose pressed against the window and watched the scenery flow slowly by under us. We then veered away from the river and I noticed a series of lakes and then a ruler-straight canal, Suez, which we followed to the sea.

The Mediterranean looked an intense and shimmering blue. I could see little wavelets on it and an occasional toy boat, which left a pearly wake behind it, like a snail. All too soon we were over land again and with a sputtering of engines and considerable creaking from the fuselage, we landed at Nicosia Airport in Cyprus. Mother and Aunt opened their eyes and removed the cotton wool and we went down the steps.

The sun was going down and it was just as hot as in Alexandria. There was dust and a foreign feeling but it felt subtly different: it was not Arab. The language was incomprehensible, although there was English spoken and there were many British servicemen about.

Aunt obtained a young porter and retrieved our luggage, organised us through immigration and customs, and procured a large American car which turned out to be a taxi. She haggled magnificently and soon we were bowling along a somewhat bumpy road, heading north into some foothills. The soft springs of the huge car imparted a nautical heaving to the body and we all felt a bit sick. But the sunset to the left was magnificent and there was merry humming from the driver (perhaps Aunt had not struck such a good bargain after all). I was fascinated by the small villages through which we passed and the whitewashed houses and little churches with round domes. The air began to smell fresh and clean. Mother was leaning back against the leather seat, an expression of suffering on her face, with small frowns every time the body of the car swooped sickeningly on a bump.

We started to climb into the mountains. There were groves of gnarly olive trees, rocky outcrops with ruins of things and occasional flocks of goats, usually accompanied by an urchin in ragged clothes, who grinned cheekily at us and sometimes waved.

It was twilight when we crested the Kyrenia mountains and plunged down a serpentine road towards the coast. It got rapidly darker and there was nothing to be seen except the lights of Kyrenia, a little port on the north coast. We drove down a narrow street and stopped outside a large building, ablaze with light and with the sign: "Dome Hotel". We had arrived.

I was tired and went to bed with a sandwich as soon as I was shown my small room. There were wooden shutters over the window and I could hear a soft lapping of water as I fell asleep.

I awoke to noises of talking and laughter outside my window. When I opened my eyes I saw bright slashes of sunlight from the slats in the shutters cutting across the room. I jumped out of bed and flung the shutters open.

There was a brittle brightness which was blinding. A cloudless sky met a brilliant blue sea; my room overlooked the water. A small fishing boat, motor burbling, was passing, and the three fishermen, dressed in colourful shirts and caps, were laughing and talking loudly. When they saw me they waved and shouted "Yaso, yaso!", so I waved back.

I washed quickly and dressed in shirt, shorts and sandals and went to find Mother and Aunt. There was no sign of them, and the receptionist, a cheerful, tubby little man, said that they did not wish to be disturbed. So I made my way to the restaurant and had a quick breakfast of fresh bread, butter, jam and white cheese, with tea, before going out to explore.

There was nothing of immediate interest round the hotel, except a small, rather boring swimming pool, with reclining chairs beside it and a dusty garden. But round the corner there were steps leading down to the sea. Mr Kostas, the receptionist, said that it was perfectly safe to swim, so I got into my bathing suit and, running down the steps, plunged into the blue water of the Mediterranean.

It was wonderfully cool and clear. The bottom, some twenty feet down, was of white sand and reflected the light. The brown rocks of the coast, on which the hotel stood, were excitingly perforated with little caves and holes both above and below water. I explored the immediate surroundings and saw many coloured fishes, of all sizes, some crabs and a gigantic slug, making its way majestically along an underwater rock. There were also clumps of seaweed, swaying in the gentle current. In the sunlight one could see for at least thirty yards under water, even without a mask, and I determined to get one as soon as I could.

When I returned to the hotel, after about an hour's swimming, Mother and Aunt were just finishing a breakfast of fruit and coffee. I told them ecstatically about my swim but Mother gave a little shriek and said: "You will be drowned ... what danger ... the sharks ..." I assured her that such perils did not exist locally and begged for a mask. Aunt said I could have one if it was not too expensive and I rushed off to my new friend Mr Kostas to enquire. He did not let me down, and produced one from under his counter, for a modest sum.

For the next few days, I spent most of the day in the water, returning only for meals and sleep. Mother and Aunt did not mind: they spent their mornings in swimsuits, heavily oiled, reclining on the deck-chairs around the pool, with leaves on their eyes; they said that sunburned eyelids could be fatal. They never actually went into the water and when I suggested they join me in the paradise of the sea, they shuddered and said that it was much too dangerous.

They had found two bridge-playing companions, an old English Colonel and an Egyptian lady of advanced years, with whom they spent their afternoons, sitting at a little square table in the lounge under a slowly turning fan, and muttering about two no trumps and other arcana. I was content to be left alone.

The other guests at the hotel were a curious wartime mixture: there were old ladies and gentlemen, mainly from Egypt and Palestine, on holiday; there were some British and French officers and also Greek families, which kept very much to themselves and were shunned by the others. The children were mostly young and there was no one of my age.

Two weeks passed in an idyllic idleness and freedom to swim and explore. But then, one day, there was a roaring outside and many raised voices. I went to the entrance and saw a bus and two jeeps draw up in a cloud of dust and a large group of American servicemen come pouring into the hotel.

They were all laughing and joking loudly and so earned themselves frowns and scowls from the residents. When they had dispersed upstairs, Mr Kostas told me that they were coming, from now on, for arr and arr, (whatever that was), and would be changing over, like sentries, every fourteen days. Mr Kostas said it was very good for the hotel and he was happy because, he said, they tipped well and would liven the place up.

My first encounter with the Americans was that afternoon. I was already well disposed towards them, remembering their kindness during the capsized dinghy incident, and wondered how to establish contact. Mother and Aunt, at lunch, had said that there would now be an intolerable noise all the time: "They are very loud, you know," said Aunt. "Such a young race. They do not have the European culture and manners ..." If the existing guests were any guide, I thought, especially the old Colonel who was boring and unintelligible, the newcomers should be a great improvement.

I was chatting with Mr Kostas when a hand clapped me on the shoulder. "Hey, kid," said a nasal voice, "what's cooking round here, huh?"

I looked round. There was a very tall and thin American soldier grinning at me and holding out a packet of chewing gum. "Gum?" he asked.

"Thank you," I said, taking a stick. "Nothing is cooking, but the sea is wonderful if you like swimming. I can show you where."

"My name is Chuck," said my new acquaintance. "Who are you?"

"I am Andrew, and I am here on holiday with my Mother and my Aunt," I said.

"O.K., Andy," said Chuck. "So show me the ocean."

"It is not an ocean," I said severely. "It is an inland sea."

"Sea, shmee," said Chuck. "Let's go."

This was much better than old Colonels and small Greek children.

We were joined by two of Chuck's friends, Bo and Cowboy, who said he was from Texas. I had never met a cowboy before, but was impressed when he said he was a friend of Roy Rogers and always wore his six-shooters at home because of the Indians.

I showed my friends the steps down to the water and also the special places I had found. We all swam around and I enjoyed myself as never before.

"Say, Andy, have you been to the beaches around here?" asked Bo. He was a large, beefy man who moved and spoke slowly and deliberately, unlike Chuck and Cowboy, whose movements were abrupt and alert. "And where are the girls?"

"I haven't been out of the village," I said, "and I haven't seen any girls."

"OK, we'll fix that," said Cowboy. "Life is nothing without girls."

The following morning, Chuck said that they had got a jeep and would be going on a 'recce', and did I want to come along. Mother and Aunt were down at the pool as usual, and I thought it would be unkind to disturb them, so I said "OK" with a mouth full of chewing gum.

Cowboy said that the people looking after the Americans in Kyrenia had provided several 'comforts' which they could use, including jeeps, fishing and SCUBA gear (I found out that this enabled one to swim underwater for a long time), candies, barbecue equipment and all sorts of magical and wonderful things. I asked what arr and arr was and Bo explained that this was Rest and Recreation, because they had been fighting a war and were tired. I asked where they had been fighting but none of them wanted to talk about it.

We jumped into the jeep and went roaring down the road out of the village. Chuck drove and Cowboy sat beside him, with his feet in their ornate boots (he always wore boots) perched on top of the windscreen. I sat in the back with Bo, and we were bounced around like dice in a cup; it seems that jeeps did not believe in springs.

After a while, we passed a farm, with placid cows grazing in a field.

"Hey, stop, stop ..." Bo sat straight up with excitement. "Listen, those are like the cows back home." He turned to me. "My folks got a farm like that but bigger. I want to go talk to these people. Go in there, Chuck."

Chuck good-naturedly turned into the farm and we stopped outside a whitewashed house. An old gentleman came to the door.

"Say, Mister, you get good milk from them cows?" asked Bo.

"Is good milk and butter," said the old gentleman, with a strong Greek accent. "My is best good cow here in Cyprus. Is very clean," he added.

"I got some in the States," said Bo. "Can I go see them and say Hi?" he asked. The old gentleman said "Ne, ne, you come I show. How you call cow? My cow are lovely."

"Just a couple of minutes, you guys. I ain't seen a cow for months. Wait for me," pleaded Bo and went off towards the field with the old gentleman. We noticed a girl peeking out of the window, so Chuck and Cowboy began to preen and were not averse to waiting.

But the girl did not appear, and after a while the old gentleman and Bo returned, holding hands and grinning at each other. Bo was carrying a tin pail in his other hand. "Hey, look what I got ..." he said when he got near.

What he had was half a pail of frothy milk, which he had just milked from one of the cows. He also had a pannikin and we each had a good drink of the milk. It was absolutely delicious, sweet, fresh and invigorating. It was the best milk I had ever drunk.

The old gentleman stood smiling. "Is best milk," he said. "You always come to Papadopolous when you near and drink good milk. You good, Bo, have cows in America."

We thanked him and Cowboy gave the old man some cigarettes and gum and we drove off waving. We often stopped there during the coming days whenever we went to the beaches on that side.

The presence of the Americans made an enormous difference to my holiday. As the only European boy in the hotel, and one who got to know the area, I became the mascot of the groups of American soldiers as they rotated every fortnight, with the departing group handing me over to the newcomers. This meant I could use all the 'comforts' provided for them, was driven to all the best beaches and ruins in the area, had all the candy and gum I could manage, and above all, had warm and friendly companionship from men who missed their own families and treated me as an equal, not as a child (as was the habit of the British). They missed their families very much and were forever showing me snapshots in their wallets, of wives, children and sweethearts. Many also had photographs of dogs and cats, houses and cars, and all the things which were precious when one was far from home. When I heard that they had not seen their families for two and three years, I decided that, seeing mine every nine months, I had nothing to complain about.

They also organised an autograph book for me, which they filled with their names and addresses back in the States, and fervent invitations to 'come on over and stay as long as you like'.

But the best times were the first excursions with Bo, Chuck

and Cowboy. There were splendid beaches up and down the coast, with marvellous swimming. The water was warm and a happy memory was sitting up to my neck in the gentle surf while munching huge slabs of watermelon; the mixture of the taste of the fruit and the salty water was delicious.

We fished and had picnics and climbed and explored and swam. Mr Kostas told us that Bellapaise Abbey, on a mountain peak just behind the hotel, was well worth seeing and he said the climb was easy. So one morning we packed a rucksack (Bo was elected to carry this) with water and provisions and spent six hours painfully climbing up to the Abbey. The slope was steep and was composed of red, barren rocks with very little vegetation. There were patches where the climb was vertical and after a short time we were all puffing and panting and Chuck was remarking that "this dumb place better be worth it if we live to get there".

We finally reached the abbey, a collection of broken ruins with some little huts dotted about, and were regarded with astonishment by a number of black-robed clerics in tall round hats, who were standing around. We noticed cars and buses, with sightseers. There was, it seemed, a perfectly good road going to the monastery from the valley on the other side – we could have had an easy drive up in the jeep.

We roared and bellowed at Mr Kostas when we got home, but he just giggled and said: "Practical joke, practical joke ..." until we all laughed and admitted his success.

We also explored the castles of St. Hilarion and Buffavento, built by the Crusaders and in ruins. It was exciting to sit on the broken stones and imagine the knights, baking in their steel armour, living so far from home; it seemed to me that soldiers had always had to leave families behind and fight in far away places. I mentioned this to my American friends and they agreed. From the mountains, the coast of Turkey, some fifty miles away, was clearly visible; one could sometimes even see it from the hotel if there was no heat haze.

There were several incidents with girls. This was hardly surprising, given the long period of girl-starvation of the GI's and the attractions of merry and rich young Americans, with gifts of nylon stockings ('the best girl-bait ever invented', I was told by Rick, a particular friend of mine from the second group) and other goodies. The young Greek girls were attractive but under a rigid discipline at home, so meetings were not easy to arrange; although some were managed. The liaison tended to end with fathers and brothers appearing at the hotel with shotguns, to the consternation of the staff and the less adventurous guests. But no blood was actually shed, to the best of my knowledge.

The war seemed distant, until the memorable day when Rick suddenly rushed out of his room, where he had been listening to his radio, and announced in a loud voice: "The war is over and the Jerries have surrendered. Now only the Japs are left!"

The news spread like wildfire through the hotel. Although the tide of war, by now, barely lapped on the Cypriot coast, everyone got very excited and the hotel produced bottles of champagne 'on the house'.

Mother and Aunt embraced each other and me and Mother burst into tears and said: "At last, we have survived ... we live ... but all the family, all the friends ... dead, dead, dead ..." and she ran to her room and slammed the door.

There was a big impromptu party that evening and the Colonel told us yet again about the end of the First World War, while the Americans kissed every female in sight and danced to the music of a gramophone one of them had. I kissed two young Greek hotel maids who giggled at me; I enjoyed it.

Thus passed the holidays, all too quickly. Mother accused me of using strange American words and Aunt said I was beginning to talk 'like in the films'. But I was happy with my friends and looked forward to each new day. All was well.

We returned to Cairo in the same creaking cat's-cradle plane. My parting from the Dome Hotel was nostalgic, especially the farewell from Mr Kostas; he gave me, as a farewell present, a tasselled Greek cap, which I insisted on wearing all the way to the hotel in Cairo.

Mother and Aunt bade me goodbye, pressed three £E5 notes into my hand and put me into a taxi to the station. Mother wept a bit and said she had so much enjoyed being close to me all summer. My journey back to school was uneventful and I was glad to be with Chak and Rid again in my familiar dormitory, even with the Whipper's scowls.

The winter term passed without any special excitements, except that I found that, more and more frequently, I would involuntarily honk when I spoke. My voice was uncontrollable and my friends laughed at me. Then it happened to Chak and we went to see Matron, fearing we had some dread disease.

Matron laughed. "It happens to all boys," she said. "You are becoming men and leaving childhood behind you. There is no harm in it and there is no medicine that you need or that I can give you."

But we were getting more and more interested in girls, and listening to the older boys when they told each other stories of what they had been doing. Some of the things were incomprehensible and there was no opportunity to experiment.

Christmas came and two other boys, both Sudanese, remained at the school with me for the holidays. We were not invited to the Headmaster on Christmas Day, but had a slightly special meal in the eating hall, of chicken and a small cake. Hassan, one of the Sudanese boys, had some money and we got a school servant to bring us some ice cream from outside.

Letters from Mother came regularly, and regularly contained no special news. She spoke of the same busy social life, the same parties and picnics and of her work with the Indian Red Cross. There were increasingly frequent mentions of Mr Arnold, who seemed to be spending a lot of time with her. She said I was sure to like him a lot when I knew him well.

Easter term was notable for another swishing. Chak, Rid and I were caught by a master while relaxing with some cigarettes behind the eating hall. Naturally, he reported us to Whipper who gave us three; not too bad. It was distressing that the tale-telling master found himself glued to his chair in class a week or so later. Rid narrowly avoided an honour fight; it was over an unfortunate comment by him referring to another boy's honesty in a game of marbles. The other boy was known to be a liar and a thief and could not find anyone to be his second, so there was no fight.

The holiday came and went and there was a momentous letter from Mother.

"My darling son," she wrote out of the blue. "I have given you a new FATHER. Mr Arnold has married me last week and we are happy. I am sure you also will be happy with us." Then there was quite a lot of incoherent writing which expressed her joy and satisfaction. The main message seemed to be that we now had someone to look after us, that we no longer had to depend on Uncle Max's generosity and that I must remember to be always extremely grateful to Mr Arnold and behave well and invariably to do as he said. If I didn't, he would leave us and we would again have nothing and nobody.

Mother also said that Mr Arnold, who was divorced from his previous wife, already had a son and a daughter, roughly my age and was it not wonderful that I would suddenly get a brother and a sister.

All this needed a lot of thinking out, and Chak, Rid and I sat down after lunch that day so that we could examine the situation. Chak had an aunt who was divorced and Rid had a brother and a sister, so they could give me advice.

"Of course, he's not your father," said Chak. "More a sort of uncle or friend, if you like him. Father has to be same blood."

"… and not real brother and sister," Rid chimed in. "If you are the eldest you can be the boss; it depends if they are friendly."

"But it says that I have to do everything this Arnold says," I protested. "He will order me about and I have to be careful or Mother and I will have to be on our own again. Anyway, I'm sure Uncle Max did not mind looking after us. Perhaps I should make trouble and Arnold will go away again?"

"Then your Mother will be unhappy," said Chak. "A woman needs a man," he said seriously. "That's what my Father always says to my aunt, who has lived with us after her divorce. He would be very happy if she got married again and went away."

"It needs a lot of thinking about, too," I said. "I suppose Mother will be Mrs Arnold the Second, and I will still be Kronman. So this Arnold has stolen our name. It's all very complicated."

We agreed to talk about it next term, when I could report on the situation, and could tell them what Mr Arnold was really like. But I could see that this was going to be a big event in my life and for the future.

The end of the summer term came, and I said goodbye to all my friends. As before, I had to go to Cairo to catch the airplane to Baghdad and this passed without any trouble.

When we landed, Aunt and Uncle Max were at the airport to meet me; Mother was not there.

"How you have grown," said Uncle Max, as he hugged me. "You are a proper person now." He stood back and regarded me with a smile, while beating his drum.

Aunt also hugged me and said: "Your Mother has gone off to Abadan with your new father, and you will be joining them in a few days. Until then, you can stay with us, as always." She smiled. "Entah has been asking when you are coming and is very excited."

"Where is Abadan and what is it?" I asked, as we drove home. "Is that where I will be living from now on, not in Baghdad?"

"Abadan is the biggest oil refinery in the world, and it is not so far away," said Uncle Max. "It is in Iran, just the other side of Basra, near the Gulf."

"I can't live in a refinery," I said. "You live in houses."

"Abadan has quite a big town attached to it," explained Aunt, "with thousands of people. Ronnie Arnold (your new father) is an important manager at the refinery which belongs to a British company called the Anglo-Iranian Oil Company. You will live in his house with your mother."

"He is not my father," I said. "He is just Mother's husband and he stole her name."

"Na, na," said Uncle Max, "Don't make up your mind before you see how everything is. Your Mama is very happy and you should be, too. But we will miss you," he added softly. I grabbed his hand and held it.

The house was unchanged, and Hussein, Entah and Ali were lined up to welcome me. Even old Ibrahim, the gardener, came and grinned at me, showing his one tooth. Entah was hopping up and down on one foot with excitement.

I settled down to my usual routine. Things were changing, as the end of the war meant that the troops were going home and business was booming. Mr Ginger and his family were going home to England and the boys were full of excitement about their English school in a town called Kent.

Entah and Hussein told me all about Mother's wedding: there was a huge party in the garden, after the ceremony in which Uncle Max 'gave Mother away'. I thought this was a curious way of putting it and asked him later why he didn't keep her. He beat his drum and chuckled and said he couldn't even manage one wife let alone two.

Anyway, the party was in the garden and a great success and Society in Baghdad spoke of nothing else for weeks, both before and after. Entah said that Mr Arnold seemed a nice man and had given all the servants large sums of money after the party, as a thank you. I thought this was good.

Finally it was time for me to go to Abadan. My few belongings went into two suitcases and I had to leave my bicycle behind, though Uncle Max said he would try to send it down to me by river steamer (Abadan was on the *Shatt al-Arab*, or Arab River, which was the confluence of the Tigris and the Euphrates before they flowed into the Persian Gulf).

It was only a short flight, mostly following the Tigris, and just as we could see marshes and a large expanse of sea, we landed at Abadan. Mother and Mr Arnold were there to meet me at the little airport and I could see the many silvery towers and tanks of the refinery in the distance.

I was still upset at having to leave Uncle Max and Entah and everyone else at what I had considered to be my home for more than five years. I was used to it, just as I was used to the Club, the town, Fizz and my farmer friends on the banks of the river. I wondered if I would ever go back.

Mother clasped me to her scented bosom and cried: "My DARLINK! Here you are and here is your new Father. Is it not too wonderful to be a family again ..." She seemed embarrassed and babbled slightly.

Mr Arnold, who was dressed impeccably in a white suit and hat, shook hands with me and said: "Ah, Andrew. How nice to see you. I am glad you are here to help me look after your

Mother. I do hope you approve of our marriage."

I thought this was a very decent thing to say, and it made a good impression on me. "I am very glad that Mother will have you to look after her while I am away, Sir," I said. "If she and you are happy, so shall I be."

"Good, good," said Mr Arnold, while Mother fluttered about. "Don't call me Sir; my name is Ronald but this is awkward, since it is an anagram of Arnold. Call me Ronnie, like everyone else."

I was pleased that Dr Mish had told me what an anagram was and I was glad that Ronnie did not insist on my calling him Father, since I didn't want to.

We all got into Ronnie's car, and were driven to his house. This was a big bungalow in what seemed like an enormous town of bungalows. It had a large garden, which was amazingly tidy and organized, full of flowers and with palm trees and lawns and terraces. I discovered later that several thousand people worked in the refinery and that the foreigners, mostly British, all lived in what was a whole town, with clubs, shops, tennis courts, swimming pools, riding stables and sailing boats on the river. There was even a hospital. The refinery itself was some distance away, and at night was lit up with a myriad lights, festooned like necklaces on the steel structures. There were also always flames gushing out of nozzles, here and there, high up in the air, called flares.

At the bungalow, we were greeted by a small, rather wizened servant, dressed very correctly in black trousers, a white jacket and a dark red cummerbund, who bowed and said "Welcome, welcome."

"This is Mohammed," said Ronnie. "He has been with me and looked after me for many years, first in Iraq, in Khanaquin and Baghdad, and now here. He is in charge of the house."

Mohammed smiled at me and said: "You are welcome, Master Andrew. If there is anything you want, please to tell me and I will get." He took my cases and went inside. There was also a cook and houseboy, as well as two gardeners, but they did not appear.

The bungalow was cool and dark. I followed Mohammed to my room, where he left me. It was large and had big windows opening onto the garden. I could hear trickling water and there was a refreshing breeze. I sat on the bed and thought to myself that everything, so far, seemed all right.

After dinner that night (this was a formal affair, at a long, shiny table with candles and silver) we sat in the comfortable, large living room and had a Discussion. Ronnie always had Discussions if there was something important to talk about, information to be given or decisions to be made. This Discussion was to tell me that I would not be returning to school in Egypt, but that arrangements had been made for me to go to a boarding school in England for what Ronnie called a proper education.

"Victoria College is all very well," he announced, "but if we are to get you to Cambridge it is essential that you are properly prepared." I was not quite sure what Cambridge was, but thought it best to listen. I also was very conscious that I should not make any difficulties or problems, or Mother and I would find ourselves on our own again.

"I have been able to find a place for you at Berkhamsted School, where an old College friend of mine is a master. I am told it is a good school, and anyway, things in England are still so disorganised after the war that we are lucky to find a place at all."

"Where in England will you and Mother be living?" I asked. It would be wonderful to be able to go home for the holidays, like other boys.

"Well," said Ronnie somewhat uncomfortably, "we will actually be staying here for a bit and after that I don't know where the Company will want me to go." I looked at Mother, but she was gazing at her husband with a smile.

"But you don't have to worry," Ronnie added. "My very best friend, Archie Chisholm, who lives in London with his family, will look after you. I am appointing him your Guardian and he will act in my place. He has a nice family, with two baby daughters (I am Godfather to one) and you will really enjoy living with them in the holidays."

"But when will I be with you?" I asked. "Will I be able to come here? Or possibly I could spend the summers with Aunt and Uncle Max?"

"Perhaps you will be able to spend a holiday with us sometimes, depending on where we are. Of course, we may be in England occasionally. You can be sure that we will do our best."

"You will not have to worry about me, darlink," said Mother. "I will be with Ronnie and he will look after me. It is so wonderful …" She gave a big contented sigh. "And you will be in a wonderful English school and become a proper English gentleman, like your Fath … I mean Ronnie."

There was not a lot I could say. The decision had been made, as had the arrangements. There was, of course, a bright side to it: I would see London, and speak proper English with everyone and maybe this Chisholm would be a reasonable person, and at least there would be somewhere to spend the holidays.

Then I realised suddenly that I would not be seeing Chak and Rid and Beast any more. But I would write to them and tell them everything. And no more Whipper; that was a good thought.

The time in Abadan passed quickly. I spent some time at the swimming pool in the Club, but the English boys there had a tight-knit society and would not let me join their games. They bullied me: called me 'Wog' when they found I spoke Arabic, pushed me into the pool and hid my clothes while I was swimming.

This was not good. I decided to make them stop it by fighting their leader, a boy rather taller than me, who was the most aggressive. He seemed not to know proper fighting but pranced around with his fists raised, while the others stood round, menacingly. I did not have my knife, so I kicked him firmly between the legs and twisted his arm sharply as he fell, breaking his collar-bone. The boys stopped bullying me after that.

When I got home, I told Ronnie what had happened. We had a Discussion, but I convinced him that I had fought a group of bullies in self defence, so he agreed to let the matter drop. He did say that English boys fought with their fists, and did not agree when I explained that boxing was a sport, and fighting was something altogether different. I believe the injured boy's father complained, but nothing more was said.

The servants and people in general spoke Farsi, rather than

Arabic, so I could not communicate very easily. Mohammed was very kind to me; he did speak Arabic, though with a strong Farsi accent, so we had a good time theorizing on his favourite subject, which was astronomy. Many stars had Arab names and he told me about them. He would stand with me in the garden at night, and point them out, and introduce them to me like his friends. He was both astronomer and philosopher and a good companion. He also gave me wonderful food and spoilt me in general.

The time came to make my epic journey to England, and I was very excited. During a final Discussion, Ronnie explained that the airplane would take two days to get to London, with an overnight stop in Rome. In London, when we landed in Northolt, Archie Chisholm would meet me and take me home. I would have £5 for emergencies, though Ronnie said he was confident that nothing could go wrong. Mother was sniffing in a corner, saying that England was very far away and she would be miserable without me.

On the day, carrying my suitcase and dressed in a grey suit with long trousers, I made my way to the airport in Basra, by launch, accompanied by Ronnie and Mother. There stood a huge, four-engined airplane which Ronnie said was called a York. In fact, it was a Lancaster bomber, adapted to carry passengers. There were brief farewells, tears from Mother, a handshake from Ronnie, and I climbed into the plane. There were rather uncomfortable seats, with very little padding and when the engines started, the noise was tremendous and the whole plane shook and rattled. We bumped onto the runway and, with an even greater bellowing and thundering, we were off. Another adventure had begun.

In Cairo aged 11

Mother just after her
second marriage

Ronnie Arnold,
my new stepfather

From my school photo, Victoria College,
Alexandria, Egypt

Joe, Me and Saïd,
Alexandria, Egypt, 1945

In Uncle Max's garden,
Baghdad, 1945

Holiday in Cyprus, 1946,
De Havilland Dragon,
Flight Cyprus to Cairo

Swimming Team, Berkhamsted School
(I am centre front row)

Rugby Team, Berkhamsted School, 1950
(I am holding rugby ball)

I become an English officer
(I am on left)

With guitar,
ready for Cambridge

King Faisal II,
1954

CHAPTER SIX

England – School

As my ears gradually became accustomed to the roaring of the engines, and the noise turned into a deep background drone, I dozed off, to be awakened by a cheerful man in a white coat who gave me a paper plate of sandwiches and a glass of milk. This was very welcome, since we had been flying for several hours.

"What is our altitude and when are we landing?" I asked in a knowledgeable sort of way.

"Oh, angels one eight, and ETA Castel Benito eighteen hundred," replied the man, grinning broadly.

This was cryptic and I realised I had been outmanoeuvered. I decided to surrender gracefully and asked: "Sorry, what happens next?"

"We are flying at 18,000 feet, young fellow, and we will be landing on the coast of Libya at six o'clock." The man winked. "We have to refuel, you know; she's a thirsty old beast."

I looked at my watch; it was a rather boring one which Mother had got me since my old one had never recovered from its immersion in the waters of Alexandria harbour.

"Remember to alter your watch," said my new friend in the white jacket. "We are chasing the sun and although we won't catch him, the time changes. Put the hands back two hours."

"It makes a longer day, but we still get paid the same." He winked again and went forward to serve others.

This was an interesting concept. Perhaps if one could catch up the sun and pass it one could get younger. Or, as was of more interest to me, one should go very fast the other way and grow up in a hurry. Now that was something.

Just before six, the engines changed note as we began to lose height. The sun was still up. I could see yellow desert out of my little window and, as we banked, the sea, bright blue, came into view. It was the same sea in which I had swum in Alexandria, but that seemed far away and a long time ago.

We hit the ground quite hard and rolled along a bumpy runway, with the plane gradually assuming its nose-up angle as the tail came down. We taxied to a collection of huts which Castel Benito, an RAF refuelling base, offered the transit passenger. I got out to stretch my legs, but there was nothing to see and soon we were off again, to Rome.

My white coated friend told me that we would be spending the night in Rome. "They will take us all into the city, in a bus, and we will sleep in a hotel. Then, early tomorrow morning, after breakfast, we will take off again, for London."

We landed in Rome after about three hours' flight. As we circled to lose height, I could see a great glittering spread of lights, winking and glimmering below me. Rome seemed huge, reaching from horizon to horizon and the darkness was pushed away by a glow which spread, like a golden cupola, over the land.

At the airport terminal there was a lot of jabbering and waving of hands. My friend from the plane made sure I was on the bus with the other passengers and we drove, through bustling streets, full of cars which honked and dashed to and fro in short bursts, like lizards chasing flies.

The hotel was very splendid. There were huge glittering chandeliers, and a shiny marble floor. Everyone working there wore black and white suits or uniforms with gold braid. I was shown into the restaurant, seated at a little table for one and given some spaghetti for supper and a glass of red wine which tasted sour. Soon, I was taken to a small room at the very top of the hotel, which had a chair, a washbasin and a hard, narrow bed. I suppose young boys were not expected to demand much luxury. Still, I was tired, so I washed in a token sort of way, and went to bed and to sleep.

I was wakened in the middle of the night by a soft knock and the door being opened. I turned the light on and saw, from my watch, that it was two in the morning. In the open door there was a pretty young maid, in a black dress with a white apron, smiling. She had dark hair and eyes and particularly white teeth. Her dress was unbuttoned down to her chest.

"Does Signore need more towel or soap?" she asked in a husky voice. "Can I do something for Signore?"

I could not imagine why anyone should wish to wake me in the middle of the night to give me towels or soap. Besides, both had been in the room when I got there.

"No, thanks," I said. "I just want to sleep, please."

The girl stared at me for a bit, sighed, and then went out and closed the door. I turned the light out and went back to sleep, though with a feeling that somehow there was more to the visit than I understood. I would ask my friend in the plane about it in the morning.

After breakfast, we all went back to the airport in the bus. My friend laughed very much when I told him the story of my nocturnal visitor and said, between guffaws, that next time could I please tell the maid that he was always short of soap and towels. So I ended up no wiser.

We flew on, roaring through the sky. We swept over what my friend said were the Alps; a marvellous sight, with snow on the summits, like cakes with cream. It was the first time I had flown over mountains and I wished the windows were a little bigger.

I was beginning to feel weary; the noise and the constant vibration, to say nothing of the bumpiness whenever there were changes in the terrain beneath, were beginning to take their toll. My British companions talked to each other, making curious British neighing noises – some of the ladies had their faces buried in brown paper bags. I began to think about London. My knowledge of it was limited to my games of Monopoly and I wondered if Fleet Street was really scarlet, and if Bond Street had so many gardens that it looked green. I was determined to explore at the first available opportunity.

My white-coated friend came to my seat, bringing with him a young lady in uniform and a smart hat. "This is Lily," he said.

"She is an air hostess and she will make sure you will be all right and tight when we land in London."

"I am certain I will be met," I said. "It has all been arranged. It's my guardian in England; his name is ..." My mind was a blank. I could not remember the name at all. Roberts? Melville? Holmes? What was it?

"When we land, stay behind until the others have got off," said Lily. "I will come and get you and we will make sure your guardian is there." This made me feel a little more confident. What was the name ...?

It got darker and darker, and as we lost height, we flew through a rainstorm. Then there was thunder and lightning and the ladies gave soft little screams. There was a rumbling chorus of "There, there ..." from the gentlemen.

It was quite dark outside now, and we suddenly landed. I was not expecting it and gripped my armrests in sudden terror, but soon recovered and said to myself: "Arrived in England. The end of the road. Here I stay."

There were muffled announcements on the loudspeakers and the engines died. The door was opened, and a cold wind came into the plane with a smell of damp soot and engine exhaust. The passengers gathered up their coats and luggage and slowly disembarked. I sat and waited for Lily.

After a while, she appeared and said: "Well, here we are in Northolt. London is very close. Come on, let's go down."

We climbed down a staircase which had been rolled up to the airplane. There was a hot smell from the engines which were ticking as they cooled. A hazy mist hung over the airfield, which made halos round the yellow lights and removed the sharp edges of things.

"Is the weather always like this in England?" I asked Lily.

"Some of the time it is," she said. "But it changes every day. That's why we talk about it all the time."

I had noticed that about the English. When you met one, he asked how you were, but didn't expect a reply. He then said something about the weather. My Arab friends thought this was funny.

We got onto a little bus, where the pilot and some other

members of the crew were already sitting, and drove to the terminal. There, Lily saw me through immigration and customs. The immigration man, who had a hard face, stared at me for a while and said: "Hmm, Polish, is it? Why are you coming to England?"

"Sir, to go to school, sir," I replied. "I have a place in Berkhamsted, which is a very famous English proper school."

The man smiled; it was a bit like ice splintering on a frozen lake. "Good, good," he said. "I hope you like England and your new school."

We went through to where people were waiting for the passengers. We looked around, but there was nobody who looked like a guardian. Lily said to wait there while she went to ask if anyone had left a message. I sat down on my suitcase and watched as gradually everyone went away and I was sitting there alone. Lily came back and said there was no message. We looked at each other; I was feeling a bit worried. What to do now? And what was the name of the guardian?

"Now then," Lily said. "What are we going to do with you?" She saw the pilot about to leave the hall. "Captain, Captain," she called. "Have you a moment?"

The pilot turned and came towards us. He was a cheerful-looking man with a big moustache; he reminded me of Dogvoice.

"What's up, Lily?" he asked. "Hullo, young fellow. No one to meet you, eh?"

"Please, Captain," I said. "My guardian is not here and I can't remember his name and I have only £5. I don't know what to do."

"Well," said the pilot. "Better that you come with us to our hotel and then tomorrow morning we can try to find your guardian. The main thing is to get some food and a bed to sleep in and you will feel better. Things always improve in the morning."

We drove through the damp darkness towards the middle of London. There were lights everywhere and quite a lot of traffic. Eventually we stopped outside a large building.

"Here we are," said Lily. "This is our hotel. We are in Piccadilly, in the West End."

Piccadilly! I looked round, but it was not particularly yellow, like in Monopoly, though the lights did shed a sort of golden glow on the damp pavements.

At the reception desk, the Captain and Lily were trying to explain about me to a very doubtful-looking managerial person, in a black coat.

"Just take him in for tonight," Lily was saying. "He has £5 and anyway, I am sure his guardian will come tomorrow and settle up anything owing. Where do you expect him to go, anyway? He can't sleep in the street." She glared at the manager.

For a moment I thought of using Mother's method and becoming the Prince of the High Tatra, as in Rome. But without Mother it probably would not work.

By then the other members of the crew had gathered menacingly round the manager and had made him agree to put me up for the night.

"All right, all right," he said. "But he goes into the annexe, not the hotel proper. And he can have some sandwiches."

I thanked Lily and the Captain, registered my name and followed a smirking bellboy to my room. We went down passages, through a kitchen, across an alley and up several flights of stairs, rather grubby and badly lit. Eventually, we ended up in a little attic room – an attic again – where the bellboy, muttering under his breath, left me.

I sat on the bed and wondered what would happen the next day. I had handed over my £5 (in those days £5 was a princely sum, more than enough to cover the cost of the room). I still could not recall the guardian's name, but I did remember he worked, like Ronnie, for the Anglo-Iranian Oil Company and that I could always try to telephone them in the morning and tell them that Mother was married to Ronnie. I was sure they would know about him, and Abadan, and Baghdad and everything.

By this time, a young waitress had brought me some rather unappetising sandwiches and a cup of tea. I disposed of these and fell into bed and a troubled sleep. I dreamed of multicoloured streets and refineries and a guardian without a face.

I woke with the sun shining into the room through the

window and the door banging open. A tall man, beautifully dressed in a dark suit, with wings of graying hair and a rimless monocle glinting in one eye came into the room, followed by a policeman and the night manager, who was looking nervous.

"You must be Andrew," the tall man said. "I **am** glad to see you."

"Yes," I replied. "Are you the guardian?"

"Archie Chisholm," said the tall man. Chisholm, of course! "I've been looking for you all over London," he said. "I only realised late last night that I had got the date wrong, and should have met you at Northolt, what? But by the time I got there, you were gone, so I called Scotland Yard (I have a friend there) to track you down. We telephoned everywhere and finally found you had been registered here. I'm so sorry."

"It doesn't matter," I said magnanimously. "The Captain and Lily helped me and I managed all right. I gave the manager my £5, too."

The policeman grinned and said: "So all is well as ends well, Sir. You won't be needing me any more."

The guardian smiled and said: "Thank you, officer. You have been a big help. Everything is all right now." The policeman touched his helmet and left.

"Now then, Andrew, get dressed and we will go home. I will wait for you downstairs. I am glad to have found you." The guardian also left the room, as did the manager.

I washed and dressed and went down to the lobby.

The guardian was there and came up to me, with his hand extended. "We should meet properly now," he said, shaking hands. "I am your guardian and my name is Archie Chisholm. You can call me Archie, since we shall be seeing a lot of each other. I am Ronnie's oldest friend and he has written and told me all about you. We will go home now and you can stop worrying."

"I am not worrying," I said. "I am used to managing alone and everything has been all right. I am glad to be in London and going to Berkhamsted, the proper school."

"You speak quite good English," remarked Archie. "I was not expecting you to. You have a strong accent, of course and you are making mistakes but we will soon get it right." I was pleased about that; Archie spoke with a wonderful accent and his English, as far as I could tell, was most correct. I wanted very much to speak like him.

We went out and got into a large black car, with a driver. Archie did not have a car of his own, he simply hired something appropriate when he needed one. The sun was out and Piccadilly looked quite yellow. We drove away from the hotel. Archie asked me to tell him about the flight and how Ronnie was and Abadan, so the trip passed quickly. We pulled up before a large and imposing house in a place which Archie said was called Hampstead, and got out. The door opened and there was a comfortable looking lady who gave me a big hug.

"We have been so worried," she said. "Archie should have remembered which day you were arriving. I'm so glad to see you. I am Josephine, Archie's wife and you will be staying with us. Have you had breakfast? You must think of this as your home now."

Well, I had had many homes, and this was the latest. "Thank you very much," I said politely. "It is kind of you. No, I have not eaten." I was very conscious of not doing anything which would upset Ronnie if he heard about it. After all, what would happen to Mother and me if he were to abandon us now.

I picked up my suitcase and we all went inside. The house was beautifully furnished, with shining antique chairs and tables and rich-looking rugs on the polished floors. It smelled clean and was tidy and neat. Archie disappeared up the stairs with my suitcase, while Josephine led me into a bright kitchen and told me to sit down at the table.

"What about some eggs and bacon and kidneys and fried bread?" she asked. "And then you can have some toast and marmalade, if you like. And tea, of course."

I just nodded. I was hungry, having eaten nothing but sandwiches since my spaghetti in Rome. Josephine's proposal sounded perfect.

I ate and ate, and answered questions between mouthfuls. Josephine also told me that I had my own room upstairs, that her two baby daughters and a nanny (on the top floor) shared the house with us, and that I was to do just as I wanted and to tell her if I needed anything. Archie would be going off to the office shortly, and would tell me all about the school and the other arrangements when he returned in the evening. He would send a telegram to Ronnie and Mother from the office to tell them that all was well.

I spent a wonderfully relaxed day. Josephine was as good as her word, and left me to my own devices: I lounged around, catching up on sleep, eating and exploring the house, which was large, warm and comfortable. The two small daughters were brought down, and Anne, the elder, stared at me with huge blue eyes, while Clare, the younger, just a blonde baby, lay peacefully in Nanny's arms.

Archie returned in the evening, and we had a leisurely supper. He told me that there were some ten days before I had to be taken to school, which was about thirty-five miles north-west of London.

"We have to organise a ration book and clothing coupons for you," said Archie. "We must also fix up your school clothes and a tuck-box and sports things and pocket-money ... My goodness, this will be good practice for when my two grow up."

"I must also register you as an alien," he added as an afterthought. "Things have not yet returned to normal after the war, and it will be some time yet."

Tuck-box? Alien? Ration book and clothing coupons? Much of what Archie said was a mystery.

The following few days were a rush of activity. Archie took time off from the office and whirled me around London in a beautiful car with a driver. As we progressed, much of what he had said became clear.

England was still very much in the grip of post-war discipline. Food was strictly rationed, although the amounts had increased. Everyone had a ration book with various sorts of coupons which were cut out as food was purchased. Clothes were also rationed and the same applied. It was easy for England to import whatever was needed, Archie explained, but the country had huge wartime debts to repay, and was not earning much in exports, since industry had been largely destroyed and was anyway geared to war production, so there was not enough money to pay for everything; hence the rationing. There was no trouble getting the coupon books; Archie seemed to have friends everywhere.

A tuck-box was revealed as being a stout wooden chest, the size of a smallish suitcase, with a padlock and with my name painted on the lid, in which, at school, I would be able to keep any private provisions for myself. This seemed to be a selfish thing, and would certainly not have been acceptable in Egypt, but Archie assured me that it was normal in English boarding schools and that everyone had a tuck-box. "We'll get Ronnie to send you some good things and you will be able to keep them safe," he said. "Who knows, maybe I will be able to find a thing or two for you to put in there."

We also went to a dusty office where an old gentleman asked me some questions and gave me an identity card which said ALIEN in large letters on it. He told me to show it at the local police station when I got to Berkhamsted.

As we drove round London, I noticed many wrecked and smashed houses, like rotten teeth in what had been a beautiful mouth, and saw that the lovely parks had been dug up in places. The town looked hurt and tired and made me feel that, with the towns in my own country suffering a similar fate, I had something in common with the English. But I was also excited to identify my Monopoly streets and squares, though disappointed that, in real life, they were not colour-coded.

Life in Gainsborough Gardens was pleasant and comfortable. Josephine treated me as one of the family and spoilt me after hearing the much abbreviated story of my life, which she drew out of me bit by bit. I was quite willing to be spoilt.

The day finally came when, fully equipped with the accoutrements of an English public school boarder, we set off for Berkhamsted by car. Josephine bade me an emotional farewell and said she and the family looked forward to Christmas with me after the winter term. She also gave me a large cake and a jar of strawberry jam to put in my tuck-box.

We drove out of London and into the country. It was my first view of the English countryside and I thought it very beautiful.

There were lush fields and rolling hills and masses of trees. The impact of so much green, after years of browny-yellowy desert, was tremendous. One other thing which made a great impression on me was that there were no flies; this was truly amazing, and the air felt empty. I thought that England, in this autumn of 1946, would be a most acceptable place to live.

After an hour's drive we reached Berkhamsted. This was a smallish undistinguished town, which formed a ribbon on either side of a long main street. There were hills on one side, and what looked like fields, with a ruined castle in the middle, on the other. There was also a railway line and a canal, both of which ran parallel with the main street.

Right at a church and in through a gate to a complex of red brick buildings. This was to be my home for the coming four years.

Berkhamsted was a middle-ranking public school. Its main claim to distinction was the fact that the father of Graham Greene, the famous writer, had been Headmaster there, and the school appeared, in uncomplimentary terms, in Greene's writings. It was an old school, part of Henry VIII's endowments, dating from 1541. The crest, which appeared on our school caps and blazer pockets, included a sort of naked cherub, modestly concealing various bits with a casual hand, and with an ambiguous motto: "*Virtus laudata crescit*", or 'virtue grows with praise'. The crest caused fights with members of other schools, who mocked and made lewd remarks. The motto was, in my experience, untrue, particularly at school, where it should have read 'virtue grows by not getting caught'.

Even the school song was in Latin, and incomprehensible, though sung weekly in chapel.

As Archie and I got out of the car, we saw all round us clumps of boys, some with parents, some chattering to each other after a summer apart. There were masters swishing about in long, black gowns, exchanging greetings with boys and parents. A very tall, thin master came up to us. He had dark, curly hair and a pleasant lined face. He was so tall that he stooped and inclined his head in an attentive sort of way.

"My name is Wraith," he said. I thought he rather looked like one. "I don't think we have met."

"Chisholm," said Archie. "This is Andrew Kronman, my ward. I think it was Mr Gaussen, his step-father's friend, who arranged a place for him here."

"Ah, yes," said Mr Wraith. "John Gaussen has told me about him. He will be in my house. Gaussen is a Junior School master, you see." He turned to me. "My house is Lowers, half of School House. You should be pleased; it is by far the best house in the school."

"Of course," said Archie, and the two grinned at each other.

Mr Wraith turned and looked around. "You, Gordon," he called. A biggish boy came over. "This is Kronman. He is coming to our house. Get Roberts and Brown and show them all round, will you?"

Gordon nodded and said: "Come along, Kronman. Follow me." I looked at Archie, but he said: "Get along with you. I will be in touch. Your trunk and tuck-box will be looked after. Good luck this term." We shook hands under the benign eye of Mr Wraith and I followed Gordon towards the nearest building. I was impressed by the easy relationship between master and boy; it was nothing like the armed truce which existed between them in Egypt.

We found Roberts and Brown standing chatting by the door. Roberts, who was to become my best friend, was a tallish, well-built boy with short fair hair and a lively smile. He was the son of an RAF Vice-Marshal who was a Sir, and determined to be an RAF doctor himself. He had an older brother at school, though they were not particularly close. Nigel Roberts, or Nidge as he was known, was a good and keen cricketer and distance runner, sports at which I did not excel.

Mike Brown by contrast, was short, powerfully-built, dark-haired and an enthusiastic rugger player. He was also to become a good friend. All three of us were allocated to the Upper Fourth, the top admission form into the senior school.

"What kind of a name is Kronman?" asked Nidge. "And why do you speak in this strange way?" Mike added.

"I am a Pole, and my name is really Andrzej Kronman," I said. "I have been in Baghdad and Egypt at school and I have just come to England because there is no more war. I speak good English. Anyway, your names are nothing special." I had learned that one must establish early that one could not be pushed around or insulted with impunity. Also, I had my knife, though the atmosphere was not at all threatening.

"Well," said Nidge, "whatever you say, your name is peculiar and the Andrz ... Andzjr ... doesn't work. You look like a black porter in an American film and I shall call you Joe." I was still very sunburned. Joe sounded good; I had been called so many things that another new name did not matter.

"Come on, come on," said Gordon, who was in the fifth form, a year ahead and somewhat superior. "Don't waste time. Follow me."

He took us on a tour of the house. The main building was old, though newer bits had been added on as the centuries went by. It all looked a bit shabby and threadbare, and the facilities, such as heating, were primitive. Of course, the war had meant that nothing much had been done, in the way of maintenance, for six years. It smelt strongly of furniture polish and cabbage, a compound odour which seemed to be endemic in boarding schools and which made me feel at home.

The upper floors had the dormitories (Uppers on the second floor, and Lowers on the first). These were long rooms, with ten iron bedsteads on each side, every bed within a shoulder-high cubicle open at the front, to give a false illusion of privacy. There was a small bedside chest, and some hooks on the wall. I noticed that the beds had only two thin blankets, and that, in spite of the cold, the windows, which ran down the side of the room, were slightly ajar. There was also a huge, iron pipe which ran round the wall, low down, and which alternated between being too hot to touch and ice-cold, so that the temperature of the room swung violently between tropical and arctic.

There were several dormitories. There was also a small washroom on each floor and Gordon said the baths were in the basement, enough for each boy to have an obligatory bath once a week. After rugger, the teams bathed communally in a miniature sort of swimming bath, also in the basement.

There were a couple of studies for the senior boys upstairs

and Mr Wraith's small flat, where he lived alone. Gordon said he was known as Streaky, and that is what we called him, though not, of course, to his face.

On the ground floor there was the Old Hall, dating back to the 1540s, with rows of battered, ink-stained wooden benches and tables, carved with initials, facing a master's desk on a dais. This was where the most junior boys spent their time, and where boys not senior enough to have studies did evening prep. Here also there was a roll-call every evening. In keeping with the age of the building, I suppose, the calling out of one's name was answered in Latin, by '*adsum*', meaning 'present', though as one progressed up the hierarchy this was gradually elided to a drawled 'aaaad', to show that one was an old hand.

A door at one end of Old Hall led to the Headmaster's spacious apartments, where he lived with his family. He was never far away.

Finally the basement, full of intricate passages, little rooms, boiler and kitchen areas, all festooned with gurgling pipes and with the light of bare bulbs glaring off the whitewashed walls. Some of the little rooms were occupied by middle-ranking boys, who peered out of their studies like rats out of nests. A row of claw-footed white enamel baths without partitions, a wooden chair beside each, stood on brown linoleum in a room at one end of the basement.

By this time it was getting dark. The parents had departed and we were called on to assemble in the Old Hall. Streaky and his counterpart for Uppers each made a little speech, welcoming us to the House. Then there was a sort of administrative period, when dormitories and studies were allocated, lesson timetables distributed and ration books and clothing coupons collected by Matron, a pretty, youngish lady. After a scrappy supper, we found our beds and tried to sleep. There was a lot of talk, however, after 'lights out', and Streaky came and shouted at us.

I was jerked out of a sound sleep the following morning by the ringing of an extremely loud bell, like a small church bell, which was hanging on a bracket on the wall just outside the dormitory window, beside the black iron fire escape. It was seven a.m. on a grey autumn morning, and it took me a few seconds to realise where I was. I sat up. One or two of the boys were stirring, but mostly they had covered their heads and were trying to go on sleeping. I got a towel and my washing things and went to the washroom. I heard a loud voice in the dormitory as a senior boy, who I was told was a prefect, stripped the bedclothes back on each bed and caused the occupant to jump out, protesting bitterly.

Breakfast was very lumpy porridge and some reconstituted eggs in a rectangular block. There was bread and a tiny smear of what looked like butter. We were instructed to choose our rationed two-weekly pot of jam. Each boy wrote his name on his jar, which was private and sacrosanct – one of the worst possible crimes in the school was to steal jam from another's pot.

Breakfast was followed by a short free time, a brief service in chapel, and lessons.

I found the school routine much like that of Egypt, though the whole atmosphere was gentler and relations between staff and boys were more friendly and less hostile. In fact, I stopped carrying my knife after the first week. The system of prefects helped, since they formed a buffer between masters and boys.

There were House prefects with powers only in their own house, and School prefects with jurisdiction over all boys. They helped the staff with administration and discipline. At Berkhamsted prefects were not permitted to beat boys but they had a wide armoury of sanctions: extra study, household tasks, running round the quad and so on. They settled quarrels between boys in peer-group courts, prevented bullying and kept most misdemeanours from reaching the ears of the masters.

Gordon explained 'fagging', the system whereby the youngest boys acted as menials to the eldest: cleaning shoes, tidying studies, washing up plates, running errands and so forth. The work was done on behalf of a group in a study, not on a one-to-one basis, as in most other schools, so felt less like real servitude, more like almost public service.

The least popular duty for a fag in winter was to sit after breakfast on the seat of one of a row of outside toilets, which were largely open to the elements, and warm it for a senior boy. I mostly managed to hide, be allocated other tasks, or run mythical errands for masters, to escape this duty.

I gradually realised that what looked like humiliation of younger boys was quite intentional.. The whole education system in England was geared to producing the "English gentleman" of legend, by building a boy up to a position of authority, then knocking him down to the lowest social level on his next move, through junior and senior schools, military service, university and first job. This roller coaster ride, reinforced by peer pressure, was supposed to build character, and prevent un-British bragging, conceit and self-advertisement.

Sport was important at Berkhamsted: rugby football in winter, running and athletics in the Easter term, a choice between cricket and swimming in summer. Other sports, such as boxing, fencing, gymnastics and many others, fitted into the cracks. Team sports were highly rated and those featuring individual effort were somewhat downgraded.

My introduction to rugger was rather traumatic. I trudged up to the playing fields, on a gray, drizzly afternoon, with the rest of the school. The boys in my year were made to line up while the Captain of the First XV (an immensely heroic and god-like figure), and some of his team came to cast their eye over the new intake. Since none of us new bugs had much idea of rugger (I had none), choices were made solely on physical attributes.

"You!" said the Captain, and threw at me a lozenge shaped football. I caught it. "You look a prop type. What is your name?"

Prop type? Propeller? Proposer? "Kronman, sir," I replied. The Captain grinned. "Don't call me sir. Foreigner, are you?"

"Yes, er ... Captain," I jiggled the ball, which was leather, heavy and slick with rain. "What is a prop type?"

"Front row of the scrum," he said. "You will find out. You have the right build."

I was of only average height, but my body was quite wide and deep. It seemed these were attributes necessary for a prop type; more so than skill.

My form mates were variously allocated to field positions. The master in charge told us that the purpose of the game was to move the ball by any means, preferably fair rather than foul, to the far end of the field and that we could learn the rules as we went along. My first scrum was a painful experience but I then learned how to adopt the proper posture and to take the weight of both packs on my neck and shoulders, which was apparently what props did.

After a strenuous two hours, we all went back to school, bruised, filthy and covered with mud to shed our football kit and leap naked into a steaming communal bath, with much shrieking, horseplay and splashing. It did not enable us to wash particularly thoroughly in the chocolaty water, but was much fun. I discovered that Nidge had been designated a three-quarter, and that this would not require any amputation or physical reduction.

Classes were interesting too. There was the usual list of subjects, though, unlike Egypt, there were different 'sets', to which boys were allocated depending on ability and knowledge. I found I was in the top set for everything, but my complacency was shaken in the English (language and literature) set, where my greatest interest lay, and where my accent and ignorance of literature let me down.

This set was presided over by a Scotsman called McLeod (and known as Mac). He was a big man, with a big voice and movements like a whirlwind. His reddish hair was always untidy and his long, black gown was frayed and torn. He habitually wore hairy tweed jackets and was totally outspoken and blunt. He made his own rules, both for behaviour and teaching. We worshipped him and produced good results.

My first meeting with Mac was on the second day. We were sitting at our desks when the door was flung open with a crash and Mac came striding in. "Ho," he cried in a booming voice. "My new lot of whelps; grist to my mill; lambs to the slaughter..." He guffawed loudly. "Now then, who are you all, whence and whither? I'll read out names and you stand and tell us about yourselves."

We were seated more or less alphabetically and stood up in turn to introduce ourselves. I sat next to Nidge. When my turn came, I explained briefly that I had escaped from Poland, lived in the Middle East and had come to England the previous month. Then Nidge said that he had come from a prep school in Kent and that he was an Englishman.

Mac grinned. *"You from the Polack wars, and you from England, are here arriv'd ..."*, he declaimed and clapped his hands with glee. I discovered that he knew much of Shakespeare by heart and that few things gave him more pleasure than to find apt quotations. He was an Elizabethan character, larger than life, who gloried in using archaic language and almost unknown phrases. I found this fascinating; he was the first person after Dr Mish who really enjoyed words.

"Go on, next bantling. Expound unto me, boy." We continued. There was a variety of boys, from different backgrounds, about twenty in all. I was the only alien.

We found that the masters were a curious mixture. There were some older men, brought out of retirement during the war to replace the masters who had been called up, and some younger ones, demobilised early, who had returned to teaching after five years in the Forces. We tried to make these latter tell us of their experiences, as gory as possible, but they were always reluctant to do so.

Our French teacher, Mr Hollycombe, was an elderly, white-haired Englishman whose impeccable French was so correct and classical, and so far removed from every-day speech that a real native would have found it difficult to understand. The accent, hard for an Englishman, was produced through agonised contortions of his lips and face, copied faithfully by the class. Seen through a sound-proof window, we would have looked very odd, as though in the grip of spasms and seizures.

Nidge wanted to do medicine, and spent much time cutting up frogs. My other close friend, John Bradman (nicknamed Don after the famous cricketer), wanted to be an electrical engineer and busied himself with batteries, wires and resistances. This was useful, since he was able to put together, for the significant sum of seven shillings and sixpence, a 'crystal set', a simple radio in a cigar box, with a battery and a 'whisker' which was adjustable on a crystal. On this, through a headphone, one could pick up the BBC. At one stage, he had quite a production line going.

We listened, most illegally, in bed after lights-out, under the blankets, to 'Much Binding in the Marsh' or 'It's That Man Again'. Wearing the headphone meant it was not possible to hear the approaching footsteps of Authority: innevitably we were caught, in spite of a system of sentries and alarms, and a complicated web of string attached to the listeners' toes. The greatest blow, of course, was the confiscation of the 'crystal set', since its prohibitive cost meant that nobody could afford more than one per term.

As an alien, I had to report to the police station once a week. The first time, I was rather nervous, and persuaded Nidge to accompany me. We went to the Police Station and found a Sergeant, with huge moustaches, sitting behind a desk.

"What can I do for you boys?" he asked comfortably. He had a small fire going in the iron grate and there was a large, steaming mug of tea in front of him. On a notice-board there was a poster exhorting the reader to keep his lips sealed since the Enemy Is Listening. It seems the contents were not often changed, since the war had been over for quite a long time.

"I am an alien," I announced importantly, "and I have come to tell you so." Nidge snorted and turned away. The Sergeant raised his bushy eyebrows.

"Is that so, young feller-me-lad," he said. "And just what kind of alien are you supposed to be?"

"I am a Pole," I said firmly, "and I am an allied alien, not an enemy; I am a friend." I thrust my identity card at him. He took it and examined it closely.

"Ho," he said after a while. "I don't believe you represent any great danger to this country. But we must follow the law and register you." He pulled out a large book from under the desk and, biting his tongue, carefully copied the details from my card into it. "Kronman, is it?" he said. "Right. Come back every week and report. But now we know who you are." He turned to Nidge. "What about you?"

"I am Roberts, an Englishman and a Man of Kent," said Nidge. "I came to say that Kronman is a friendly alien and that he should not be locked up." He stood on tiptoe. "I VOUCH for him," he said grandly.

"That's fine then," said the Sergeant, grinning, "if you vouch for him, he must be all right. Now cut along back to school, you two, and tell Mr Wraith that everything is in order."

In subsequent weeks the Sergeant, whose name was Garner, and I became good friends and I would stay in the Station for a few minutes, drinking hot, sweet tea and joking with the policemen who came in and out.

But the mind plays strange tricks. There had been some minor thefts from the Headmaster's House and the police had been called in. Nidge and I happened to be walking across the quad when a black car drew up and two men got out. It was drizzling and they both wore dark raincoats down to the ground and dark hats. They looked at us.

Without any conscious thought at all, I avoided making eye contact and my legs, seemingly of their own volition, took me at a run straight up to the dormitory, where I sat on the bed, with my eyes closed, panting and shaking. I did not fully understand what had happened, but when I opened my eyes, I found that Nidge had quietly followed me, and was sitting beside me without saying anything. I was glad he was there, though we never spoke of the incident.

A letter came from Mother. It was just like all the others and adjured me to 'behave like a good boy' and 'make Ronnie proud' of me; above all, not to cause any trouble since we Owed Him So Much. Towards the end of the letter, Mother also casually mentioned that the Company had posted Ronnie to Hong-Kong, and subsequently to Shanghai, as Chief Representative, and that would mean that they would not be coming to England for a while. I must confess that the letter had not much effect on me, and I wrote back (as we were obliged to do once a week, on Sunday afternoons) that I hoped all would be well, that I hoped the Chinese would be friendly, and that the odd ten shilling note would not come amiss. This last comment earned me, in the next letter (from Hong Kong) a short, sharp note from Ronnie, enclosed with Mother's meandering message, to the effect that begging was demeaning and that it was important to live according to one's means. I could see the shadow of a Discussion looming.

By the end of term, I was wholly comfortable in my new

environment, and was happy. The other boarders, especially the ones in my House, were my new family, and it was a supportive, loyal and friendly group. We were sorry for the day-boys when, at the end of the school day, they had to leave all their companions and make their way home to parents and siblings, while we could spend the full twenty-four hours among our friends. This feeling was seldom understood by the parents of boarders, who felt their children must miss them terribly. By common, though unspoken consent, the boarders encouraged this useful fiction, and their parents' feelings of guilt and pity, when short of cash or when the tuck box was getting empty.

Archie wrote once and telephoned once to enquire if all was well, and expressed himself pleased when reassured. He sent a ten shilling note, quite unsolicited, which showed him to be an understanding and compassionate person.

Money was not of enormous importance, since the tuck-shop, where one could purchase one's ration of sweets, or the odd Chelsea bun or packet of biscuits did not present a great choice. But the circulation of illicit, though relatively harmless comics, bottles of ginger beer and mildly romantic books on the flourishing school black market, as well as bribes to other boys sometimes to do one's chores and the cost of replacement "crystal" sets, did strain the purse.

Christmas with the Chisholms was fun and both Archie and Josephine did all they could to make me feel at home. It was all very traditionally English and I was glad to have had the Christmas experience with the 'Groups' in Cairo, which prevented me from making a fool of myself. We had a Christmas tree, and holly and mistletoe and a splendid lunch with turkey and even pudding. British housewives had become expert in making the somewhat sparse rations go a long way and were geniuses at improvising in all sorts of ways. I gave Archie a special pencil with a multicoloured lead for the office and for Josephine I managed to get a small packet of needles. My present from them was a magnificent water pistol which, sadly, was confiscated within the first week of the new term when inadvertently used in the sight of Streaky.

It was, however, easy to get bored in the holidays. Archie went off to the office every morning and only returned well after dark; Josephine had her own life to lead and was busy with the household and with caring for her two daughters, who were much too young to be companionable. My pocket-money was minimal, and did not permit any real frolics in London. I therefore determined to explore and find all the streets on the Monopoly board, visiting all named streets, the four railway stations, the electric and water companies, the free parking and Wandsworth Jail. I remember feeling somewhat cheated that, having done all this, there was no square called Go where I could collect my reward.

I then resolved to explore London more thoroughly. I accomplished this by catching a bus in the central part of town, riding it out to the terminus in the suburbs and walking back. Josephine approved, and gave me, every morning, a packet of sandwiches and a thermos of tea, which I carried concealed in a small briefcase.

I got to know London very well and found the different districts diverse and fascinating. The East End, with its seedy houses and shops; the City, with dignified and rather snobby-looking banks and big companies, the West End, full of theatres, smart shops and restaurants. I had never been in such a varied and interesting town.

The scars of Hitler's bombs were very evident and yet, even in England's murky December weather, and with rationing, the people in general were cheerful and friendly. I spoke to many and while some were rather suspicious of my accent, they were not unpleasant and did not take advantage of my ignorance. The best fun was when one of the thick and impenetrable London fogs, a 'peasouper', descended on the town and people had to grope their way round, avoiding the blinded, slow moving vehicles, and peering at street names.

The holidays passed and it was time to return to school. This was a real pleasure: I looked forward to seeing and being with my friends again. Josephine kindly gave me new supplies for my tuck-box and I had a new scarf.

The Easter term was devoted principally to athletics and was considered to be the dullest of the three terms. I had a strong dislike of running, since I could see no merit in leaving a place in order to see how quickly one could return there. I was also lazy.

Nidge, Don and my other friends, however, seemed to enjoy slogging up hill and down dale, in the mud and pouring rain. I managed to persuade Mr Wood, the games master, that I had a great interest in the physiological mechanics of running and wanted to become the long-running team's physio-therapist. Trustingly he arranged for me to go on a course with the local St. John's Ambulance Brigade to learn about muscles. massage, exercise and so forth. Thus I could accompany the team on away matches, with all the fun this entailed, while not exerting myself in any way. I actively encouraged a wholly spurious myth that I was able to cure strained and cramped muscles by a simple laying on of hands.

Thanks to my stocky build I was 'volunteered' to put the weight. This was not very onerous and I gradually worked my way up to the school team.

Academically, lessons continued as before. Mac addressed me as *"Most excellent imp ... thou proper stripling"* when, on returning from a week's absence with influenza, he entered the classroom, proclaiming: *"A untimely ague stay'd me a prisoner in my chamber ..."* and I was able to say *"Henry VIII"* which fortuitously I had been reading that morning.

He continued to inspire me and I became more and more determined to lose my foreign accent, and to get the highest possible marks for English in both School and Higher certificates.

I joined the Junior Training Corps, a cadet group pretending to be the Army, under the command of an ancient master who was a veteran of the First World War. Once a week we wore scratchy uniforms, with webbing, belts, pouches, gaiters and packs, and marched up and down carrying heavy Lee-Enfield .303 rifles. There was brass to clean, but since the alternative was joining the Boy Scouts, the JTC was definitely preferable. We had a summer camp under canvas, where we could shoot our rifles. I rose from Lance-Corporal, in four years, to Senior Under Officer, which enabled me to wear leather gloves, carry a swagger-stick instead of a rifle, and strut about giving orders. Though I would not have admitted it, I thoroughly enjoyed the discipline and the tidiness of thought which seems to characterise the military mind and organisation.

To my great delight, Nidge's parents invited me to spend the Easter holidays with them. They lived in a modest house in northern Kent, not far from a major railway junction. The men of the family, that is Nidge, his Sir father and his elder brother were all train enthusiasts and would spend much time together collecting locomotive numbers and ticking them off in little books they had. I knew about this curious English hobby, as I had spent hours at Berkhamsted with Nidge, often in the rain, standing in a field by the railway and waiting for the trains to go by. I had little enthusiasm for this past-time, but felt that solidarity demanded I support my friend.

So during the holiday we all went down to the junction, and I got to know what saddle-tanks were, and what a 4-6-4 was, or a 'Schools Class' engine. I had much more fun playing with an extremely elaborate model train layout in the attic, with controls for three people, yards of track, stations, signals. bridges and tunnels. Lady Roberts (or Mumlady as the family called her) was a very understanding person and put up with the curious habits of husband and sons with great understanding. The mystery of why an eminent RAF family should be so interested in trains was never solved. It seemed more suitable that at school Nidge was forever making flying models of aircraft out of balsa wood.

During the first evening, when we happened to be alone in the kitchen for a moment, Lady Roberts said: "You seem to be Nidge's best friend, Joe, and he has told me about you. Do please call me Mumlady, like the others. I am so glad that you are spending these holidays with us. I hope that you don't mind about the trains; I don't, as I am sure there are worse hobbies and it keeps them out of mischief." I wondered what mischief an Air Vice Marshal could get up to, but did not like to ask.

It was a warm and happy atmosphere and it occurred to me, sometimes, that perhaps I could also have a family like this. The people I had spent time with, the Groups and others in Egypt, the Chisholms in London and now the Roberts, all seemed to get so much pleasure out of being together.

The summer term was the best. Almost everyone (including me) played cricket but my main interest was swimming. There was a shortish indoor pool at the school, which smelled strongly of chlorine, and everyone swam a bit. There were swimming matches against other schools during the summer term. My Middle East years, and all the days spent in the pool there, led to a place on the school team. I even swam for England, unofficially, (I was a Pole) in two minor junior internationals. Nidge and Don were cricketers rather than swimmers – Nidge achieving the glory of the Ist XI. My best memories are of warm, lazy afternoons and evenings on the playing fields, or swimming 'away' against other schools, singing in the bus going there, seeing how other schools were run, the excitement of the races, the huge teas, the triumphant return. It lulled one into a sense of well-being and careless of the end of year examinations which then suddenly pounced on us.

My first exams at Berkhamsted (the following year I would take School Certificate), were not as bad as I had feared. In English, especially, I enjoyed myself and, to everyone's astonishment, came first. This drew a thunderous clap on the back from Mac, who roared: *"Thou hast the spirit of a youth that means to be of note ..."*. He spun round, with tattered gown flying and went on: " *"Fasten your ear on my advisings"*, you have done excellently well. Sort out your accent and we will have a go at a Cambridge scholarship. How about that, looby?"

I was immensely flattered, and determined, there and then, to beat the English at their own language. I was sure Dr Mish would have approved.

Term ended and the Chisholms told me that they were going to spend part of the summer in the Sussex town of Seaford, by the sea. Archie would come down at the weekends and the women of the household and I would stay at a small, rented villa on the cliffs.

Time passed slowly. There was not a great deal to do and no one to do it with. I went down to the beach when the weather was reasonable and read when it was not. Then Josephine kindly arranged for me to go 'cubbing' one day with the local hunt.

I was told to report to a stables in town, early in the morning. There I saw a mass of children, some only five or six years old, and dressed splendidly in riding outfits with jodhpurs, boots, whips, hats and cravats. I was wearing a pair of flannel trousers and a shirt with a pullover, and felt a bit out of it. The older girls eyed me and giggled.

A resplendent lady, with a loud neighing voice, explained that we would all proceed, keeping our horses to a walk, to a field beyond the cliffs, and there certain mysteries would be made known to us on the subject of the ceremonial killing of foxes. We then all went to our mounts.

The horse to which I had been allocated ("Never ridden before, what? Well, Dolly is like an armchair; just sit there and hang onto the reins ..."), was an immensely fat, elderly mare, with a cunning look in her eye. I patted her on the head, negligently, and she bit me, not very hard, on the arm.

I was helped into the saddle and found that sitting astride caused acute pain, Her back was so broad I was almost doing the splits. So, having worked my way to the very rear of the cavalcade, I took my feet out of the stirrups and sat cross-legged on top of the horse, which I thought was fun.

We proceeded in a prudent way up through the narrow streets to the open fields above the town. We then turned off into a narrow lane between high hedges.

The Horse-lady suddenly shouted: "Trot, trot ..."

The cavalcade began to trot and since I was still sitting cross-legged, I immediately fell off. As soon as she felt I was gone, Dolly turned briskly in her tracks and trotted back to the stable. When I picked myself up, I saw the main group bouncing off in one direction and Dolly disappearing in the other. I therefore made my way to a pub, not far away, and spent the sixpence I had been given on a large lemonade and a bun. I sat in the sun and pondered on the folly of mankind, and then meandered slowly home.

Josephine asked if I had had a good time, and I thanked her and said I had, without volunteering any information. The Horse-lady did not report on the incident, so no more was said. This was my only involvement in hunting.

Archie appeared at the week-end and said: "I have your school report," in an ominous way. But then he grinned and patted me on the back. "It's a good one, Andrew. Well done. We shall have a cake to celebrate, eh, Josephine?"

Sure enough, at teatime, there was a small chocolate cake (not easy in the grip of rationing), and I was solemnly toasted by everyone, with a slice.

Later, there was a letter from Mother; she also congratulated me on the results of the exams, but again there was a short note from Ronnie, which said: "Not bad, but I am sure you can do much better if you work". I did not know it then, but this would be his attitude to whatever I did, good or bad, for the rest of our life together. At the time it just made me determined to earn his unqualified praise.

The summer holidays passed peacefully and I eagerly awaited the beginning of the new term. It was a great relief to be back with Nidge and Don in surroundings which were now familiar and, importantly, no longer to be the very lowest in the school but a rank up from the fags.

Rugger occupied much of my attention, though I was also an enthusiastic supporter of the House in the singing competition – I liked singing. I became a member of the English Society (presided over by Mac) and the French Society (I wanted to understand what Mother and Aunt were saying when they made private remarks in front of me). I also took up fencing.

I had, at Ronnie's suggestion: "You should learn to defend yourself", an unwilling go at boxing. Naturally, Ronnie was unaware of my adventures in Egypt, and I could not very well tell him, so there was no way of avoiding the boxing without appearing cowardly.

I was very heavy for my height, and for my first skirmish (or sparring bout) I was matched against a friend of mine, a dayboy by the unlikely name of Sam Weller. He was a fraction over six feet tall, slim, but the same weight as me. His muscles (as I knew from the rugger field) were like whipcord. We squared up to each other and there was a flurry of uneducated punches.

When I came to, I was lying on a bench beside the ring and the Sports Master, Mr Wood, was pouring water on my face. Sam was distraught: he kept telling me how sorry he was, and how he had tried to knock me out as gently as he could.

"I think, boxing at this weight, you are going to have trouble reaching your opponent," Mr Wood said with what I thought was a cruel smile. "You'd better stick to rugger and fencing ..."

Thus honour and good sense were both satisfied.

There were no half-term holidays at Berkhamsted, but parents were permitted to visit once or twice a term and take their offspring, plus two guests, out to lunch at a local hostelry. When Don's parents came, he invited Nidge and me out and Streaky duly gave permission.

Mr and Mrs Bradman were very friendly, pleasant people, from the Midlands, where Mr was in some sort of industry. Mrs. was an extremely thin, tall lady with a high-pitched giggle but went immediately into my good books since she had brought me, as a gift, a pot of jam for my tuck-box, as well as one each for Nidge and Don. This was major largesse and unexpected.

For our lunch, we were taken, in Mr Bradman's modest Hillman, to a small hotel in a neighbouring village. This was famous, not so much for its food or ambience, but for the 'Evangelical Parrot'.

We entered the lobby, which had a small reception desk, a couple of armchairs, a bookshelf and, in one corner, a tall, narrow brass cage. In the cage was a garishly coloured parrot which turned its beady eye on Don, Nidge and me, as we approached it.

"Sinners repent!" it screeched suddenly and very loudly. "Repent! Repent! Watch and pray!"It then cackled with maniacal laughter.

We were startled and retreated rapidly. The parrot eyed us cynically and hung upside-down on its perch.

The landlord appeared, grinning, and explained that the parrot had belonged to an old lady in the village, now deceased, who had been much given to reading the Bible aloud, hymn singing and bursts of religious fervour. Having no other companion, she had talked a lot to the parrot. She had behaved rather strangely towards the end.

"Just look at this," our host pointed with glee to the hotel register which lay on the desk beside inkwell and dip pen. It seemed very ink-stained and the signatures in it were mostly wildly erratic.

"Strangers don't know about the parrot, you see, and we make a point of not warning 'em, as we get a good laugh when he makes 'em jump. Makes a bit of a mess of my register, but most come round to seeing the funny side of it. Folks round here call it the Evangelical Parrot."

We had a good hearty lunch, and could hear from time to time high-pitched phrases like: "Everlasting bonfire!", "Love Jesus!", snatches of hymns and hoarse laughter. None of the other diners, who were probably regulars, so much as looked round. We were all disappointed that no unwary strangers arrived to sign in.

For some time after this lunch, we three would suddenly shout to each other "Watch and Pray" followed by loud cackles and screeches This greatly bewildered our other friends. Sadly we never made another visit to the Evangelical Parrot.

My English continued to improve and I paid particular attention to my accent, practising various words when I was alone. Mac noticed the improvement and, after a meeting of the English Society one evening, said: "You are doing well, Kronman. Keep it up. This is a good school, you know, and one day you will be grateful to it."

A 'care parcel' arrived from Mother. It contained a tin of cheese, two bars of chocolate, a large, tinned fruit cake and, for reasons unknown, a jar of mustard.

Nidge, Don and I, having made sure we would be undisturbed, opened the cake tin. There was an immediate and powerful smell of spirits. It was a rich fruit cake, well soaked in brandy. It was quite a big cake, but we wolfed it down at one sitting, unfortunately just before supper, on empty stomachs. Don soon complained of feeling queasy and Nidge was giggling in a strange way. I found it difficult to focus my eyes.

As luck would have it, Streaky appeared and looked at us suspiciously; in fact, he peered closely at us in his short-sighted way and sniffed loudly. "Now then, what is this?" he said. "Have you ghastly boys been drinking?"

"Oh, no, Sir," we chorused, although Nidge went on giggling. "My Mother sent me a cake, and we were eating it, that is all," I added, blinking. "See, Sir, here is the tin."

Streaky looked at it and sniffed. "Hmmm," he muttered. "Perhaps not the letter of the law, but certainly the spirit ..." He turned and marched away. He was an understanding man.

There was also a letter from Uncle Max. It was typed, presumably by his clerk at the clinic; this was just as well, since his writing was totally illegible except, probably, to pharmacists. I also had the impression that the clerk had edited the contents. It was in English, and read:

"Respected and Beloved Nephew,
It is long since we had the pleasure of speaking. You and I are both far away although our hearts are one. Your Aunt says that you are happy and the school is good. I am glad because school is of much important, and learning is for a virtuous life. Here we live as before but there is much beggaring and leprosy which we help. Everybody remembers you and is your friend. Faisal is not happy. I send a small gift.

Your loving uncle
Doctor Max Makowski Pasha MD".

Enclosed was an enormous, white English five pound note. I was rather scared by it; it was a huge amount of money and I thought it best to hand it in to Streaky to look after. But it made me wealthy for a whole term.

I was sure that Aunt was not aware of the letter or the gift and puzzled how I could thank Uncle Max without giving the game away. I eventually wrote, addressing my letter to both Aunt and Uncle, reporting that I was well and happy, that I had unexpectedly made five wonderful new friends who had come from abroad and that I was lucky and thankful to have them. When I next met Uncle Max, after a couple of years, he told me he had understood my code and Aunt was none the wiser.

Archie announced that he would be coming down to take me

out to lunch and I could bring a couple of friends with me. This was kind of him, since I was constantly beholden to my friends and their parents for their many invitations which I could not return. It was with much pleasure, therefore, that I was able to invite Nidge and Don to lunch.

On the appointed Sunday, dressed in our best and with freshly brushed shoes and caps, we stood in the quad and awaited Archie. There was a number of other boys waiting for their respective parents and some of the masters were also wandering about. Suddenly, there was a collective gasp as an enormous black Rolls Royce nosed its silent way through the gates. I should mention that the status of a boy depended in no small measure on the sort of car his father drove.

Everyone peered with interest to see who this personage may be. The car slid smoothly to a standstill, the chauffeur (in gray uniform, with polished high boots and a peaked cap) hurried round to open the door and the personage descended.

To my astonishment, it was Archie. He was dressed in soft, brown tweeds, with gleaming brown brogues on his feet, a brown deerstalker hat on his head and a shiny brown walking stick in his hand. His monocle gleamed as he looked round at the staring crowd.

"Ah, there you are, Andrew." He walked over to me and we shook hands. I was somewhat dazed, but introduced my guests, Nidge and Don, who were standing with their eyes popping and their mouths open.

"If you are ready, we can go," said Archie, turning to the monstrous car. We all climbed in gingerly, patting and stroking the beautiful upholstery, highly polished wood and admiring the cut-glass decanters, reading lamps and, above all, the telephone to the driver.

"I thought we could have a picnic, instead of going to some pub or hotel," said Archie. "Much more fun, and we can eat what we like."

We drove silently up the hill towards Ivinghoe Beacon and stopped beside a field, with a small grove of trees. "This will do very well, Charles," said Archie into the speaking tube. "Be kind enough to bring out the picnic."

So while we stood and stared, Charles produced, from the cavernous boot, a collapsible table and chairs ("Rugs on the grass are such a bore; ants and dew and so on ..." remarked Archie), and a huge wickerwork basket, which he unpacked to reveal a snowy white tablecloth, gleaming silverware and shining glasses. There was a whole cold roast turkey, salads of various kinds, some smoked salmon, cheeses, biscuits, slices of ham and tongue and other things. We gazed in wonder as more and more food appeared on the table. How Archie had managed this with rationing we could not guess, and were too awe-struck to ask.

We sat round the table and Archie said: "Well, don't stand on ceremony. I was a schoolboy once and I remember what the important things are. Help yourselves."

We did. We ate until we could eat no more, although, at the end, Charles produced fruit and a chocolate cake and we somehow found extra room. Archie presided over the meal, telling us stories of his wartime adventures (he was a Colonel in Intelligence and was much decorated), although he managed to do it without boasting. It was a truly magic time, and the lemonade we drank (Archie had champagne) might easily have been champagne as well, so intoxicated were we with such a perfect adventure.

We returned to school, bearing paper bags full of everything that was left over, to an admiring and jealous crowd. My stock had gone up a lot, and as Archie said goodbye and acknowledged our profuse thanks, he winked at me and said quietly: "There we are. I hope you all had a good time. A Rolls Royce always helps, doesn't it!" He climbed back into the car, and with a whisper of the engine was gone.

Then there was the matter of girls. Where relations with the opposite gender were concerned, let alone sex, we suffered a mixture of lust and ignorance. In the Forties, there was no sex education, no explicit films, magazines or books, and an aura of great secrecy where relationships were concerned. It was reprehensible to show interest in sex and virtually impossible to acquire any knowledge.

The school was boys only and our contact with girls was, to

all intents and purposes, non-existent. Naturally, during holidays, some of the boys managed to gain valuable though superficial experience, which was eagerly shared with friends who had not been so lucky. The reported activities were usually so exaggerated however as to make it hard to know what to believe.

The racing hormones, the ignorance and the then current gentlemanly code of putting females on a pedestal, because women were pure and fragile, a "weaker sex" to be protected, caused us great confusion.There seemed to be a basic incompatibility between the idea of a *'preux chevalier'* who cherished and defended women, and the ruthless Casanova who pursued them, which long and earnest discussions could not reconcile. We therefore decided that there was only one answer: experience.

This, however, was much easier said than done.

Towards the end of my first term at Berkhamsted, the head boy, an Olympian figure I scarcely knew, had suddenly left, and the very pretty young matron had also vanished. It was rumoured that they had been found in bed together, though we never knew the truth. But obviously any amorous adventures had to be undertaken with extreme care, since to be found out, it seemed, would mean instant expulsion.

In Berkhamsted town there were two sorts of girls. Those who attended the local State schools, who were free to roam the town, and those who boarded at Berkhamsted Girls School (a more exotic selection) in an establishment parallel with, and similar to our own, though not under the same management then, though I believe it is today. The division was thus of specimens from a game park versus those from a zoo.

The problem was how to approach the game and bag it.

We had two school dances a year, and our partners were from the BGS only. Having been painfully taught the 'one-and-two-and-three-and …' as well as the 'slow-slow-quick-quick-slow…', while dancing awkwardly with another boy, we felt barely competent to cope with real girls. In common with the vast majority of British Public School boys of the time, we were all painfully shy in the presence of the opposite sex, while loud, boastful and foul-mouthed among ourselves.

The dances were held in the gymnasium, attended by large numbers of beady-eyed staff from both schools, who did not dance, but patrolled the dance floor, enforcing the rule that the only contact permitted with a partner was to be one hand lightly clasping hers, and the other lightly placed on her waist. There must be NO MOVEMENT WHATEVER of the hand on the girl's waist, and there must be A LARGE GAP between the bodies of the dancers.

The music was provided by a gramophone and there was only the strictest tempo in the selection of pieces: waltz, quickstep and fox-trot. The dance began with the arrival of a large group of giggling girls, trying very hard to be sophisticated. They stood at one end of the gym. The boys, meanwhile, shining from their oil-anointed hair to their highly-polished shoes, milled about at the other end. The music started, the staff scattered to their observation points, and nothing much happened for a bit. Then the braver girls began to dance with each other and steered a course closer and closer to the terrified boys, who pretended not to notice. It was usually a girl who broke away, pulled a boy onto the floor and began to dance with him. The ice then gradually broke and soon the wooden floor was full of ill-assorted pairs shuffling round and round, most of the boys wearing a look of grim concentration on their faces, while the girls looked long-suffering.

Refreshments consisted of sandwiches and lemonade, and boys were expected to serve their partners, who sat on chairs which lined the walls.

The last waltz was a special occasion, since the lights were turned down a bit and a romantic atmosphere was attempted. This was largely spoilt by the increased vigilance of the prowling staff, whose minatory barks punctuated the sentimental music.

After the dance, there was a major post-mortem discussion among the various groups of boys and a minute dissection of obviously untrue reports of conquests and assignations.

At the time, I had the uncomfortable habit of falling in love with every girl I met, though this feeling was not reciprocated and girls tended to say that they would wish to know me much better before having any feelings whatever. Still, there was one exception.

Beatrix was a medium sized blonde, with freckles, a luscious mouth and a figure which was, if not stunning, at least promising. Her blue eyes were guile-less and her manner pleasant and friendly. I managed to grab her for the last waltz and rapidly told her my name while getting hers. I told her I had been watching her throughout the evening (true), to the exclusion of all others (not quite true), that I ached with love for her and could we please, please correspond. She laughed and said that we could write to each other and be friends. I had to be content with this, though friendship, in my plans, was subsidiary.

Sure enough, a week later, I got a letter from her, telling me, among some boring chit-chat, that she looked forward to getting a letter from me. I immediately wrote back, professing undying love and asking if we could meet during the holidays. Her reply was that I must not talk of love and that we could, perhaps, meet in the holidays.

We corresponded in this way, my letters passionate, hers increasingly ardent, until almost the end of term when Jack Godley, an older boy in a different House, sought me out to tell me that his sister, who was at BGS had mentioned to him that my lovely Beatrix normally read my letters out to a large group of friends, who roared with laughter and helped her to compose a suitable reply. He felt that I should know this, as the honour of the School was at stake.

My heart was broken, I thought, for ever. Mac noticed my mood and, after class, enquired why I appeared whey-faced. I recounted my story and he clapped me on the back and said: *"That love is merchandized whose rich esteeming The owner's tongue doth publish everywhere."* I was grateful that he did not laugh and having got a new perspective on girls, decided to put the episode behind me.

Having failed with the zoo, I determined to try the game park. There was a pretty young kitchen maid who worked at the school. Her name was Rosie and I caught her looking at me quite frequently. When I managed to speak with her, she showed interest and I fell in love again. The problem was where and when to meet.

I called my friends into conclave and we eventually worked out a plan. A favourite place for local swains and maidens to meet at night was in the local churchyard, which adjoined the school building and which the window of our study overlooked. Since there was an iron fire-escape beside my dormitory window that term, we decided that I could make an assignation with Rosie in the churchyard at midnight. Nidge would keep "*cavey*", or watch, from the study window and flash a torch if there was danger so that I could hurry back. Don undertook to stay awake and ensure that no-one shut the fire escape window while I was out. The scheme seemed to be foolproof.

Rosie, who was very biddable, and somewhat older than me, readily agreed to meet me as we planned and I spent several days in a fever of excitement.

On the night, at a quarter to midnight, I got dressed in the dark, making no noise so as not to wake the slumbering boys in the dormitory. I checked with Nidge and Don that they were ready. The window creaked slightly when I opened it, but no one stirred. I climbed the rusty stairs down to the quad and quietly made my way out of the gates and to the churchyard. A memory of Cairo stirred; it seemed so long ago.

In the churchyard, I made my way to the far wall, the place of our assignation, trying not to stumble upon any of the intertwined pairs of bodies among the gravestones. There were suppressed giggles and grunts all round me.

I waited and waited. It was now almost one o'clock and no Rosie. I was beginning to lose hope when suddenly there came a series of flashes from the study window.

I rushed back to the fire escape and up to the dormitory window. The lights were on and Streaky was sitting on my empty bed.

"Welcome back," he said coldly. "I hope you have had an interesting time. Perhaps you would be good enough to accompany me to my study, where we can explore this matter further."

I followed him out of the dormitory, through a gauntlet of

staring eyes, some gleeful, some sympathetic. Nidge and Don looked sorrowful and worried.

Streaky's study formed part of the small flatlet where he lived. His pride and joy was an enormous concert grand piano, which he played very well. The room was lined with books and had comfortable, worn furniture; it felt familiar, since it was here that the French Society met every fortnight.

"I am disappointed in you, Kronman." Streaky sighed heavily. "I thought you had more sense than to break bounds at night. I suppose you were meeting a kitchen maid in the churchyard ..."

I gaped at him. It was uncanny. How could he know? Surely Nidge and Don had not betrayed me.

Streaky looked sad. "You are not the first and you will not be the last. Of course, I am going to beat you. But since this is your first major crime, I won't mention it to anyone. I want your promise that you will not do it again; I assure you, it is not worth it."

He hated beating people, and assuaged his unhappiness, when forced to cane someone, by offering them a small glass of sherry after the punishment, while he played a short piece, of their choice, on the piano, as they stood and drank.

He gave me six. The cane was a fairly thick one and Streaky had nowhere near the sinews, accuracy or enthusiasm of Whipper, so it was not too bad. He gave me the glass of sherry and I asked for the first movement of the Moonlight Sonata, which I liked and which I knew he also enjoyed. I then made my way back to the dormitory where I recounted the story to Nidge and Don, who had managed to sneak back to bed without being observed and who were much relieved that their involvement remained unknown.

Rosie disappeared from the kitchen. I do not know how she was discovered, but I did get a message from her saying she was sorry and that I was not to worry about her. There was no explanation as to why she had failed to come to the churchyard.

Contrary to a commonly held view, homosexuality was not rife at school though there were exceptions. One of my friends, Simon, was a homosexual. I knew this only because he had told me about it. I do not think he told anyone else, and if he was a practising one, he must have been very discreet, since he made no reported overtures to anyone, least of all to me. He was a kind, caring and sensitive person, very musical, who had no enemies and who was always prepared to help and listen to any tale of woe. At the same time, he was not too sensitive to play rugger for the Second Fifteen. I was very sad when he was killed, driving his sports car, in his first year at Oxford.

A letter came from Mother to say that Ronnie had been posted back to England, and that they would be returning in time for the summer holidays and that they would buy a house. I was thrilled. At last I would be able to invite my friends to my own house, and have my own room and be like all the others. Perhaps my step-brother and my step-sister would come to live with us. Suddenly, life presented an exciting prospect and the impending School Certificate examination took second place.

This was an important exam. In order to achieve Matriculation exemption to Oxford or Cambridge Universities, you had to obtain, at one sitting, a minimum of six Credits and a Pass, in predetermined major subjects. I took English Literature, Language, French, History, Latin, Maths, Physics, Chemistry and Additional Maths, got three Distinctions, five Credits and a Pass, and so all was well, and I could concentrate on my new home. Mac was particularly pleased at the Distinctions in the two English subjects, and he invited me, together with a couple of Sixth Formers, for an illicit pint of beer, in a local pub, on the last day of term.

Mother and Ronnie returned, and wrote to tell me that they had bought a house in Chipstead, in Surrey, from where Ronnie could comfortably commute to the office in London. Ronnie had also bought a small car, and they would come to pick me up on the last day of term.

They duly arrived at lunchtime, and said that they were in a hurry and that we had to leave as soon as possible. Mother was all dressed up, in hat, veil and high-heeled shoes; she was just as I remembered her, golden hair and painted face. Ronnie was immaculate in tweeds.

In front of all the boys and masters milling about in the quad, Mother pressed me to her scented bosom and said loudly: "Ach, my little son! How you are grown and becoming a man! Now we are together ..."

I struggled to free myself, and could see everyone within earshot looking away with broad grins on their faces. "Not now, not now ..." I hissed at Mother, "let go."

She looked slightly injured, but stepped back. Ronnie shook hands with me. I wanted to introduce Nidge and Don, who were standing close by, but did not have the chance. I explained where my suitcase and tuck box were, and we went to fetch them.

Ronnie suddenly stopped and stared at me. "Good Heavens, Andrew; your accent has gone and you sound quite English. I am astonished and pleased. Well done."

An unsolicited compliment! I was glad to have surprised him. Of course, I had not seen or spoken to him or Mother for two years, so the change in me must have been striking.

Ronnie said that there would be future opportunities to meet the masters and my friends, and we drove away to the new house.

On the trip, Mother babbled incessantly of their life and experiences in China and Hong Kong, and how happy she was and how I had grown and how glad she was to be in England and to have a proper home and and and ...

The house turned out to be a modest, three-bedroom affair, tile-hung and standing in a leafy lane with a fair sized garden. It was called The Knoll. I was shown to the smaller of the two guest rooms, with sparse furniture but a pleasant garden outlook from the small window.

"This will be your room when you are at home," said Mother proudly. "When you are at school, we will pack all your things away so we can use it for guests; you are a kind of guest, aren't you?" This made me a bit sad.

Life at home was very formal. Clothes had to be neat, room tidy, shoes polished, table manners impeccable. Ronnie was very kind, though he set high standards of behaviour. Mother adored him and seemed happy. This made me feel secure, since it absolved me from the burden of responsibility for her. Ronnie seemed to love her, in spite of her retained Polishness, which he found charming: the accent, the fluttering femininity which concealed the steel core known to me, the caressing endearments, and the new interest in those things which interested Ronnie. She was the perfect wife of the Forties, living to please and support her husband.

They both seemed disinterested in my school life and asked only a few desultory questions. Ronnie was an enthusiastic gardener and spent every moment of his spare time in digging, mowing, fertilising, weeding, clipping and planting. I was instructed to help and, having little interest in nature (I much preferred to read) was bribed with small sums to do the heavier work.

Mother, who, to my knowledge, knew nothing about gardens and cared less, suddenly developed a passion for flowers. Ronnie knew all their Latin names, she mostly did not know even their English one, but would wander about the garden saying: "Ach, the violets, how beautiful!", while clasping her hands to her bosom and casting her eyes heavenwards or "The roses, the roses, what an artist is God!"

Ronnie thought this was wonderful and even uprooted a small group of pansies when Mother said that their faces were following her round and she was frightened that they were souls of dead people.

My step-brother Andrew and step-sister Felicity came for a week-end. I was to remember (Mother informed me in a confidential whisper) that their mother, Ronnie's divorced first wife, probably felt unhappy that her husband had married a foreigner who had a son, and that I should be careful how I behaved.

In the event, they both seemed perfectly pleasant people and, while not becoming close friends, we got on well together. They were younger than I, by a year or two, and I could see that they considered Mother as some sort of exotic creature, hard to understand and one to treat with caution.

Mother tried hard to make the weekend a success. She was effusively welcoming and more Polish than ever, while, at the same time, exercising her new-found English expertise in the serving of tea with scones, or speaking of the roses and violets in the garden.

Andy, a brawny lad who was at Gordonstoun school, a very physical establishment and Fizzy, a slim English schoolgirl, who was at Sherborne, must have been puzzled. After they had gone, I wondered what sort of report they would make to their mother, and what sort of lady she was. I speculated also why she should have wished to divorce Ronnie, who seemed a wonderful husband and a kind and thoughtful man. I hoped however that my relationship with my step-brother and step-sister might in time develop into that of true siblings, and so it has, in spite of the differences in our background and upbringing.

We went to Northern Ireland for a two week holiday. The crossing was appalling, in a full gale, and we stayed, as genteel 'paying guests', in a large manor house in Armagh. Mother and Ronnie spent their time playing bridge with the hosts, a dried up, ancient couple whose interest did not extend to teenage boys, or they visited local gardens, in which I had no interest. As a result, I was bored to distraction, since there were no books and the primitive, wind-up gramophone only had two records, both of religious music.

There was, however, a fair-sized lake, and a local boatman, who was an old, rather drunk Irishman, called, unsurprisingly, Paddy. His delight was to thrust in one's face his left hand, which lacked a little finger, and to tell the tale of how a giant pike, which lurked in the lake, had amputated it years ago. The owners did not permit fishing, so Paddy and I would row on the lake, while he took periodic gulps from his bottle of indeterminate spirits and told me improbable stories of giant fish, and of leprechauns, the 'little people', in whom he firmly believed.

I got to know Ronnie much better during these holidays. He was reasonably pleased with my exam results, although I was told that I could have done better. He was a man of immense authority and rectitude, whose whole character appeared impeccably proper. Mother said that he had studied hard at school, and had worked his way through King's College in Cambridge (a most unusual achievement at the time), by teaching in the King's College Choir School. He had then joined the Anglo-Persian Oil Company (as it then was) and was to remain with it all his life, through its metamorphosis into the Anglo-Iranian and finally British Petroleum. Certainly, he was, in a more inconspicuous way than Archie, the very epitome of an 'English gentleman'. I think that Mother felt that I should aspire to be one too, though I never could manage it.

The one surprising facet of his character was his understanding and love of art and, to a lesser extent, music. I was persuaded to accompany him and Mother to the Tate Gallery in London, where Ronnie spoke with knowledge and passion about the various paintings he liked. I later learnt that he had longed to be an artist, and gone to live in Paris in his youth, but that common sense had prevailed, and he had joined an oil company instead. When visiting galleries Mother had found a useful phrase (as was her wont with subjects in which she was less than expert), and repeated it frequently. It was: "Ach, the texture, the texture ...", delivered with rolling eye and a deep sigh.

In a way, I suppose it was a relief to get back to school. I had no friends in Chipstead, and Mother and Ronnie seemed almost hermetically self-sufficient. Also, I was now in the Sixth Form, Secretary of Rugger, Captain of Swimming and a prefect, as well as Under-Officer in the Training Corps.

Nidge, Don and I had our own study on the first floor, which we called the "Bear Garden" and which had battered armchairs, desks, and an open gas fire where we could make illicit toast. I learnt to play a ukelele-banjo, which I had acquired for two shillings from a boy who was leaving.

My various posts all involved responsibilities, and life was busy. After a discussion with Mac and Streaky, we decided that I should concentrate, for my Higher Certificate, on English and French, as well as Latin and History as subsidiary subjects, with a view to trying for a scholarship to Jesus College in Cambridge, where Mac had some connections. Ronnie was disappointed that I did not want to follow him to King's, but it had, at the time, a reputation for effeminacy in its undergraduates, and so Jesus sounded a better bet. There was fierce competition for every place at Oxford and Cambridge.

At school, drama seemed to be the fashion of the moment, fomented by a keen master and by pressure put upon him by

Mark Boxer, a fellow boarder. Mark was a gifted actor and an even more gifted artist, and his caricatures were funny and wicked. He was a person of great charm, and was the moving spirit in school theatrical performances. He was to go on to cause quite a stir at Cambridge, editing Granta magazine, continuing his acting and barbed cartoons, and when rusticated (sent away for a term from Cambridge) enjoying a scandalous mock funeral staged by his indignant friends. Later years saw him become a famous magazine editor and a darling of London society.

When I showed interest, I was immediately recruited to 'carry a spear', in a splendid production of 'St.Joan', in which Mark took the part of the tortured maid and also in an English translation of Aristophanes' 'The Birds', in which Mark again took the principal role. I was, in the surprising company of Streaky, a Triballian god, cast in the part because Mark said I looked like a thug. The part entailed prowling round the stage, dressed inadequately in a fake tiger skin and carrying a balloon, camouflaged to look like a deadly club.

On opening night, with parents, staff and local dignitaries present, a particularly obnoxious boy, who was being one of the 'birds', surreptitiously burst my 'club' with a pin. The sudden explosion made me jump, which dislodged the tiger skin and revealed me, to a hysterical audience, clad in socks and underpants. I made a dignified exit and did not again act at school.

I was now playing serious rugger, and Ronnie and Mother decided to come, take me and friends out to lunch, and watch a match.

They arrived as planned, and we went to a local hotel for lunch. Ronnie got on well with my friends, who were under strict instructions not to volunteer any information about our activities, but only to talk in generalities.

On return to school, I went to join the rest of the team, who were getting changed and preparing for the match, which was against a nearby school. Ronnie and Mother were invited by Streaky to have coffee with him to discuss my future.

The match started normally. It had been raining, and the

ground was muddy. It soon became apparent that the teams were reasonably evenly matched, and that the result would depend on luck and physical effort. The scrums, rucks and mauls became more and more enthusiastic and, at one stage, I found myself under a heap of damp, steaming bodies, with someone's boot digging into my back.

Suddenly there was a loud shriek. I could see, on the edge of the heap, a pair of high heeled shoes, with one stamping up and down in a rage. A shrill voice was shouting, in the sudden silence: "My darlink! They will kill my SON! Get off, get off, murderer, villain ... Oh my God, he will die ..." and so on.

It was, of course, Mother, who had escaped from Ronnie's restraining hand and run onto the pitch to save my life, as she thought in her ignorance of rugby football. She was indiscriminately lashing out with her umbrella, hitting players, referee and even one of the linesmen who were trying to restrain her. Her hat was askew and her face pink with rage.

I wanted very much to die, there and then. How would I ever face my friends again? Eventually, Ronnie took Mother away and the game continued. I was enraged by our smirking opponents, who were saying, *sotto voce*, but audibly: "Poor lamb! Does diddums want his Mummy, then? Careful with the precious baby ..." and so on.

Fury lent me superhuman strength. I picked up the ball, put my head down, and ran for the goalposts. I think people tried to tackle me, but I was an irresistible force, a steam roller, a locomotive. I was going to score a try if it killed me. Through a red mist I saw a goalpost and dived for the ground. There was a sharp pain and everything went black.

I regained consciousness in the Sanatorium, an hour or so later. I had fractured my collarbone and got serious concussion scoring, while running into a goalpost, what turned out to be the winning try. This meant that I was off school for four days, that my heroism went a long way to cancel out the public disgrace of Mother's behaviour, and that Ronnie promised never to let her attend a match again.

Christmas at home was fun and adult. As was to be the family habit, on Christmas Eve there was the 'Polish Christmas', with traditional Polish dishes – barszcz (beetroot soup), fish in aspic, makowiec (poppy seed cake) and so on – and everyone dressed up, Ronnie in dinner jacket, Mother in an evening dress and I in my only suit.

Christmas Day was English, and slightly more informal, with a splendid traditional turkey, pudding and mince pies for lunch. I was given a bicycle, which gave me mobility and enabled me to explore the neighbouring towns and villages.

During the Easter term there was a major upheaval in my life. Streaky called me one morning and said I was going home for two days to be 'naturalised'. I asked him what this was and would it be painful, but he just grinned and said that I would find out.

When I got home, Ronnie was there and said that he had decided officially to adopt me, which made it much easier and quicker for me to obtain a British passport. As it was, Mother had one, through her marriage, while I just had my rather grubby piece of paper from the Baghdad Polish legation. A major problem was that I had no birth certificate (all our records had been destroyed in Poland during the war), and the only proof of my existence, name, age and gender was a minor entry in Mother's now extinct Polish passport. So by adopting me as his son, Ronnie gave me an official identity, though my lack of a birth certificate was to prove a troublesome burden throughout my life.

Although I was not consulted, I expressed my gratitude to Ronnie for his generous gesture, but pointed out, in the politest way possible, that though I agreed to have a British passport, this would not make me less Polish. He smiled, said that he quite understood, and hoped that I could combine the best characteristics of the two nations.

The following day, we went to London together, to the office of Ronnie's lawyer. It was a dusty, dark room, with a stale smell. It was lined with bookshelves. There I had to sign numerous documents, and accompany the lawyer and Ronnie next door where an impressive, very fat gentleman, who was a Commissioner for Oaths gave me a worn Bible and made me repeat what he called a Great Oath of Loyalty, whereby I pledged myself to be loyal and true obedience bear to His Majesty, King George VI, his heirs and successors, according to law. Everyone then shook hands and I was British.

One of the by-products of this was that I got a shiny, new British passport and that I could stop reporting weekly to Sergeant Garner at the Berkhamsted Police Station. We were old friends by now and his moustache was greyer than when we started our weekly meetings. He examined my new passport carefully, professed himself delighted, shook my hand warmly while welcoming me to his nation and produced a bottle of ale from his desk, which we shared companionably, while toasting the King. He also ceremoniously crossed my name through in the Register of Aliens.

Four months later, another change occurred. Following a number of Discussions, we (Ronnie, Mother and I) decided that it would make very good sense for me to change my name to match that of my parents. I thought about it for some time, feeling that perhaps I would be betraying my real father, but it did seem a practical thing to do. My English was now good enough for me to pass for a native and I was tired of having constantly to explain why I had a funny name and why it was different from that of my parents.

We went back to the lawyer and again I signed a series of documents, involved in the deed poll, renouncing the name Andrzej Michal Kronman and adopting the name Andrew Michael Arnold. The order of events was to prove a great nuisance, since the certificate of naturalisation was in the old name. Verifying who I was in the future was therefore always immensely complicated.

A final problem to be resolved was the conundrum that my step-brother, whose names were Charles Andrew, was also known as Andrew Arnold. There could not be two Andrews in the same family so we tossed a coin to decide who would change. I lost, and became Mike.

It would be dull to list the problems of a boy who, in the middle of a Sixth Form year at a boarding school leaves in the middle of term, to return two days later with a different name and nationality. There was great confusion, with masters, boys, examination authorities and everyone else unsure what to call me and forgetting who I was. My friends continued to call me Joe, so that was all right. Streaky called me "Whatever your name is today" while Mac boomed: *"What's in a name? that which we call a rose By any other name would smell as sweet".* "A singularly inappropriate quality for a schoolboy!", he added.

Ronnie telephoned and said: "I want you to come up to London on Tuesday morning. Max is visiting and King Faisal is here to go to Harrow. We will go to see them at Claridges, so meet me there at eleven. I have arranged everything with Mr Wraith."

Uncle Max in London! Wonderful. I had not seen him now for several years and could not wait to meet him again. Of all people, I missed him most.

And Fizz. I wondered if he had changed much. And if perhaps Sergeant Abdulla was there; and maybe the Regent.

Streaky gave me some money and told me to be back in the evening. Nidge and Don were very impressed when I told them I was going to meet my friend the King.

I found Claridges Hotel without any trouble, arriving there on the stroke of eleven. Although I was dressed in my best finery (which was not saying much), I felt overawed by the splendour of the porter, the doorman and the collection of formally suited staff in the glittering lobby.

Fortunately Ronnie was already there, and we went to the desk and announced that we had the promise of an audience of King Faisal II of Iraq.

We were led, by an imposing personage, up plushy stairs, past velvet curtains and alcoves and down thickly carpeted corridors to a set of high, white and gold doors. These opened to reveal a vast room, richly furnished and full of people. There were splendid uniforms with lots of gold braid, men in morning coats, men in dark suits, men in court dress; there were no women. At the far end, and in the centre of an attentive group, was the still diminutive figure of Fizz, with an expression of utter boredom on his face.

Ronnie and I approached, and he bowed deeply. I just stood

there; I had never bowed to Fizz in my life, but Ronnie dug me in the ribs with his elbow and I bent at the waist.

"Your Majesty," said Ronnie. "It is a great honour that you grant us this audience."

"Hullo, Fizz," I said. He looked at me and smiled. "Your Majesty, I mean," I added, noting the horror on a number of faces.

"You are big now, Andrew," said Fizz. "I am glad you came to see me. I am much more busy now than before, but maybe we will be able to talk later." We bowed, and were ushered to one side to make room for the next visitor.

A hand patted my shoulder. I turned to see Uncle Max, with a huge grin on his face, beating his drum. Disregarding protocol, we embraced and he took me to the very back, where we could whisper to each other.

We exchanged news, both talking at once and ignoring everyone else. Then Ronnie appeared and Uncle Max said: "Why you not leave Andrew with me for the lunch and I will make him go back to school after. We have much to say. Maybe Ina and I can see you tomorrow with Isabel. Today I can see the young man."

Ronnie smiled and nodded. "Very well, Max. I leave him to you. But we will spend tomorrow together." He turned to me. "Make sure you get back to school in good time, and behave yourself."

Fizz seemed very busy and it was clear he had no time for me. I looked around, but there was no sign of Sergeant Abdulla or of the Unimportant Ones. It was obvious to me that Fizz was now a different sort of person and that we had grown too far apart to remain as close as we had been.

Uncle Max led me to the restaurant, where he insisted I have huge amounts of the best food there was. We talked and talked, and he told me all about what he had been doing, and that Hussein was still there, but that Entah had gone to be a taxi driver. He said the clinic was working well, but that there were bad political problems coming and he hoped that Faisal would be all right.

In turn, I told him what had been happening to me, and

272

explained about my school, and my new name and nationality. "So now I call you Mike, huh?" Uncle Max grimaced. "I say '*do widzenia*' (goodbye) to a Polish Jedrek and '*ahlan wa sahlan*' (welcome) to an English Mike ... The world is strange." We still spoke our mixed up language; nothing had changed.

We both ate a lot and I did not even notice the huge dining room, with elegant people all around, impeccable service and splendid food. Eventually we ran out of things to say and just sat there companionably, grinning foolishly at each other, very content.

After a while, Uncle Max took a flat case out of an inner pocket, and gave it to me.

"This is for you," he said. "A small present after much time and because you are now a man. It is good to give presents when you have friends who you love."

I opened the case and took out a wonderful watch, which was a stop-watch and which showed day and date and phases of the moon. I vividly remembered the last time Uncle Max had tried to give me a watch and how Aunt took it away.

"Wonderful. Thank you very much," I said. "What a marvellous watch! Will Aunt let me keep it this time?"

Uncle Max nodded like a Buddha. "Yes, she will. You are now old enough and anyway you are not in my house any more."

We went into the lobby and there saw Mother and Aunt, who had just come in. They descended on us in a flurry of scented furs and hats with half-veils. Both were in full war paint and looked sophisticated and blonde and beautiful. Aunt gave me a great hug, while Mother beamed with pride beside her. I was glad I had the watch in my pocket and not on my wrist.

We sat and I had to recount to Aunt what I had been doing and it was only by pleading that I had to get back to school that I got away. There were more embraces, a powerful hug from Uncle Max, and I went back to school.

I would only see Fizz once more, on a visit to Iraq some years later, not long before his murder. We had not much in common by then, except some nostalgic memories. He had made new friends in Harrow School and our time together as small boys was long ago. When I married, I invited him to the wedding: he did not come. He did, however, send me a handsome wedding present, of two silver vases engraved with his cipher in Arabic and the Royal crown, which are on a shelf beside me now, as I write.

There were now two momentous decisions to be made, one concerning university and the other my two years' National Service, which I could elect to do before or after my three years at university.

There were people to advise me about University: Mac, Streaky and Ronnie, all of whom had been to Cambridge. Mac strongly suggested that I should sit for a scholarship exam in English at Jesus College, in Cambridge, since he knew the English dons there and said that they were very good.

"Even if you don't get a scholarship or exhibition," he said, "you can be awarded a place. It's the only way to get in. They have the exams in December, so you can try it before your Higher Certificate next summer and stay on an extra term to have another go next year. "*O this learning, what a thing it is!*" But I have hopes for you, ecdemic lobcock!"

December soon came and I was told to go to Cambridge to sit the scholarship exam. A number of other boys were also going up, to take exams at different Colleges, but I was the only one for Jesus.

It was bitterly cold when we got off the train at Cambridge, and a wild wind was blowing across the Fens. The ancient buildings of the University, though impressive and beautiful, did not extend any sort of welcome nor did they look anything but gloomy. We were all too nervous to appreciate anything.

I made my way to Jesus College, a little outside the centre of town and went down a long passage from the street to the large doors. The passage, I later learned, was known as the Chimney. Just inside the gates was a large window into a porter's lodge. There was an impressive and dignified personage, in a black suit, leaning on the counter.

"And what may I do for you, Sir?" the personage enquired.

"I have come up from Berkhamsted to take the scholarship exam," I replied, putting down my small overnight case.

"Ah yes. One of the scholarship gentlemen. I am the Head Porter and my name is Captain Austin," said the personage.

"Welcome to Jesus," he added, without any irony.

He called a minion (a minor replica of himself) and instructed him to show me to my rooms.

We walked through a number of quadrangles and through narrow open arches. Eventually we came out into a large open area, with a single, two-storey building running round three sides. Every ten yards or so there was a staircase We went into one, about half-way round and up to the first floor.

The 'rooms' turned out to be a little suite of sitting room, bedroom, tiny kitchen and minuscule hall. There was a double door: a thick, outer one ("This is called the Oak," said my guide. "It is inviolable. When it is closed, you are said to be 'sporting your Oak' and no one may disturb you.") and there was also a normal door inside the Oak.

As evidence of the rooms' normal occupant, there were some books, an ornate ashtray stolen from a Viennese hotel, a hockey stick and some clothes, including a bedraggled, black gown which I immediately tried on and in which I pranced around before the full-length mirror in the bedroom.

The evening meal was in Hall, an imposing great room, like a church, lit by candles, with portraits of dour-looking former Masters of the College on the walls, and long, dark wooden tables, with benches, in longitudinal rows. Across the top, forming a T, was the High Table, where dons and distinguished visitors sat.

The Hall was almost empty, since the undergraduates were on vacation and only the scholarship candidates were present. We all sat down, and eyed each other with great suspicion. These were the competitors, I thought, and I tried to size them up. Apart from a handful of spotty, weedy studious-looking types with glasses, whom I considered alien and obviously the greatest threat, the others looked normal, and I soon struck up a conversation with a chap from Merchant Taylors' School, against whom, it turned out, I had played rugger.

Before too long, there was a hum of conversation as nervousness was dissipated in chatter.

Suddenly there was a banging on the High Table and silence fell.

A tall and imposing don strode to a lectern and said, in a booming, bass voice: "Stand for Grace".

There then followed a four minute, largely unintelligible Grace, in Latin, while we all stood and fidgeted. My companion whispered: "It's only for our first meal here. After that, there is a short simple one they use".

The food was plentiful and standard institutional fare, served by ancient retainers in black suits. I could see that the High Table was served somewhat different victuals, and wine. We drank water.

After Hall, I went straight back to my rooms, since I wanted to refresh my mind about Chaucer. I smoked (and choked on) two cigarettes from a packet I had bought at the station and felt totally adult. But I was sleepy, and went to the small, though comfortable bed, where I immediately fell asleep, to wake at six o'clock and worry.

The examination hall was in the town, and we all sat down, with our fountain pens and blotting paper and bottles of ink. We had two three-hour papers to do that day and one the following day. In the evening we had interviews with two Jesus dons.

The written English part was not too frightening and I felt I had acquitted myself reasonably well, both morning and afternoon. Back at College, I was told to see Mr Rossiter at 5.30, in his rooms.

Mac had told me about Mr Rossiter. He was a brilliant English scholar, specialising in Shakespeare, and would test my general aptitude in English.

He was a fierce-looking man, in a study lined with books from floor to ceiling. He sat behind a desk piled high with papers and was holding what was obviously my file in his hands.

"Come in, come in and sit," he barked. "You are Arnold," he stated.

I agreed with this.

"You are from Berkhamsted," he went on. "We have had a few from there. You are taught by Mac, aren't you? How is the old reprobate? Still quoting?"

"Yes," I answered. "He is well and has told me about you, Sir. He sends his regards."

Mr Rossiter grinned. "Thanks. I won't ask what he told you."

He then spent half an hour in a penetrating interrogation which clearly showed that while I had a broad knowledge of English literature, this was superficial and clearly of school rather than university level.

Mr Rossiter seemed satisfied with my answers, however and dismissed me, saying: "Greetings to Mac when you get back. Now cut along to Mr Fisher, on the next staircase. If you do come to Jes, *"Here will be an old abusing of God's patience and the king's English"*. Good luck!"

I tried to memorise the quotation for Mac, who was delighted when I told him about it.

Mr Fisher was a different sort of man entirely. Calm and friendly, it was his job, I thought, to investigate the non-academic characteristics of candidates and assess them as potential members of the College community. He was easy to talk to and soon had me telling him an abbreviated history of my life.

"Most interesting and unusual," he remarked. "You will have to write it down some day. Also, I must say that, for a foreigner, your command of English is astonishing."

"I have my English teacher to thank for that," I replied. "Mr Rossiter knows him. When I came to England, people laughed at my accent and I determined to beat them at their own game. But English is a difficult language to learn – no rules, just exceptions!"

Mr Fisher laughed and said he agreed; he thought French much easier.

After a general paper in the morning, we all went back to school. I reported to Mac and Streaky what had happened, and both said we would have to wait for the College to tell us if I was in or not.

Just after Christmas we got a letter from Mac, telling us that I had not got an award (of which there were five in total), but that I had been placed eleventh, and thus missed a place by one. Mac added that he had been told by Jes that I should sit the exam again the following year. There was disappointment, but at least I would be given another chance.

The Higher Certificate exams came and went, at the end of the summer term. The results, which arrived during the holidays, were reasonable, though Ronnie said I could have done better. I had got a Distinction in French and English, my main subjects, and had got through Latin and History, the subsidiaries. There was a note from Mac, which said: *"Upon your sword Sit laurel victory! and smooth success Be strew'd before your feet!"*. I was delighted.

Now I had an extra term to polish myself for another attempt at Jesus. It was marvellous. Very few lessons, all with Mac. Senior position in school; I was the Grand Old Man of the rugger team, a school prefect and a cynosure for younger boys. Mac and Streaky however made sure that I did not become too big for my boots.

It was time to think about military service. Nidge, Don and the others (they had all left at the end of the summer) had made their decisions. Nidge would do his medical training in the RAF, and then be an RAF doctor as a career. (He became a doctor, an Air Chief Marshal and was knighted before sadly dying at a relatively young age).

Don went, of course, into the Royal Engineers, where he was able to mess about with engines and machines to his heart's content.

I knew nothing about the British Army, least of all about the snobbery attaching to various Regiments. No adult thought to enlighten me. The only person I found to talk to about what part of the Army I should try to join was Tom Evans, a friend in a different boarding house, who had decided that, because he liked cars and trucks, he would join the Royal Army Service Corps, which was responsible for the transport and supplies of the entire army. I did not know that it was looked down on by military snobs (it would have made no difference had I known) and, since I also was keen on cars, motorcycles and lorries, decided to follow Tom into the RASC. I therefore filled in my call-up forms accordingly and was immediately accepted. I was given a delayed entry to enable me to take the Jesus exam, and told to report to Aldershot, Buller Barracks, on January 2, 1951, a month before my nineteenth birthday.

The exams at Jesus, when they came, were a repetition of the previous year, except that my interviews with Messrs. Rossiter and Fisher were shorter. Also, I was astonished and pleased that Captain Austin, the Head Porter, remembered my name. I was later to find out that he never forgot a name or a face from the many thousands he had seen pass through his gates.

I bid farewell to the boys and staff at school, and went home early, before the end of term. My parting from Mac and Streaky was the hardest part. They had become very much part of my life and I felt closer to them than to almost anyone. I knew how much I owed them and how many of my modest successes were due to their care and teaching.

At home, time passed quickly. Since I was now over eighteen Ronnie had been teaching me to drive. I took my test and passed with no trouble, driving our Hillman Minx around with enormous pleasure.

The Jesus results were sent to us by Mac. I had not got one of the five awards, but had a place. I had come sixth, just missing an Exhibition. There was a Discussion, at which Ronnie and Mother, both pleased that I had managed to get in, announced that there was not enough money to pay for me, since there were heavy expenses connected with the school bills for Andy and Felicity, and also payments to Ronnie's first wife.

After some investigations, however, I went for interviews and form filling to Surrey County authorities, and based on the results of my Higher Certificate and a letter of commendation from Jesus College, was awarded a County Major Scholarship, which would pay my tuition and give me enough money (just) to live on.

Thus my schooldays were over. I looked forward to the Army as a new experience. I had decided that I would get better value from the University if I went there after my National Service, since I would be older, would have learned something about independent living and, most important in my mind, clearly established the break between school and university, with their completely different systems of learning and living.

Christmas was the usual family one. Ronnie and Mother were going shortly thereafter to the United States, where Ronnie had been made Chief Representative of British Petroleum, based in a luxurious flat on Fifth Avenue in New York, and there was much packing.

I felt very pleased with myself, and looked forward to my time in the Army, which I thought would be a pleasant and easy way of spending an eighteen month period, driving cars and riding motorcycles.

I could not have been more wrong.

CHAPTER SEVEN

National Service soldier

There was a cold and miserable rain falling when I finally arrived at Buller Barracks, Aldershot, where I had been told to report. Christmas was eight days past; it had been normal, elegant and unexciting, with Mother and Ronnie, at the Knoll. It was strange to think that school was finished for good, after so many countries, friends and even names. This was now a big jump, straight into being an adult and responsible to myself. No more beatings and no more pocket money. Now I would be earning and could do what I wanted, without having to answer to anyone.

As I stood outside the barracks, the rain continued to fall and was beginning to soak through my raincoat. I was wearing a trilby hat and feeling proudly very young-man-about-town-Ronnie always insisted I wear a hat since, as he put it, "What would you do if you met a lady of your acquaintance and could not raise your hat!"

I approached the little hut at the entrance to the barracks. There was a counterweighted pole across the road and a wet and doleful looking soldier standing beside it. He glared at me and sniffed loudly.

"Excuse me," I said politely, "I was told to report here for National Service."

"You was, was you!" exclaimed the wet soldier. "Another bleedin' toff come to serve 'is King. Go into the 'ut and report to the Sergeant."

I went into the hut. The atmosphere was foul: a mixture of smells of damp cloth, cigarette smoke, coke fumes from the stove and something extra, the worst of all, on the origin of which I did not dare even to speculate. There were seven or eight soggy, khaki-clad figures spread about in various slack attitudes around the stove, with the sergeant occupying a chair at a rickety, scarred desk. All the men were steaming gently, like horses after exercise.

I walked up to the sergeant: "Excuse me, Sir, Michael Arnold reporting for duty, Sir!" I stood straight and removed my hat. I was glad I knew how to report from the Junior Training Corps at school. Water dripped on the floor.

There was a hoot of laughter from the group. The sergeant cast his eyes upwards, as though communicating his perplexity to the Deity, then barked at me: "First, I am 'Sergeant', not Sir. Second, you look like a heap of dung and your hat is horrible. Third, welcome to the British Army."

He glanced at the grinning soldiers. "You, Brown," he pointed at a small, gingery man. "Take him to the new intake barracks. And come straight back here, understand!"

I followed Brown into the rain. He marched fast down the road and I tried to copy his movements, but failed, since I had my bag and my raincoat flapped round me. My hat fell off and landed in a puddle I picked it up and had to run to catch up with my guide.

We arrived at a building and went in. Inside, there was a large barrack room, with iron bedsteads on each side, some forty in all. There was a pot-bellied black stove in the middle of the room radiating tremendous heat. On the beds nearest the stove, a motley collection of young men, dressed in a great variety of civilian clothes, were sitting, lounging, standing, smoking and, it seemed to me, all talking at once. They stopped as Brown and I walked in, and turned to look at us.

"Another one for you," said Brown to the group. He turned to me. "Just wait 'ere and fings will 'appen. And you won't like them, neither."

He marched out. One of the group round the stove, a tall, dark haired man with a squint said: "Who are you, then?"

I told them my name. The tall man, whom the others called Squinty, said: "Pick a bed and put your stuff there. We was told somebody will come in a little while. Anyway, we are just getting acquainted."

I picked a bed and then joined the group. There was a wonderful mixture of accents and my companions all seemed to come from a great variety of backgrounds. I was fascinated. I had never, in England, got to know anyone outside my parents' friends and my school colleagues and their families. Here were people from farms and slums, cities and ports in the north, south, west and east of the United Kingdom. The language was interesting: rich, expressive and full of intriguing slang. Four-letter expletives padded out the sentences and lost their meaning, remaining only as a sort of decoration or frieze round the sense. I sat transfixed as the conversations flowed round and over me. Squinty offered me a thin Woodbine cigarette and I smoked it without too much choking. I was a soldier.

The group gradually assumed identities. There was Dusty (the inevitable nickname for anyone with the surname of Rhodes). He was a farmer's son from Devon, a big, slow-speaking blond man with sleepy blue eyes. Tom Smith, known as Chirpy, was a small Cockney sparrow. Squinty came from Yorkshire and was extremely chauvinist, finding fault with everything and comparing everything unfavourably with its Yorkshire equivalent. He showed strong incipient hostility to Albert Johnson, who (in Squinty's phrase) " 'ad the misfortune to coom from Lancashire, a very fourth rate county," and who seemed to me to be quite harmless.

There were others, and more came drifting in as the afternoon wore on.

We discovered that there were, including me, six Michaels. Squinty, who had emerged, through the curious chemistry of groups, as the provisional leader, said that this was "stoopid and inconvenient and 'ad to be sorted out".

Accordingly, all known forms of Michael (Mike, Mick, Mickey and so on) were written on scraps of paper, put into a hat (mine was the only one) and the assorted Michaels were invited to draw one each. Mine had Mick on it, and thus I became Mick for the rest of my life (except at home, where I was still called Mike).

The first three or four days passed in a painful, sleepy blur. We were issued with kit and uniform including 'socks, khaki, woollen, short, other ranks, pairs, three'. There was the same scratchy khaki uniform (I was used to it after the cadet force at school), improbable underwear, sports kit and a great deal of stiff, dirty webbing (belt, gaiters, ammunition pouches, straps, pack) which had to be 'blancoed' into spotless powdery khaki freshness. There was a great deal of dented brass, to be straightened, polished and eventually buffed with jeweller's rouge until it was mirror-like, back front and interior. Heavy, stiff boots, thick with grease, one pair for work and one for parades. The grease had to be scraped and burned off, the grain of the boots smoothed with the back of a red-hot teaspoon, and the toecap and back spit-and-polished until the leather looked like black glass. Even the sole had to be polished and the hobnails and horseshoe-shaped strip on the heel made to shine.

That first evening we also met our sergeant, who was to be with us for the duration of initial basic training. We were in the barracks, examining our new kit and trying to work out how it all fitted together, when there was a shrill scream at the door.

"Squa.a.a.ad! 'Shun!!" We paused in what we were doing and looked round. Just inside the door was a khaki-clad figure which was all corners. There were no apparent normal, human rounded bits on it. It stood rigidly upright, with a bamboo stick under its arm, and a pair of bright blue eyes glared at us unblinkingly. The brass shone and gleamed, the uniform was smooth and unwrinkled except that the trousers had a knife edge, the boots were refulgent and there was an air of perfection about the whole man.

"Stand up and listen!" The voice was hoarse and abrasive and you could almost see the exclamation mark at the end of each sentence. "My name is Sergeant Binns and I have the tragic misfortune to be in charge of you horrible shower! Gather round and listen!"

Sergeant Binns stood at ease; this meant he moved one foot out from the other and brought it down with such a crash that a cloud of dust rose from the wooden floor and we all jumped.

"I am your father and your mother. What is good for me is good for you. What is bad for me will be very bad indeed for you. You will obey me without question. My word is law. My decision is law. Even my whim is law. You are useless, ignorant, dirty scoundrels and I have to make something out of you, Gawd help me." Sergeant Binns slapped his bamboo cane into his hand at the end of each sentence.

"I'll show you something now. You think when I say 'Shun!' you just bring your heels together. That's for civilians. Soldiers do it like this ..." He took a hazelnut from his pocket and placed it carefully on the floor inside his left heel. "Squa.a.a.ad! 'Shun!!"

He brought his right heel, with its steel horseshoe, down onto the hazelnut with such force that when he stood at ease again there was no nut, just a smear of powder. "You will all do this when I am finished with you."

I noticed that when he came to attention or stood at ease his eyes squinted slightly and blinked rapidly, as though he were punch-drunk. I suppose that years of sudden smashing impacts on his spine must have done damage, jarring his brain.

He proved himself to be unforgiving, tough, sarcastic and we all hated him with a deep loathing. He marched us, on our second morning, to the barber, who roughly removed all hair longer than an inch from our heads. The barber also sprayed evil-smelling stuff on our remaining hair 'to kill the animals', as he put it.

We were marched to the administration hut, where we were issued with paybooks and our numbers, which we were ordered to memorise at once. I was 22446290 – so there were almost twenty two and a half million before me!

We were then marched to the medical hut where we were told to remove all our clothes and stand in single file. The Doctor (a Captain in the Medical Corps) sat at a table and we paraded naked in front of him. I suppose for me, with shame and shyness eliminated by years of boarding school where privacy and modesty were impossible and unknown, the experience was not as traumatic as for my companions. Some of them were painfully modest, and tried inadequately to cover themselves with their hands, while objecting loudly, only to be yelled at by the NCO's, whose ribald jeers and personal remarks only made things worse.

We then ran the gauntlet of two pairs of medical orderlies, having to walk between them, with arms akimbo, to receive four painful injections against Heaven knows what dread diseases.

" 'Ere, I'm not 'avin' none of that," said Chirpy. "I'm not 'avin' no needles stuck in me!" He tried to run away to the back, but a burly Corporal grabbed him and held him immobile while the needles went in, all four together. Chirpy fainted and we had to carry him to a bench where he lay, his thin little white body twitching, for several minutes.

The same day, we were issued with our rifles. These were vintage Lee-Enfield .303 calibre monsters, heavy, unwieldy and covered thickly with sticky grease. We each had to memorise the number of our rifle too.

Sergeant Binns said: "Your rifle is your most precious possession. You can lose your wallet, your life and even your virginity and I'll forgive you. But if any harm comes to your rifle, I'll have you and even your mothers won't recognise you when I am finished." He then told us there would be an inspection at 6am the following morning, of everything, and dismissed us. We knew nothing of inspections. We all had high fevers from the inoculations. We wanted to die. But we made an effort to clean the rifles and to polish the floor and our equipment, before falling on our beds and into a restless sleep, at about midnight.

Before sunup in the morning, and feeling ghastly, we stood beside our beds as Sergeant Binns stalked round examining our beds, possessions and rifles. He said not a word until the end, and then he gave a heavy sigh.

"I might have known," he said. "You miserable lot couldn't organise a fart after a bean dinner. Gather round and I will show you what you do for an inspection. I'll only show you once. After that, you suffer."

He then arranged everything neatly, in rows and piles, symmetrically and straight. We had never seen blankets folded like that, nor back-packs made perfectly straight by cardboard boxes stuffed into them. Sergeant Binns even showed us 'old soldier' tricks like rubbing the creases on our thick, new trousers with soap and then shaving them with a razor blade to make them thin, before ironing them and pressing them between cardboard sheets under the mattress overnight.

Chirpy, who seemed to be accident prone, was so enthusiastic with his trousers that the following day, on parade, they suddenly parted and he was left standing at attention with his spindly white legs showing through the strips of cloth flapping in the breeze; he had over-shaved the seams. Sergeant Binns was furious and charged poor Chirpy with the cost of a new pair.

We also had to clean the barrack room and washroom, until they shone. The brass pipes and taps of the wash-basins and urinals, and the shelves and paintwork had to be spotless. The most difficult was the floor, which was of dark wood, pitted and scarred, and which had to be polished until it shone. We tried a system proposed by Dusty, which was to let him sit on a blanket, while we waxed the floor and then dragged him up and down in his blanket. This worked quite well, and he sat there smirking until he suddenly let out a great yell and showed us a large splinter firmly embedded in his buttock. This was removed, with great hilarity, and there was no more dragging.

The food we were given was solid, which is all that could be said for it, except that it was reminiscent of school. It was prepared for us by trainee cooks from the Army Catering Corps and we were by way of being guinea-pigs. The Orderly Officer, usually a snooty young Second Lieutenant, and the Orderly Sergeant would come round and ask, *pro forma*, if there were any complaints, but we all knew better than to criticise.

An officer inspected our barrack-room on the Friday morning. He came strolling casually in, wearing a uniform which contrasted very unfavourably with Sergeant Binns', who marched behind him, carrying a clipboard and a pencil. The officer, whose name was Smith-Montgomery, had a short bamboo swagger stick and tended to poke at things with it. He was a tall, thin young man, with protuberant pale blue eyes like marbles and a small, scrubby blond moustache. He sauntered round the washroom with his hands behind his back and gazed at the windows and the floor, without saying anything. He then began to look at us and our beds. He would stand in front of the man and stare at the bed and the equipment laid out on it. He said nothing.

He finally came to my bed. He stared at me for a moment, then said: "Ah, you are Arnold, I believe." "Yes, Sir," I replied. I could see Sergeant Binns glaring at me.

"Ah, public school, Arnold?" Smith-Montgomery asked. He began all his sentences with 'Ah ...'

"Berkhamsted, Sir," I answered.

"Ah, not much of a school," he said in his drawling voice. He then walked out, saying over his shoulder: "Ah, very good, Sergeant. Better than I expected from a new lot ..."

Sergeant Binns saluted, and came back into the room. He made us stand at ease, then read out from his clip-board a long list of criticisms. Not one of us escaped, and the room itself was found to be 'dirty, untidy and not acceptable'. In particular, poor old Dusty was given one night's 'jankers' for forgetting to put his spare boots out.

'Jankers' meant you had to report to the guard-room (the only people awake), on the hour, every hour, from 11pm to 6am in battle order, wearing full equipment and with your rifle. We really needed our sleep and the day after 'jankers' was always tough. The only worse punishment was 'running jankers' where, as well as reporting, you had to run, every hour, once round the playing field (about half a mile), still in full battle order.

"It doesn't matter what the officer says," barked Sergeant Binns. "It's me you have to deal with. Sergeants run the Army; the officers are only there for show."

Our predominant activity was drill. There was a huge, paved area known as the drill square, and at any time of day there would be squads of soldiers marching, wheeling and doing weapons drill on it; 'square bashing'.

Standards varied. It was easy to distinguish the advanced squads, who had been in training for several weeks; they would be doing apparently useless movements, like 'rotate arms' or 'rest on your arms' or 'half wheels'. The less practised squads would tend to march into each other, mistaking left for right, to the gibbering, scarlet-faced fury of their drill sergeants.

Chirpy was very brave: he asked Sergeant Binns what drill was for. The Sergeant did not shout. He pondered for a moment and then proclaimed: "There are only three kinds of people in the army. There is officers: they have the King's commission because they talk proper and have education. They can't think because they don't know how, but they are supposed to lead. The senior officers tell them what to do, but if anything has to be done they just say 'Carry on, Sergeant!' Then there is us, the bloody sergeants: we run the army and we have to think for everybody, because if we didn't bugger-all would get done and we would never win a war. Last of all, there is Other Ranks, like you lot: you are not supposed to think because you are stupid and because if you could think you wouldn't follow orders or you would be a sergeant. So drill is to teach you to have nothing in your bloody mind except listen to me and then it doesn't matter if we are here or facing the Huns with bullets flying all round because you will all do as I say and follow my thinking and we will win. Is that clear?"

"What would 'appen if you was to get killed, then, Sergeant?" asked Squinty.

"We would lose," said Sergeant Binns simply. "Without me you are dead."

"And it is no good looking to an officer to save you, neither," he added. "Squa.a.ad! 'Shun!" he suddenly yelled and saluted smartly as a Captain walked by. "You are saluting his uniform and the King's commission, not him," he remarked.

The initial bout of induction training took some four weeks, after which we really got down to it. We were now fully fledged recruits of the Royal Army Service Corps and had to learn a certain amount of Corps history and recognise our Corps march. The Corps was prominent during the Boer War when its duties of transport and supply were crystallised. Thus the Corps march was the South African tune of "Wait for the Wagon". I thought the words were somewhat ironical. But we felt more at home in the army now and undertook the major part of basic training in good heart. In particular, we looked forward to our driving training, since the Corps had exchanged their Boer War ox-drawn wagons for lorries and RASC Other Ranks were known not as Privates but as Drivers.

The squad had become a team and we got to know each other. I was the only public schoolboy, but was tolerated, though with frequent sly digs for being a "toff". I "F'ed" and "B'ed" with the rest and felt I belonged.

It was at about this time that the Prof arrived. He was in his middle thirties and a man of mystery. Who he was, why he should be fifteen years older than the rest of us, why he joined us late and other questions remained unanswered. He refused to enlighten us and Sergeant Binns said nothing.

His name was White, but since he was well spoken, knowledgeable and appeared to have previous army experience, he became known as Prof. He was medium in all things: medium height, medium build, with nondescript, thinning hair and curiously colourless eyes behind gold-rimmed spectacles. He was treated just like the rest of us and kept a low profile.

In the evenings, however, during our kit cleaning sessions in the barracks, when we ragged each other, relaxed, told stories and joked, Prof had many tales to tell us: he had travelled widely, had obviously done military service though we did not think it was in the British army (Squinty thought it may have been the Foreign Legion) and seen many wonderful things. One evening he mentioned hypnotism, and we all clamoured for him to show us. He was reluctant to do so, but was eventually persuaded.

"Hypnotism is a mysterious thing," he said, sucking his pipe. "You will hear a lot of nonsense talked about it. The most interesting thing, I think, is that with it you can reach hidden parts of the brain and make the body do things which are impossible when awake."

He asked for a volunteer, promising that he would be unharmed. No one offered himself, so an affronted Chirpy was volunteered by the rest of us, much to his disgusted protests. We sat on beds and our two benches, and left two wooden chairs free for Prof, as requested. Cigarette smoke hung in a blue haze over the scene.

Prof put Chirpy to sleep without any trouble, by spinning a

pocket-watch round and round on its chain, and then showed us a number of 'experiments'. It was a somewhat eerie scene: the long barrack-room, the stove throwing out terrific heat, the bare light bulbs swinging on their wires, the wind moaning outside, the group of soldiers huddled round Prof and Chirpy.

He told Chirpy to be stiff, like a plank, and then balanced him with his heels on one chair and the back of his head on another. Then he told Dusty, who was a big, heavy man (especially compared with scrawny Chirpy) to sit on the human plank, as though he were a bench. Dusty did so, gingerly, and Chirpy did not give way at all: he really was as stiff as a board. He could not possibly have supported Dusty had he been conscious.

"You have to be careful," Prof said. "If you put too much weight, you could break his bones, because he won't give way." We all marvelled at this, and all tried to explain to each other how it was done. Prof just grinned.

In the next experiment, Prof showed Chirpy (who was still in a trance) a pencil, and said: "This is a red-hot piece of steel. I am going to touch your arm with it, but you will feel no pain at all."

He touched Chirpy's arm with the end of the pencil. We all crowded in to see better. At once a blister sprang out; a perfectly normal blister. It was surrounded by what looked like red, burned flesh. Chirpy, who had not even flinched, looked at it with interest while the rest of us were horrified, and made worried noises. Prof grinned again and said to Chirpy: "Make it better!" We saw Chirpy glance at him, then at his arm and, as we watched incredulously, the blister disappeared over the course of about a minute and the irritated flesh returned to normal. We examined the place where the blister had been, but there was no sign of anything. Even now, I can hardly believe what I saw. Had we all been hypnotised?

Prof brought Chirpy out of his trance, telling him not to remember whatever had happened and instructing him to feel happy and relaxed. When Chirpy woke, he faced a barrage of questions from us, but insisted that he remembered nothing and felt fine. When we told him what had happened, he refused to believe us.

During another session Prof asked Squinty if he remembered

his fourth birthday. Squinty laughed and said he didn't and that nobody did. Prof asked him to write to his mother and ask her if she would write back and tell him as many details as she could remember of his fourth birthday party: Squinty said he knew he had had one.

Prof then hypnotised Squinty; it took longer than with Chirpy, but Squinty was altogether a tougher character and more distrustful than Chirpy, who was good-natured and suggestible. Finally, after much twirling of the pocket-watch, he went under.

Prof said to him: "You are now fifteen years old, ... now you are ten, ... now you are six ... five ... four ..." He paused after each statement. We all watched Squinty intently, as his face gradually assumed a sort of childish expression, and, on reaching five, he began to suck his thumb and giggle. Chirpy suddenly said: "Cor, did I do that?" We all reassured him.

Prof then began to question Squinty about his birthday party. Squinty answered in a childish voice and with childish words. He told us that there were only three children at his party, including his older brother, what he wore, what kind of cake he had and what presents he got. He even remembered what clothes everyone was wearing and the colour of the jelly – it was green.

On being wakened from the trance, Squinty remembered nothing either of his fourth birthday or of what had happened when he was under. When Prof showed him the notes he had made of his answers, he scoffed and said it was a put-up job.

A week later we got the answer from his mother. The facts tallied exactly. We were amazed, but Prof said that no one ever forgot anything; they just forgot how to remember it.

We were kept busy. Apart from endless square bashing, we were taught how to take our rifles apart, into quite small pieces, and also to do the same with out 'platoon weapon', the Bren gun, a light machine gun, usually fired prone, with the gun resting on two small folding legs. We practised, in competition with each other (the slowest having to do 'jankers') until we could – and did – take our rifles and the Bren gun apart and put them together again, blindfolded, in less than a minute each.

Surprisingly, it was Dusty Rhodes who was the best, and who

represented our squad when Sergeant Binns, without consulting us, decided to challenge the squad ahead of us to a competition. If we won, the other Sergeant had to buy Sergeant Binns a dinner with beer in Aldershot. If we lost, it was 'jankers' all round.

On the day, which was sunny and spring-like, we all gathered round a couple of blankets spread in one corner of the drill square. Dusty and the other squad's representative each knelt in front of his rifle and Bren and was duly blindfolded. On the command "Start!", each took his weapons apart and put them together again, while we cheered loudly and shouted useless instructions to our champion.

It was close, but Dusty won by a couple of seconds and was hoisted shoulder high and carried round a short triumphal circuit. Sergeant Binns almost smiled and clapped him on the shoulder.

The following day, Sergeant Binns announced that he was too busy to spend any time with us before lunch, and said he would not notice if we spent the morning hanging round the NAAFI, or army shop and restaurant, drinking tea, eating buns and smoking. It was the first time off we had been given for some six weeks, apart from Church Parade on Sundays, and we enjoyed watching the other squads marching, wheeling and doing arms drill on the square while we shouted critical comments.

Then we went shooting. We were driven in a lorry some miles into the country, to the shooting ranges. The lorries bumped and whined their way slowly down little country roads; it was the beginning of spring and trees were in bud. There were flowers in the hedgerows and a great twittering of birds.

We eventually reached a locked gate, beside which a red flag flew from a flagpole. This was meant to warn that there was shooting on the day. The butts, or high banks of earth, stood behind a row of big, round targets, with four concentric rings. Sergeant Binns gave us a short lecture on how to lie prone, how to hold our rifles and how to aim. He told us that another squad was servicing the targets and not to fire if the butt flag was showing. Then the first ten were told to lie down and fire five rounds.

We were all very excited: this was real, live ammunition. You could kill somebody with one of the shiny bullets which weighed surprisingly heavy in our hands. I had a momentary flash of memory – the first for years – and wondered if it was a bullet like this which had smashed into Ryszard's forehead.

The first shoot was at only 100 yards, and so not very difficult. We all managed to hit the targets, more or less. The noise and the acrid smell of cordite were exhilarating. All went well until Smokey, a rather slow and taciturn man from Birmingham did not count his rounds and got up, leaning on his rifle, before the order came to do so. The rifle suddenly went off, with his fifth round whistling just past his ear. Sergeant Binns was furious, and stamped round in a circle before trusting himself to speak at all.

"You are not playing kiddie games now," he roared in his grating voice. "This is real; this can kill you. Next time any of you does something so bloody stupid, the whole squad goes on jankers for a month!"

But I enjoyed my shots; I was surprised at the powerful kick the .303 gave, and Chirpy had a sore shoulder for several days, with a purple bruise.

We went shooting several times. I found that I was best at the longer ranges, especially 1,000 yards. I also much enjoyed the Bren, which kicked hardly at all, and was very accurate.

But then we were introduced to the infamous Sten gun. The Bren gun was fired prone, with the gun supported by its own stand. The Sten excitingly was fired from the hip, like Tommy guns in gangster films. It also jammed frequently, was only good for close combat, and was dangerously inaccurate at anything more than 25 yards. It had an uncomfortable magazine sticking out of one side, and we all hated it. We fired it at a special range, with the squad standing in a slit trench, while the firer, up in front, shot at cut-out plasterboard human figures made to look like enemy soldiers charging with bayonets.

The Sten got its own back on us on one occasion when, in Dusty's large paws, it jammed, then, as he was turning – against orders – to ask the Sergeant what to do, fired one round. Dusty was so startled that he dropped the Sten, whereupon it went to automatic fire, balanced on its long magazine, and spun round and round as it spewed its bullets out along the ground. We were all hiding in the slit trench and only Dusty (as the man firing) and Sergeant Binns were above ground. We all roared with laughter as Dusty and the Sergeant leaped into the air every time the stream of bullets spun towards them; it was as though they were skipping rope.

Sergeant Binns was livid with rage. When the magazine was exhausted, and he could trust himself to speak, he shouted at us for several minutes, comparing us unfavourably to cretins, dog-turds, and many other unprintable objects. He gave the whole squad three nights' jankers, which we thought was very unfair. In revenge, for quite a long time, we sneaked up on Dusty at odd times of the day or night and shouted: "Jump, jump!" in his ear.

Then there was the assault course. When we first saw it, we all felt it was clearly impossible to negotiate in gym kit, let alone in full battle order with rifles.

There were high scaffolding platforms, with ropes to climb and narrow, slippery planks at the top; huge concrete pipes to crawl through while the sergeant and his Corporals harried us, throwing deafening thunderflashes (a sort of large firecracker) and firing blank ammunition at us; barbed wire under which we had to crawl, choking on smoke grenades and with the Corporals throwing buckets of cold water over us. But the worst obstacle was the Pit, which was a hole in the ground, twelve feet wide, four feet deep, full of an unspeakable putrid something, over which we had to swing on a slimy rope, catching it on the run at full speed. Those who fell in – I only did so once – had at least three hours' extra cleaning to do at night on clothes, rifle and kit, as well as needing a long and comprehensive shower before being readmitted to our company.

On one occasion I fell off the scaffolding and as I lay with my face in the mud, I noticed, some inches in front of my nose, a little blue flower, all by itself. I do not know how it survived, but as I lay there for a few seconds, I remember asking it: "What are we doing here?"

Somehow, nobody from our squad got seriously hurt (Dusty sprained an ankle falling off a wall) although it was rumoured that one recruit, a couple of squads ahead of us, fell off the scaffolding and broke his neck, dying later in hospital. There was no change to the course or the obstacles, and everyone carried on as usual. After our first few times over the course, with the encouragement of a prize for the fastest (exemption from the next time) as well as punishment for the slowest (jankers), we coped.

What was more fun was the driving. After all, our Corps was responsible for the Army's transport and, when fully fledged, we would be called Driver rather than Private, so it made sense that we should learn to drive. We were shown what we would drive: two types of three ton lorry, the long-nosed OY and the flat nosed QL. Our squad was allocated one of each and we took turns at driving them for ten minutes at a time, round and round a disused drill square, with the others in the back, smoking and jeering. Sergeant Binns stood in the middle of the square, 'observing' as he called it, while a Corporal sat next to the driver, swearing and trying to teach.

It must have been a comical sight: terrible crashing and grinding noises, as we tried to engage gear, with the lorry spasmodically jerking and stalling. Prof could drive and so could I, although a three ton lorry is a very different proposition from a car. As we got braver, we would swing the lorry in a tight circle, accelerating, while our comrades, in the back, shouted, swore and yelled as they were thrown around.

When we could just about manage, we went out on the main road in a convoy of twenty lorries, to the despair of the other traffic and discovered to our surprise that when the leader was doing a steady 20 miles per hour, 'Tail End Charlie' found it hard to keep up at 60 mph. Squinty somehow managed to ditch his Corporal Instructor, by persuading him to get down and check a supposedly flat rear tire. Squinty, leaving the corporal standing in helpless fury, drove lorry and the four friends in the back, to a local pub. This earned them all four days' running jankers, but they said it was worth it.

Most of the basic training had been a nightmare, but sustaining me was the secret which I dared not admit to the others – I had been to WOSB (War Office Selection Board) some time before, and knew I was going to be an officer.

The WOSB was held during a weekend visit to an elegant country house. There was no army discipline, no Sergeants, no shouting, no swearing. We were met at the door by a suave young Captain in the Royal West Kents, who welcomed us and showed us to our rooms – a small, civilised bedroom with a comfortable bed.

"Drinks in the drawing room at six sharp: wear mufti," he said.

Promptly at six, wearing civilian clothes as instructed, I went downstairs to the drawing room. There were some twenty-five young men, all in tweed jackets, grey flannel trousers and old school ties. There were also about a dozen assorted older men in uniform, obviously senior officers from a selection of regiments and corps (this was officer candidate selection for the whole army). We were given a glass of sherry, then one of them made a speech.

"Right," he said. (I found that all officers, when addressing more than one person, always began their opening sentence with 'right'.) "You are very privileged to be here. The King has called you to his service and we must decide if you are fit to be leaders of men and to do honour to His Majesty's commission as officers and gentlemen. As an officer, your men will look up to you and respect you, and you must live up to their trust. You must care for them and always remember that they may not have had the advantages you have of good schooling and a happy home."

This was not at all what I had been hearing from Sergeant Binns about officers; and I had a strong feeling that what he said was much more realistic. I found this officer's patronising attitude offensive. He was a little, tubby man with a bright red face which twitched nervously: he had a bristly, ginger moustache, his eyes were rather bloodshot and his cheeks had the tracery of burst veins of a heavy drinker.

"Your manners and social behaviour are as important as your leadership qualities. Life in an Officers' Mess, and how you get on with your fellow officers is what makes our army the best in the world. This evening we shall observe your behaviour.

Tomorrow we will set you some tasks, in four-man syndicates, to consider your leadership qualities. You should not see this as a competition. We see no merit in winning, only how you manage your men and play the game. A poet chap wrote a poem about it."

He cleared his throat and smiled mirthlessly. "Right, if you have finished your sherries, we will get the nosebags on."

The dining room was elegant, with tables for four. We were invited to sit three at a table together with an older officer. At my table there was a languid Honourable somebody, from Stowe school, about to go into the Dragoon Guards; and a small, sensible soft-spoken Scot with bright red hair who wanted to go into the Black Watch. Our older officer introduced himself as Lt Col James of one of the infantry regiments.

"Right," he said as we got settled. "Don't take any notice of me, chat among yourselves. Just tell me first who you are." We did so, and he wrote everything down in a notebook.

The meal was quite good, served by bored army waiters who must have seen hundreds of eager young candidates go through the same procedure. After an initial period of embarrassment, we found we could chat quite easily; Lt Col James remained silent, but went on making surreptitious notes. I realised that a full six courses were deliberately being served so that our social skills in the correct use of cutlery could be observed. I wondered how this helped to identify which of us would be able to lead men under fire.

There were two wines, and we all drank circumspectly, two glasses of each. Then the port and cigars came round. Here the rituals seemed very precise and important.

Lt Col James pointed to the decanter, which was on a sort of coaster, and said: "The port *always* goes clockwise round the table. It should never actually stop and it is very bad form to let it stand in front of you."

He poured a glass for himself, and moved the decanter round. "When everyone has filled his glass," he continued, "the President of the Mess will call on the junior officer present and say 'Mr Vice, the King!' You will all rise, and Mr Vice will say 'The King, God bless him!' Everyone drinks the King's health and only then can you smoke."

We did not let the port stand in front of us and, when the decanter had been refilled and emptied twice, staggered to bed.

The following morning, dressed in ill-fitting dungarees, we were divided into four-man syndicates. I was with my dinner companions, with the addition of a rather fat and garrulous chap from Manchester. Each syndicate was looked after by two referees and we were given a series of complicated tasks to do and problems to solve. These included crossing imaginary rivers with insufficient equipment while escorting enterprising imaginary prisoners who must not be allowed to escape; scaling a very high real wall helped only by a small plank, old tyre and short piece of rope and defending a small hillock using only three spades and one rifle. When we had done this we went back to our units. Later, I was told that I had passed and that I would be an officer. I suspect almost all the WOSB candidates got through.

One morning Sergeant Binns called me outside and said: "You will be leaving us tomorrow. You are going to the Officer Cadet Training Unit at Mons Barracks down the road. Just do what you are told and you'll be all right. If you see Sergeant Bertram, tell him I looked after you." He rubbed his nose and grinned. "You'll hate him; he is a proper bastard."

"And pay attention to RSM Brittain. He is the head of all the sergeants in the army and a great man. You will be lucky to serve him. Anyway, good luck, and remember everything I told you."

The following day, I said goodbye to the gang and, carrying my kitbag, rifle and with my parade boots wrapped in an old pair of flannel pyjamas for protection, marched down the road to Mons Barracks, to be my home for the following ten weeks.

Mons Barracks was a forbidding collection of red brick buildings grouped round a huge, paved drill square. As I reported at the gate, I could see squads marching and counter-marching all over the place, with the shrill screams of the drill sergeants punctuating the steady crump of boots.

It was here that officer cadets were introduced to special officer training. It was one of two principal centres for the whole

British army: infantry was trained at a country estate in the north, while the Corps and tanks trained at Mons.

An officer cadet was a curious anomaly, being neither an Other Rank nor yet an officer. We were distinguished by white collar tabs and a white plastic disk behind the cap-badge. We were the lowest of the low in the eyes of our sergeants, who nonetheless had to call us 'Sir' while cursing us. It was common to hear: "You 'orrible, dirty little bugger, Sir!" floating on the breeze.

As it happened, I was in Staff Sergeant Bertram's squad. He received the message from Sergeant Binns impassively. Bertram was a big, tough long time soldier with two rows of medal ribbons, including the Military Medal. Nominally in the Royal Signals, it was rumoured that he had been in Special Services, and parachuted several times into France though he never spoke of this. He was almost bald, vicious and unforgiving. His weight was muscle, not fat, and he could easily beat any of us over the assault course. He was deeply hated by all his subordinates, and held in great respect by his peers, who called him 'Half-and-Half'. This was explained by a corporal as meaning that he grudgingly gave half the credit for anything and was only half merciful about any shortcomings.

Our first meeting with 'Half-and-Half' was when we were formed up on the square, some thirty newcomers, to be introduced to him. He marched over to us and stood at attention in front.

He did not stand us at ease. For a moment he fixed us with his piggy black eyes, tiny, and lost in his enormous, pasty moon face, then he spoke. He had a harsh, grating voice, like a concrete-mixer. It came out of a thin slit where his mouth should have been, but it was difficult to tell, since he appeared to have no lips.

"You are squad 348, and you are goin' to be better than 347 past ones. You are goin' to be officers and you will set an example." He paused. "For example, you will get no rewards from me, only punishments. That is because when the things you do are wrong, I will make you bleed and when things are right I may not make you bleed. But forget happiness for the next ten weeks."

He turned smartly and began to pace up and down the front rank; we were still straining at attention.

"You 'ave come from a 'oliday camp. Now the pain will start. I enjoy that because the pain will be yours and from pain comes excellence. When you 'ave finished with me, I want you almost as good as a sergeant. AT EASE!!" he suddenly screamed. We were unprepared and ragged.

"Oh you 'orrible, 'orrible lot, sirs," he said sadly. "You make me weep." He turned and marched away.

An attendant corporal said: "You have to be wide awake with Staff. Now we will do two hours drill and see if that makes him happy." We did, and assume he was, since we heard no more from him that day.

Our routine was much as in the basic training unit, but the standards demanded were higher, the punishments tougher and we were so tired by the evening, that there was little conversation or companionship. My comrades were mostly public school boys and varied from those who were to go into the Hussars and Lancers at one extreme, to the lower end, like me, who were to go into the various Corps and service units. But misery brought us together.

My first encounter with the famous Regimental Sergeant Major Brittain was on the fourth morning. We were drawn up in squads (some 350 men) on the square, in our best uniform, for inspection by the RSM. A staff sergeant brought us all to attention and a huge figure, flanked by two sergeants, came marching towards us. The RSM was not less than six and a half feet tall and very generously built. He carried a pace-stick at the trail and came to attention in front of us. I was in the front rank of our squad and could see him clearly.

So this was the man whose voice was supposed to carry for a mile, and who was a legend. His hair was sandy and grizzled and his bright blue eyes squinted in the watery sun. His uniform was impeccable and I noticed that his moustache was waxed and extended, in two sharp spikes, some three inches out from his cheeks. It was said that he placed highly polished brass cones, held in place by elastic, over these spikes when he went to sleep, so as not to break them off accidentally.

"Para.a.a.a.de, stand at e.e.e.ase! Atte.e.e.n SHUN!" The sound the RSM made was astonishing. I saw the leading ranks sway back, like corn in a high wind.

The RSM began his inspection, walking slowly along the front rank, followed by his assistant sergeants, with their clip-boards and pencils. The RSM suddenly spun on his heel and pointed his pace-stick at a cadet in the squad next to ours.

"YOU!! You 'orrible gingery weasel bugger, sir! You just moved your eyes! When you're at attention, you don't ... move ... anything!" he emphasised his roar with rhythmic jabs of the pace-stick in the direction of the culprit. "You will work in the kitchen for the next three evenings, you nasty person, sir! Now keep still! Take his name, sergeant, take the bugger's name!"

The RSM paced on. As he passed me, I felt a cold sweat break out on my brow. I was frozen with terror and actually shivered as the triple row of medal ribbons bobbed slowly past my eyes and I prayed that they would not stop.

As he walked behind us, I heard him pause about four men past me. There came a hissing whisper, cold and terrifying, like death. It was quiet at first, but grew in a crescendo to end in a huge, deafening roar: "Am I hurting you, sir? No? Well, I should be, you bloody pansy layabout, sir, because I'm standing on your HAIR!"

The wretched man's hair was half an inch too long. "I've never seen anything like it in my LIFE!" This was his favourite expression. "March him off, sergeant, march the grisly nasty idle moron off out of my sight!"

One of his attendant sergeants marched the guilty man off, in double time, to an unknown fate. Nobody so much as twitched a muscle. We had met RSM Brittain.

The training we received was slightly more sophisticated than hitherto. We were now doing work in class, where bored junior officers would instruct us in the mysteries of 'O' groups at which one used the mnemonic of the '11 May' in giving out orders (Information, Intention, Method, Administration, Intercommunication), in enfilade fire, the movement of troops, supply lines and so forth. Finally, we were to put all our new knowledge together in a 'scheme'.

This was a 48 hour exercise on a special training ground. Our squad, 348, was to be the Green army while 347 were the Red army. We were given coloured armbands and blank cartridges and taken, in lorries, to a wilderness of scrub and moor, with small hills dotted about. It was cold and wet, and the rain ran down the back of our necks. For the first day we marched about in our dripping groundsheets, dug pointless trenches and subsisted on wet sandwiches and oily-tasting water from our water-bottles. In the evening, we had to ford a deepish stream, so we were all soaked to the skin and shivering with cold. The sergeants who were our constant companions (including Staff Sergeant Bertram) were warm and dry, having sat in strategically placed tents and crossed the stream on a bridge which we were forbidden to use.

We ended up on a large concrete slab, where we were told we would spend the night. A Colonel appeared and, after making us sit on the cold concrete, said:

"Right. You are the Green army. Tomorrow, starting at oh seven hundred hours, you will begin your task. Your objective is to capture the Red flag, which will be flying outside Red HQ, on top of that hill ..." he pointed into the gathering darkness. "You are free to accomplish your task as you wish. You, Pemberton, will be in command; appoint some lieutenants."

Pemberton was a short, fat and very outgoing person, whom we all liked and who was notorious for his indiscipline and cheek. He had very black hair and a huge mouth, like a frog. I wondered why he had been chosen.

"The scheme will end at fifteen hundred, and we will analyse the results the next day and see how much you have learned," the Colonel continued, wrapping his dry, warm greatcoat more closely round him. We went on shivering, and I could hear the chattering of teeth. "There will be referees watching you, and they will tell you if you are dead or wounded, when you should go back to the lorries and wait. I think that is all; carry on, sergeant."

As the Colonel marched away, Staff Sergeant Bertram came to the front. He looked at us and a small smile crept uncomfortably out of the corner of his mouth.

"A soldier fights best when he is angry," he said. "I'm going to make *you* angry, so you better win tomorrow, or *I'll* be angry."

"Now, then," he continued, marching up and down, with his boots ringing on the wet concrete. "First, I have cancelled the hot meal which they were going to bring you tender pansies; in battle, the enemy could cancel it. Second, I have told them not to bring the tents and blankets which you were going to 'ave; a real soldier doesn't need tents and blankets. Third, there will be no fires and you will sleep on this concrete area. A hard bed makes a hard man. Now you are on your own. Remember, I'll be watching you tomorrow."

He turned on his heel and marched off with his two corporals, to a large tent about a hundred yards away, where we could see some lights and hear the hiss of portable heaters.

Pemberton climbed to his feet and said: "The bastard has done it again. No use moaning. Who wants to be a lieutenant?"

I put up my hand as did two others. "OK," said Pemberton. "I commission you. Now gather round, everybody, and listen; this is my plan, but you can argue when you have heard it, if you want." This was not like any of the lectures we had heard on leadership.

"We have been lectured that in war there are no rules – all that kind of thing went out with redcoats and stopping for tea. We have been told that the scheme starts at oh seven hundred hours. Fine. I propose we start at oh five thirty hours and attack the enemy at oh six hundred, when they are still asleep. With luck, we will be back at the barracks early and dry off. What do you think?"

We sat there stunned. Well, why not? "Terrific!" a voice came from the back. "That's right," said another, "if we live that long." "That will show the bastard sergeant ..." and so on.

Pemberton divided us into three squads, each under a new 'lieutenant'. My job was to attack from the left flank and another squad attacked the right. Pemberton himself would lead the third squad straight to the enemy HQ, 'massacre' the sleeping troops and capture their flag.

We huddled down on the wet concrete, shivering, put our heads on our soaking packs and wrapped ourselves in our groundsheets. Then we lit up comforting cigarettes and eventually fell asleep. Though nothing was ever said, we discovered some time later that Jones, a thin, little Welshman, who was so quiet and shy that no one really knew him at all, caught pneumonia that night, and died a week later in the hospital. We all felt that Staff Sergeant Bertram had murdered him.

At oh five thirty, we were woken by the sentries that Pemberton had sensibly posted and fought our way to our feet. We were stiff, cold, hungry, wet and extremely bad-tempered; that part, at least, of the Staff Sergeant's strategy seemed to be working. We loaded our rifles with blanks, and set off.

The plan worked. By six fifteen we had 'killed' all the sleeping enemy, captured the flag and won the war without the Reds firing a shot. We marched to the officers' camp, woke the Senior Referee, a Major, and presented him with the captured flag.

He stood there, in his striped pyjamas, spluttering: "What the hell do you think you are doing? The scheme hasn't started yet. I haven't had my breakfast! You are cheating. You will all be punished. You will never make officers, any of you ..."

The Colonel suddenly appeared from his tent, dressed in a bright blue dressing gown. "What on earth is going on, Major? What are these lads doing here?"

"They have wrecked the scheme, Sir," said the Major. "They were clearly told it did not start officially till oh seven hundred hours, but they started earlier, so the others were not ready. They have brought the flag. I have told them they will be punished ..."

The Colonel raised his hand. "What have you to say, Pemberton?"

"Sir, you have told us that an officer should show initiative. If the Major can tell me of a single instance in the last war when the Germans told our troops at what time they were going to attack, I will hand back the flag and apologise."

The Colonel thought for a moment, then a big grin appeared. "I'm afraid he's got you there, Major! Well done, chaps. I accept your win and I like the reason. Off you go back to barracks and get warm."

We went off to the lorries and climbed in. Staff Sergeant Bertram came round and said: "I suppose you think that was clever. Well, I'll let you get away with it, because the Colonel said it was all right. But don't try any of your tricks on me or you'll be sorry."

One day it was announced that we would learn how to throw grenades. This was done on a special grenade range, not far from the shooting butts.

The grenade range consisted of four chest-high trenches, in a line, on a flat piece of ground. The squad waited in the first trench on the left, next man up waited in the second, the thrower, with Sergeant Bertram occupied the third, and those who had thrown waited in the fourth at the far right. The grenades were in a box in the second trench, and you brought one with you when going to the throwing trench. You were only allowed to move when the Sergeant yelled: "Change!"

The grenades looked harmless and it was a shock when the first was thrown and exploded near a sand-filled drum used as a target some thirty yards away. There was a big bang, sand and earth thrown up and smoke. We all had our heads down as there was shrapnel flying around. The grenades had a four-second fuse, which started as soon as the spring-loaded lever – held in place by a pin for safety – flew off.

A weak sun was shining and we were enjoying ourselves; those who had thrown were smoking in the far trench and commenting on the accuracy of the thrower. Those about to throw were pretending they were not tense.

A nervous cadet called Jelks (inevitably nicknamed 'Jelly') was next to throw. He was a big, simple man, with a bad stammer, a round, spotty face and pale hair that stood on end. He lacked confidence and was constantly mocked for his shyness and abject attitude. We were all puzzled how he had managed to get through WOSB and keep up in his basic training; he was with the Royal Engineers.

Sergeant Bertram yelled "Change!" and Jelly took a grenade and ran to the throwing trench, where he jumped in beside Staff. At the same time, I scrambled to the waiting trench and jumped in; I was next in line.

"Right, Jelks," said Bertram. I could hear him clearly from my trench, some ten yards away, and I stuck my head up to see Jelly throw. "Pull out the pin, but don't let go of the handle. Then throw at the drum."

Jelly seemed to be shaking and was very pale. He pulled out the pin and stood looking at the grenade in his hand.

"Go on, sir," said Staff, "throw the bloody thing ..."

Jelks looked at the Sergeant and said "I can't!" and dropped the grenade. The handle sprang off, activating the fuse as the grenade rolled along the floor of the trench.

Moving very quickly for such a big man, Sergeant Bertram threw himself on the grenade, covering it with his body. "Heads down," he yelled. We all ducked. Jelly just stood there.

There was silence. We all waited, holding our breaths. Nothing happened. After about ten seconds, the Sergeant scooped up the grenade and, in one swift motion, threw it out of the trench. There was no explosion.

"Change!" yelled Sergeant Bertram, standing up and brushing his uniform. "Get along with you, lad," he said to Jelly, who scrambled across to the last trench, to be greeted by a stony silence. He was crying.

I threw my grenade without incident and, shortly afterwards, we finished and went back to barracks. We were all chattering about the incident and news of it spread quickly around the camp, but Sergeant Bertram never mentioned it, and Jelly left soon afterwards. His was the only dud among the thirty five grenades we threw that afternoon.

At about this time, I decided that it would be manly to smoke a pipe. I therefore got one, and after breaking it in with brandy and rum, began, to everyone's disgust, to smoke a local mixture, called Aldershot Black Shag.

The time at Mons went quickly and, after the passing out parade, we were returned to our units. For me, this meant going back to Buller Barracks, but to a different, slightly better barrack block.

We were now Officer Cadets of the RASC and, after a further period of training, would become proper officers. We had a new sergeant to look after us, and he turned out to be quite a decent man – certainly not as fierce as Staff Sergeant Bertram. This final part of training was essentially no different from Mons, except that it focused more on our Corps interests, namely transport of troops and supplies. We were taught, in the classroom and on the road, convoy theory, battle planning, storage and transport of fuel, food, ammunition and infantry.

But we still had to do at least two hours of drill a day, as well as keeping ourselves and our kit in perfect condition. There was the continuing stress of the assault course, the route marches of twelve miles in three hours and unarmed combat. We also played rugger and I have a splendid scar on my eyebrow to remind me that Army rugger is very different from school. To stress our inferior status, we scrubbed floors, peeled potatoes and cleaned latrines.

One of our tasks was mounting guard at night, twice a week, at the RASC Headquarters Officers' Mess. This entailed spending the night in a nasty little hut, behind the grand building which housed the Mess, and taking a two-hour turn at standing as a sentry around the Mess. The worst place to be allocated was beside the main entrance. Here you had to be on the lookout for officers going in and out, saluting according to rank (butt salute or presenting arms), and putting up with the inevitable taunts, insults and wisecracks from the younger officers who, not long before, had been doing this sentry duty themselves.

The sentry posts round the back were better, but it was a firm rule that if you were caught sleeping on duty, you were removed from the cadet group, and returned to the ranks. There was no second chance. But it was, at least, possible to sit down surreptitiously from time to time.

It was hard to sleep in the hut. There were no beds, the iron stove threw out great heat and a poisonous smell and taste, which irritated the throat and eyes. The worst thing was that the next day you were sleepy and your eyes were stinging, though no allowance or concession was made in the training demands.

One day, some three weeks from the end of training, I was called into the Adjutant's office. He was a pleasant and seemingly civilised Captain of the regular – rather than the

National Service – army. He had the reputation of being rather absent-minded, which was an odd attribute for an Adjutant.

I marched smartly into his office and saluted. He winced as my heel came crashing down. He was sitting behind a desk cluttered with a great deal of paper, with overflowing wire baskets and files.

The Captain was a small, compact individual, with a single row of medal ribbons and a brown, seamed face. His thinning, mousy hair was slicked down onto his head and he looked harassed.

"Arnold or something, isn't it?" said the Adjutant. "What do you want?"

"I was told to report to you, Sir. I don't know why."

He rummaged among the mess of papers on his desk and came up with a list. "Right, here we are." He looked up and smiled.

"I am glad to tell you that you have been selected as 'Best Cadet' of the course and that you will be commanding the passing out parade."

I was thunderstruck; the thought had never occurred to me. "Yes, Sir. Thank you, Sir", I answered automatically. This all needed thinking about.

"All right, you can go. You will be told later about the parade and so on ..." I saluted and turned, when he said: "By the way, coming top means you have first choice of the postings available for your lot. The list will go up tomorrow and you can let me know which one you want."

I marched out and went back to the barracks to think things over.

Commanding the passing out parade. I was amazed. I did not think I was particularly good at any of the military subjects we had to learn, but my shameful secret, concealed from the others for fear of awful retribution, was that I really enjoyed drill. The disciplined choreography of platoons, the satisfying synchronised movements and the total power of command I found, to my astonishment, exciting and fulfilling. Now I was going to march a parade of some eight hundred cadets and a full Corps band past the General taking the salute, in front of all the doting parents and families in the audience. The thought was exhilarating. I was terrified.

The day arrived soon enough. Everyone else was thoroughly fed up with endless drilling. I would have liked several hundred more rehearsals. Astonishingly, Ronnie and Mother said they wanted to come and, what is more, were going to bring my step-sister Felicity. We would all go home after the parade for the traditional week's leave before joining my new unit. I was somewhat apprehensive about what Mother might do, but was pleased that they wanted to come.

It was sunny and quite cold. The parade was at eleven o'clock and there was the final frantic polishing and preparation to be done. I had managed to obtain an officer's second-hand uniform and hat, and had put a pair of shiny 'pips' into my shoulder straps in readiness for after the parade. I had bought an old and well-polished Sam Browne belt. By now I understood the British tradition of not wearing anything which was showily new and would also identify you as only recently commissioned. The whole outfit had cost £7, which was all I had.

We formed up outside our barracks and marched to the parade ground. The cadets had their rifles, but the Under Officers did not. I took up position in front of the parade; the band was on one side.

I could see the General on a dais opposite, some hundred yards away, and the multicoloured audience of families on either side. I spotted Mother, who was waving a large white handkerchief.

I offered up a small prayer to RSM Brittain. Here we go …

"Para…a…a…de! Atte…e…e…n…SHUN! Slo…o…o…pe ARMS!" So far, so good. Now then …

"General Salute…Pre…e…e…sent ARMS!" A satisfying rhythmic crash of hands on rifles and heels on tarmac from behind me. The band struck up a short tune. I saluted, as did the General. The audience stood, and I could see that Ronnie had removed his hat.

When I had brought the parade back to 'attention', I strutted – as I had been trained – up to the General and saluted. He produced a swagger-stick, a short bamboo cane with a silver band with my initials on it, and handed it to me. He muttered: "Well done, old chap. Best Cadet, eh? Jolly good show ..." I distinctly heard Mother say in a piercing whisper: "MY SON! MY SON!" I saluted again and marched back to my position in front of the parade.

We then marched past the General, with a smart "Eyes Left", arms swinging and band playing and off the parade ground. It was over, and we were officers.

We 'fell out' and rushed into the barrack room to change into officers' uniforms. In record time, out I came, kitbag over my shoulder and cane under my arm, and headed for the car park, where I had arranged to meet the family. I was very conscious of the new 'pips' on my shoulders.

Sergeant Binns was waiting outside the barrack room. He came to attention and saluted me smartly. I was so astonished that I froze for several seconds, before dropping my kit bag and returning the salute.

"Well done, Sir," he said, grinning. "You're a proper officer now and no mistake. Remember what I taught you, but if you forget, you can always say 'Carry on, Sergeant!' with the best of them. Good luck to you."

We shook hands and I went on. The family were waiting. Mother trotted to me and embraced me, saying quite loudly: "Ach! My little boy is an officer. He is a soldier and will defend us all!" Ronnie managed to detach her from me, and I could see Felicity weak with laughter. I hurriedly got into the car. Thankfully we left for home before anything else could happen.

Of course, there was a fly in the ointment; there always is. At my moment of greatest happiness, Fate struck with a thunderbolt.

I had been told that as top cadet I would have first choice of available postings. Obviously, I wanted to go where there was action and excitement, rather than to some boring, administrative unit. The excitement at the time was in Korea, where there was a full scale war; in Kenya, where there was Mau-Mau terrorism; and Malaya, where there was a guerrilla conflict. On the list of open postings, the only 'active' vacancy was in Kenya, so I applied for this.

The day before the passing out parade, I was summoned again to the Adjutant's office. I marched there, full of excitement, ready to find out when I was to leave for Kenya.

The Adjutant was sitting at his desk, with the same piles of paper, and the same expression on his face as the last time; I wondered whether he had moved at all since we had last met. I saluted, but he did not look up.

"Under Officer Arnold reporting as ordered, Sir," I said loudly.

"Ah, yes, hmmm ..." he muttered, still without looking up. He went on writing.

I waited. After a minute or so, he stopped writing and said: "The Army is a very big and complicated organisation, you know."

He looked at me and passed a hand over his slicked-down, gleaming hair. "Sometimes things don't happen just as we want..."

I began to feel worried. What was the man leading up to?

"I may as well tell you straight out," the Adjutant said. "The posting to Kenya which you should have got has been allocated to Arnott, another cadet, in error, I'm afraid. The names are similar," he added, unnecessarily.

"So what happens to me, Sir? Can't the allocation be changed? I do have the right to the posting of my choice ..." I was devastated.

"Nothing in the Army can be changed after it happens," he said. "The Army never makes mistakes. You will now get the posting requested by Arnott. He lives in West London, so he asked to go to the Motor Transport Unit near Hounslow. At least you are unlikely to get a spear in your belly there," he laughed without humour. "You will report to 405 Company (MT) in eight days' time, to take up your duties. I suppose I should say I am sorry," he said.

"But ... but ... but ..." I began. "Dismiss!" said the Adjutant. "Go away! NOW!"

I saluted, turned and marched out, broken-hearted.

My leave came and went. There were some difficult moments since Mother kept on asking that I wear my uniform, especially at a cocktail party she gave for the neighbours. The last thing I wanted was to wear army clothes – I had been doing so for months. She also kept making embarrassing remarks. So I was really not sorry to kiss her goodbye, shake hands with Ronnie and set off to my posting in Hounslow.

I later heard that Arnott had been killed while on patrol two months after arriving in Kenya.

I had a railway warrant (first class as befitted an officer) and got as far as Houslow station, then a taxi deposited me at the entrance to the camp of 405 Company (MT).

I stood in the rain, with my kit-bag and guitar case at my feet, and looked at the camp. There was a huge paved area, like three football fields, with rows and rows of lorries, vans and jeeps in neat lines parked on it. On two sides there were huts and what looked like barracks, at the far end there were workshops and on the fourth side offices and a sprawling brick building. The whole place gave an impression of great neatness and order, and there were whitewashed stones marking everything out. A sentry stood at the open gate and I picked my luggage up and made my way towards him.

He shouldered arms and slapped the butt in a salute, which I returned.

"Is this 405 Company, soldier?" I asked.

"Yes, sir." He paused. "Sarn't!" he suddenly yelled.

A sergeant came out of the guard hut at the double. He skidded to a halt and saluted. I saluted back in a casual and, I hoped, practised way.

"I've come to join the Company, Sergeant. Can you get someone to help with the luggage?" I was getting very wet.

The sergeant called one of the guard, and accompanied me to the brick building, which turned out to be the Officers' Mess. There was no one about – the camp looked wet, miserable and deserted. The soldier dumped my luggage at the entrance to the Mess, then he and the sergeant saluted and marched smartly away. I had arrived.

I pushed open the scarred wooden swing door and found myself in a square hall, with doors on three sides. There was a coat rack, empty, on one wall.

One of the doors creaked slowly ajar and a small, round face peered round it. It looked like a girl, and was topped by a carroty red mop. It looked at me with some caution.

"Come in, then," I said with authority, just like an officer. "Don't skulk there."

A small person came slowly into the hall. It was a girl of about eighteen. She was tightly encased in the uniform of the Women's Royal Army Corps. She was plump and rosy faced and had very blue eyes, which she blinked nervously at me.

"Well, who are you?" I barked in the approved way.

"Please, Sir, I am Funkley, Sir." Her voice quivered slightly.

"Well, I am Second Lieutenant Arnold, and I have come to join this unit."

"Oh, Sir, Lieutenant Arnold, Sir, I was ordered to wait for you." She gulped. "I am your batman."

"WHAT?" I roared. I was in no mood for jokes.

"I am your batman, Sir," she quavered. "We are all girls here and all the batmen are batwomen reely." She paused. "Those that isn't drivers, I mean ..."

I was stunned. Had I made a blunder and gone to the wrong unit? Had the Army made another of its ('we never make mistakes') mistakes?

"What is this unit, Funkley?" I asked in a reasonable voice; she was quivering and poised to flee.

"Please, Sir, this is 405 Company, Sir. There is about three hundred girls and about fifty men. We have men and lady officers here in the Mess, Sir."

We stared at each other. She advanced further into the hall.

"Will I show you your room, Sir?" she said. "And then I can get you a nice cup of tea and something to eat if you want. There's no one else in at the moment."

"All right, Funkley," I said. "Lead on and thank you."

She conducted me to a room off a corridor. It was not large, but looked comfortable, with an iron bedstead, a washbasin, a wardrobe and a desk. It was painted in various shades of gray.

Funkley dumped my luggage on the floor and said. "When you are ready, Sir, come to the sitting room, and have your tea." She paused in an embarrassed sort of way. "Everybody calls me Flunkey, Sir. It's a joke." She blushed to the roots of her carroty mop. "I'd be pleased if you call me that."

With that, she rushed out of the room. I sat on the bed to think things through.

I looked at my guitar case; at least I would have that.

In my last year at school I had bought, for two shillings, a ukulele-banjo, to accompany our singing in the study and the rugger songs in the bus on away matches. It was relatively simple to learn and I became quite proficient. At that time, guitars were rarely played by amateurs, being almost entirely confined to Spanish virtuosi, American blues players, jazz rhythm sections and a few folk singers, like the Ink Spots and Burl Ives.

But the limitations of my uke-banjo soon became apparent, and I bought a second-hand guitar, with case, for four shillings, when I was commissioned. Having two more strings, it was much more difficult to play and I was not making much progress. I was determined to practise and here there might be an opportunity.

I went along to the Mess sitting room. It was a large, square room, with weather-beaten, overstuffed furniture, in appalling condition. Scarred side tables held large ashtrays and there was a worn rug on the floor. There were reproductions of famous landscapes on the walls and a hatch, closed, which led through to a bar where drinks could be served. It was a dingy scene, very different from my expectation of polished mahogany, shining Regimental silver and an air of opulence. This was obviously a hard-working Mess.

Flunkey was there with a wooden tray on which rested a teapot, milk jug, sugar basin, cup and a plate with a huge, doorstep cheese sandwich.

"I hope this is all right," she said. "There's not much in the kitchen."

"Thanks, Flunkey," I sat down in an enormous, leather armchair. "That's fine." She scurried out.

I had just finished the sandwich, when there was a shrill noise from the hall and the door flew open. A large female person irrupted, loudly singing a tune unknown to me. She noticed me and stopped dead, staring. She was a middle aged lady, shaped like a traditional beer-barrel, filling out a khaki uniform with a captain's pips. Her face was red and round and she had a halo of untidy brown hair.

"Ho!" she said loudly. "What have we here?" She advanced towards me, holding out a large hand. "I'm Myrtle. Who are you, boy?"

I stood up and shook hands. She had a grip like a blacksmith. "I'm Arnold. Just joining today."

Myrtle grinned. "The girls will like a new face," she said. "You do know what sort of unit this is," she went on. "Mixed, if that's the word."

I was confused. "Why 'mixed', Captain?" I asked. "Mixed duties, do you mean?"

There was a roar of laughter from Myrtle and she slapped my back, hard. It hurt.

"Don't call me Captain, lad," she roared. "I'm Myrtle ... Myrtle MacPherson. When I say mixed, I mean the camp is shared by about 50 blokes and 300 or so girls. You've fallen on your feet ... by the way, what do we call you?"

"I'm known as Mick," I said.

Myrtle spotted Flunkey peering round the door. "Flunkey!" she bellowed, "bring tea, chop chop." Flunkey fled. "Yes," Myrtle continued, "we have a large detachment of WRAC girls to drive our vehicles. We are responsible for Eastern Command and War Office transport and we have lots of cars, utilities and lorries. We have some men here to pick up heavy things and to repair the transport. Otherwise they are not much use ..." she roared with laughter.

She paused to drink the tea in my cup. "The Mess is small. There is Major Ponsonby-Walker who is the Officer Commanding, and three Lieutenants, one chap and two girls. You will even things up. I am second-in-command and responsible for the girls, so be careful." She banged my empty cup down. "Where is that dratted girl with the tea?"

Flunkey came in with tea. She gingerly put it down and scuttled away.

"Do you play games?" Myrtle boomed. "I mean cricket and things?"

"Not very well, I'm afraid," I said. "I play a bit of rugger, but swimming is my real sport."

Myrtle snorted. "Swimming!" she said derisively, "that's not a sport. At least, not a British sport!" I found out later that she had played cricket for England.

There were voices in the hall. The door banged open and two girls came in, wearing uniform, followed by a thin, stooping figure. This turned out to be the other male junior officer, Peter Trevelyan. All were subalterns.

Myrtle introduced me noisily, adding: "Be nice to him; I think he's shell-shocked, har, har ..."

The girl with good legs, slim waist and blond bob was called Blossom. She was marginally prettier than the other, Shirley, who was plump, with a rosy round face and mousy hair. Blossom said: "How very nice to have another man to balance things out. Poor Peter has had to look after us all on his own ..." Peter sighed. He had strange long, narrow ears; he resembled a spaniel.

I did not quite know how to interpret Blossom's remarks, and smiled rather weakly. I thought that the circumstances into which I had fallen were a far cry from anyone's idea of National Service with the King's commission.

The final member of the Mess then came in. This was Major Roderick Ponsonby-Walker, MBE, the Officer Commanding, or OC.

He was a small man, about 5'4", who looked as though he had been polished all over. His hair was a shining black helmet, smoothed with some form of cream, his uniform was impeccable, his Sam Browne belt and shoes shone with a patent leather brilliance. His hands were particularly noticeable, being long, slim, white and with manicured, shining nails. He had a little rosebud mouth, which he usually kept pursed up in a grimace of disapproval.

He looked at me in a discontented sort of way, as Myrtle introduced me. "Arnold, is it?" he said in a soft little voice. "There is plenty for you to do, so don't think this is where you can skive ..."

"I am glad to be here," I said diplomatically. Myrtle snorted loudly.

The OC looked at me suspiciously. "You are the junior, so you can be Mr Vice," he said (the junior member of an Officers' Mess was always the Vice-President, general dogsbody and proposed the King's health on Mess nights). He called for tea and took off his Sam Browne belt; only the Orderly Officer wore a belt in the Mess.

So began my sojourn at 405 Company. I was made responsible for a number of duties, not least of which was Bar Member of the Mess, which entailed making sure that the right drinks were always available, that everyone paid their monthly bills, that the stock could be reconciled (the two bar stewards were crafty and thirsty) and that all accounts balanced. They never did, and balancing them came from my meagrely supplied pocket.

I was also given responsibility for the maintenance of a group of luxury limousines which transported high ranking officers about; there were wonderful Daimlers, Humbers and a solitary Rolls-Royce, for the C-in-C.

But my greatest pleasure was the motorcycles. These were huge, heavy and lumbering BSA 500cc monsters, or lighter Matchless 350's, painted a uniform, dull khaki. Fortunately, my Sergeant was a fanatical motorcyclist, and we spent many happy hours tinkering and testing. I volunteered to do the 'confidential despatch' ride every other day to Horse Guards Parade in London, and felt very superior with my green crash helmet with a star on the front, especially when the guardsmen on sentry duty in Whitehall saluted me. There were also happy muddy days in cross-country 'scrambles', at which I was fortunate to win a number of prizes. I also acquired, for a princely £8, a ramshackle Velocette motorbike which ran most of the time.

To my great delight, I discovered that I was, *ex officio*, a certified and approved Government Driving Examiner. I had held a driving licence for cars since I was old enough, and possessed a provisional licence for motorcycles. Now I officially passed myself (after a series of comprehensive tests on which I piously got my Sergeant to accompany me), in all groups of vehicles. Also, being the Official Examiner and since most of the girl soldiers in the camp were training to be drivers, I had conscientiously to examine them all before they could hold a full licence. These individual examinations took up a lot of my time and were most agreeable.

I quickly settled into the routine of camp. The days were predictable, since the Army has spent centuries in reducing life to basic essentials which could be controlled, foreseen and enforced. Morning parade, training, driving, inspections, interspersed with standard meals, jokes, and tall stories. We were fortunate in getting on well together in the Mess, the lieutenants behaving like siblings, Myrtle like a cheerful aunt and the OC like a headmaster. Fortunately, he lived 'out', in married quarters, with a huge wife who dwarfed him, and thus we saw little of him after about 5pm. He was a nasty, sarcastic little man, who loved his power over us, and stocked up on small victories to comfort him at home where, I suspect, he was mercilessly bullied in his turn.

Our fortnightly Mess Night was a rather miserable affair. Far from a display of gleaming regimental silver, fine wines, outstanding cuisine and ancient traditions based on a myriad battle honours, we had to make do with a silver-plated candlestick, second-rate port and a somewhat everyday menu. As 'Mr Vice' I had to propose the Loyal Toast (after which we could all smoke, and did) and get gently drunk on the port. Myrtle was notable in having a huge capacity for alcohol and for smoking large cigars, while Blossom and Shirley got rather giggly and Peter, a miserable man, whined about his bad feet and unkind mother. Altogether a far cry from traditional elegance.

Once an ancient Colonel friend of the OC's came as an honoured guest. He was a red-faced caricature of a retired Colonel and bored us to tears with endless and pointless stories of mule trains in Afghanistan. He fell asleep just after the Loyal Toast and had to be taken home.

One evening, most exceptionally, I received a visit at the Mess from my Sergeant. He looked excited and, after apologising for disturbing me, said: "I just heard through my brother-in-law, the one as lives just down the road, that his neighbour 'as killed hisself."

I was puzzled. "I'm sorry to hear that. Is there anything I can do?"

"No, no, Sir," he said. "It's like this." He took a deep breath. "It was a Shadow, see!"

Still at a loss, I said: "Start at the beginning and explain."

The Sergeant looked at me pityingly. "He killed hisself on his new Vincent Black Shadow, only a week after he got it. His widder wants it out of the house straightaway and will accept twenty-five quid! I thought you would want it." He paused, sadly. "I haven't got the money to get it."

A Black Shadow! The most wonderful motorcycle in the world. Raw power and amazing engineering. Every boy racer's dream.

We dashed round to see the widow. She did not seem very upset and gladly parted with the gleaming black and chrome monster in exchange for my cheque for £25. (I had to scurry round the next day to borrow the money, since otherwise the cheque would have bounced.)

"Easy now, Sir," said my Sergeant as I straddled the beast preparatory to riding it, illegally, back to camp. "Start in second, and very gently, or you will end up upside down ..."

Sure enough, it was all I could do to keep the front wheel on the road. I took the beast home and sat up all night polishing and adjusting and reading the handbook. Sometimes I just sat and looked. I had never been happier.

I rode many wonderful miles on my Shadow, at up to 130 mph – there were no speed limits in those days, except in towns. I kept her for two months, becoming ever more daring, until I had a couple of narrow escapes which badly shook me.

The first was one evening in London, in the pouring rain, just outside the Ritz Hotel. Revving the bike for a fast getaway from traffic lights, as I started to go forward my back wheel skidded on a metal stud, and the whole bike flipped into the air, and fell over, with me underneath. A double decker bus stopped a few inches from my back wheel.

On the second occasion I was on the A4 and doing well over 100 mph when my back tyre blew out and I was extremely lucky to finish up in the hedge. I might easily have shared the fate of the previous owner. With enormous regret I swopped her for a more civilised and docile Triumph Thunderbird, which I took to Cambridge when the time came.

Another exciting event was a telephone call, out of the blue, from Barry, a school friend with whom I had lost touch. Barry was a tall, gangly youth, destined for the Church (he was the youngest of three brothers), from a family of minor landed gentry in the Midlands. His father was a Sir.

After an exchange of pleasantries, Barry said: "Can you take this weekend off?" It was Thursday.

"Listen, Barry, old boy. In the Army you don't take weekends off. If it is something really important, I could go and grovel to the OC, but nothing is guaranteed. What's up?"

"Well, I've been invited for a weekend in Yorkshire at Gallan Hall, by my girl friend's dad, Lord Mannan, and she said I had to bring an extra bloke or not to bother to come. Please come, I will take you up and down and everything. Bring a dinner jacket or your uniform or something. Yes? Yes?"

I agreed, subject to the OC's permission. He gave it, grudgingly, when I said I had been invited by a Lord; he was a great snob. So I found myself, on the Saturday morning, seated beside Barry in his luscious, delectable MG TC, bowling northwards along the A1 with the top down.

Gallan Hall, not far from Driffield, was a huge country mansion, approached by a mile-long drive. It was surrounded by parkland, gardens, orchards and a home farm. Lord Mannan, to whom I was introduced, was a white-haired, very well-spoken aristocratic-looking man, in well-worn tweeds and with a pince-nez. He shook my hand in a vague sort of way, muttered: "Pleasure, pleasure. Have a good time ..." and wandered away.

Barry's girl friend, the Hon Georgina (the youngest of three daughters), was a plump little thing with, apparently, a will of iron, since everyone seemed to do what she told them. I was paired off with her best chum – momentarily without a boy friend – who turned out to be very pretty, very stupid and requiring a week-end escort rather than a new paramour. Her name was the Hon Ysolde Perriman-Wakehurst and she was not going to waste any time on me, when she found out my antecedents. I therefore abandoned Barry, who was mooning about after his beloved, and made friends with the eldest son, and heir of the Noble Lord, my host.

The Honourable Jeremy turned out to be a thoroughly good sort, if somewhat spoiled. He was between Eton and the Guards, and had just been given, for his eighteenth birthday, a superb Jaguar SS100 to join the marvellous Aston-Martin DB2 which he already had. Jeremy, or Remmy as he was known, was mad about motor sport and racing, and was a member of a local club which met – and raced – on a nearby disused airfield.

I told him about my Shadow and the scrambling wins and how I had always wanted to do something in cars, and he said: "Well, why don't you come along tomorrow to the track and we'll get you a drive."

I could hardly believe my ears. "Oh," he added. "You may as well race the Aston. I'll be busy with the Jaguar ..."

My cup runneth over, I thought to myself. Life can offer nothing more. But how to escape from my duties towards Ysolde. I asked Remmy.

He grinned. "Easy," he said. "Just tell her you have a disfiguring and chronic skin disease and can feel an attack coming on ..." I stared at him. "It works," he said. "I've tried it. Just make it clear you will be avoiding her for her sake, not yours."

Dinner came. We were all seated at a huge table, all 36 of us, seventeen on each side with the Lord and the Lady at the head and the foot. Sixteen chaps in dinner jackets, with fresh faces and drawling upper-crust accents (and me, in my uniform), interleaved with seventeen very English debutante-type maidens in off-the-shoulder gowns and, to my mind, somewhat immodest décolletage. There was a lot of neighing, whinnying and snorting, rather like in a stable. I was seated in the middle of one side, as being very unimportant and the girls on my two sides (Ysolde was one) presented me with their white, freckled backs, so I was free to daydream about the morning and the Aston. I vaguely remember course after course, served by white-gloved servants, several different wines and the atmosphere of gleaming napery, silver and crystal (this was how Mess nights should have been). It seemed the Lord gave a ball like this twice a year for his children. It all seemed innocent and naive.

After dinner we danced in the ballroom, in a haze of cigarette smoke, until the wine began to take its toll of the younger guests and we retired to our bedrooms. These were in the East wing of the building (the West was reserved for the Lord and his own guests, when there were any). The East wing consisted of an immensely long corridor, with pairs of rooms facing each other, and the odd bathroom here and there, Both boys and girls were in pairs, two to a room; I shared with Barry.

The house gradually became quiet. I was nearly asleep when I heard Barry get out of bed and tiptoe to the door. I took no notice. He quietly opened the door and went out. At the same time I heard creaks, slitherings and padding footsteps outside.

I went to the door and stuck my head out. All up and down the corridor there were pyjama-ed figures, both male and female, flitting back and forth across the passage. Soon it was all over and the house settled back into its night-time peace. I went back to bed and slept soundly until woken at about six o'clock by Barry creeping in. I trust that at least one of the maidens (presumably Ysolde) got a good night's rest.

I was up early, unable to sleep because of the coming excitement. I found my way down to the dining room, where I discovered a solitary Remmy tucking into a heaped plate of assorted breakfast dishes.

"Hullo there, Mick," he mumbled with his mouth full. "Help yourself to a good breakfast – we may not get much lunch ..."

I looked at the sideboard: there was everything there, in silver chafing dishes, on hot-plates. Bacon, eggs (of different sorts), tomatoes, kidneys, sausages, hams and then there was fish, haddock, kippers, trout, and even kedgeree. I loaded my plate and sat down. On a separate sideboard, on a large hot-plate, there were jugs of coffee, tea, milk and chocolate; all over the table there were different breads, toast, butter and a myriad jams, preserves and honeys and, rather oddly, tureens of stewed prunes. I was completely overwhelmed by the variety, but managed to do justice to my host's largesse.

When we had finished breakfast, we went round to the garages. I fell immediately in love with the Aston. It was a British Racing Green fastback model, with the six cylinder engine tweaked and modified to give some 200 bhp. I was shown the controls by Remmy and gingerly followed his Jaguar down the road. The wonderful burble of the exhaust, the huge wood-rimmed steering wheel, the punch in the back on acceleration – the adrenaline was coursing trough me.

We arrived at the disused airfield after about a half hour's delightful driving. There were already some cars there and more were arriving all the time. Ferraris, Jaguars, other Astons, Morgans, Mercedes … they were all there. There were also some proper racing cars: I noticed a Maserati, some Gordinis, and others which I did not know.

"Go on, Mick," said Remmy. "Have a go round the circuit. It's pretty forgiving and not too difficult. Just don't prang the car."

Off I went, slowly at first, but then faster and faster as I became familiar with the car's performance and the track. It was about two miles of not too twisty asphalt, with plenty of room to pass, and a good flat-out straight on the old runway. I was having the time of my life, especially as fewer people were overtaking me and I was actually beginning to overtake them.

We had formal races of about ten laps, in various configurations. The Grand Prix cars were the most exciting to watch, especially one driver, a blond chap with an almost permanent grin. He was superb.

Remmy came up to me between the races and said: "Do you want to have a go in a racer?"

"Oh yes, Remmy, please," I could not believe my ears. "Can you fix it?"

"Sure," he said carelessly. "Come along."

I followed him to where the cars were lined up; he stopped beside the Maserati. "Climb in and take her round a few times," he said. "But take it easy; you will find this is a different sort of driving. Don't worry, I fixed it up with Monty, who owns her and is a pal of mine."

I climbed in. It was a tight fit, and the cockpit held me like a fist. I adjusted the goggles which Remmy had lent me and started the engine. If there had been room, I would have been blown out of the car; there was a colossal bellow and howl from the engine. I sat there, stupefied for a minute or two as I made myself familiar with the cockpit. There was a giant rev counter in front of me and assorted temperature gauges. The stubby gear lever was comfortably to hand.

I cautiously went into first gear and blipped the throttle; the wheels spun in a cloud of blue smoke and the engine screamed. I saw Remmy and his friend watching me with big grins on their faces.

I tried again, more gently, and before I knew what was happening I was on the track and the scenery was flashing by. I changed gear and came thundering up to the first bend. I applied the brakes normally and found I had stopped dead with a stalled engine. Amazing. Really a different sort of driving, like a racehorse compared with a donkey.

I eased my way round the circuit and did some laps, which got faster and better as I got used to the beast. Eventually (I could have gone on for ever) I obeyed Remmy's signals and came in to the parking area (there were no pits).

"Pretty good, young Mick," said Remmy. I climbed stiffly out; my body felt bruised. "Monty thinks so too." I shook hands with Monty and thanked him effusively.

"You were driving well," he said. "better than a beginner." He scratched his chin. He was a tall, gangly young man, with dark hair and very blue eyes. "My arm is not too good; I fell off a ladder yesterday. Do you want to race her in the next race?"

I was dumfounded. "Am I ready? I'll come last. Are you sure?"

"Oh, go on," he said, grinning. "You don't have to win to have fun." Just then we were joined by the blond driver I had been admiring.

"Oh, Mike," said Monty. "I'm going to let Mick drive in the next race. Be nice to him."

"The fool won't introduce us," said Mike. "I'm Mike Hawthorn. You were doing pretty well at the end. Where have you raced before?"

I probably blushed. "This is my first time," I mumbled. Was this THE Mike Hawthorn. Yes, it was.

So we raced. Mike won. I came in seventh out of eight. Then we raced again. Then I raced the Aston. I won. It was a wonderful day.

During this weekend, my first exposure to British aristocracy,

I decided that the men were admirable and the girls were frightful. I didn't fall in love with a single one and it was all I could do to be polite as Barry sang Georgina's praises all the way back to London. Remmy invited me back to race a few more times: it was always exciting and exhilarating but never as magical as that first time.

The problem with girls was becoming acute. At least, not the problem with girls but rather the lack of them. This may seem ironic, given that I was sitting in the middle of hundreds of them and even sharing the Mess with some. But I was crippled by the deeply impressed code of chivalrous behaviour both from school and Ronnie, which stressed that one should not "take advantage" of these delicate helpless beings. All females clearly were not delicate and helpless. After all, Myrtle was a female, and she was anything but gentle or delicate. But the code insisted that one's intentions should be honourable, and the outcome marriage.

Another problem was my lack of a permanent place of my own, where I could establish my very own home, or base. Fizzy and Andrew had their own place with their mother, and I always felt like an interloper when I stayed with my mother and Ronnie. Since my only other experience of a home was staying with the happily married parents of school friends, guided by the code I presumed that I had better get married, though I had no real notion of what marriage and children were all about. I therefore looked at all girls primarily as possible wives.

This attitude led me, for a considerable time, to fall in love with and propose to a number of girls, from daughters of Sirs to barmaids, corporals in the camp and, on one occasion, to Ethel, a blonde conductress of a Hounslow bus. My offers were refused, mostly with great mirth, by all. I was somewhat bewildered by these attitudes.

I did manage to make friends with a charming Lance-Corporal WRAC driver, and we used sometimes to take General Templer's Daimler out 'on test' to London on a Saturday night, to go to a show and have a modest dinner. Naturally, I insisted on paying, so these very pleasant excursions were limited by my low income. It was also not permitted for Officers to fraternise in this way with Other Ranks, and so we had to move secretly: for example, to drive in and out of camp with my companion concealed under a rug in the back seat.

One morning the OC called me to his office. I racked my brains to think of what he may have found out, but could think of nothing. I marched in and saluted punctiliously.

He looked up suspiciously. "Ah, Arnold," he said. "I seem to remember you mentioned once that you were on your school's shooting team ..."

"Yes, Sir. It was the .22 indoor range. Nothing special," I replied.

"Well, I've volunteered you for the Southern Command championships, to show them that we are not all girls and lorries here. I thought the .303 rifle with open sights at 600 yards would be suitable."

I was aghast. At 600 yards you could barely see the target and with no telescopic sights, and wind and the likelihood of having to face the OC after missing everything the prospect was bleak in the extreme.

"I suppose they had nothing a bit closer ..." I ventured.

"Don't be such a poltroon," the OC snapped (he liked using words like 'poltroon'). "You are an officer in an honoured Corps. Behave like one."

I gulped, saluted and marched out. My mates in the Mess were not very sympathetic. "Ho, ho," chortled Myrtle. "You'll miss everything and the O.C. will have you for breakfast."

Peter grimaced and said: "Well, thank God it's not me. I can't see anything beyond a hundred yards." Blossom and Shirley just giggled.

I went to see the Sergeant-Armourer, who was in charge of our few weapons. He was a grizzled veteran of the war, with a string of campaign ribbons and, I believe, good at his job though I had no way of telling. I related my problem.

Sergeant Flibber (for that was his unlikely name) scratched his head as he thought round the problem. "Arrr," he said pensively. "The OC done that last year to young Mr Oliver." He sighed heavily. "Mr Oliver was not very good and did not hit the target once." He scratched his head some more. "The OC got rid of him pretty quick and dirty."

I did not ask what that meant; I did not want to know.

"I suppose I can zero a rifle in for you in the workshop," said Flibber after a while. "At least it will shoot straight, so it will be up to you. But six hundred yards ..." he shook his head. "Mr Oliver had a go at three hundred ..." He walked away, muttering.

The dreaded day came, and I reported, with my special weapon, to the ranges, some miles away, in Surrey. There was a large crowd of people, mostly young soldiers carrying an assortment of handguns, machine guns and rifles. There were also senior officers, supporting their units (the OC did not come) and Sergeants of all sorts organising the shooting in a busy way.

I found my way to the right butts and reported to a Sergeant-Major who appeared to be in charge. "Mr Arnold, is it?" he said loudly. "That will be that girls' transport company in Hounslow, I dare say ..." The group of sergeants standing around chuckled and smirked. "Well, I suppose it takes all sorts ..."

He explained that we would be shooting prone, with a sandbag rest and an observer with a telescope beside each shooter. "You can have two 'sighters' to sort out the windage and so on then five rounds which count. We will see if you managed to hit the target, and then you can go home to the girls!" He laughed loudly.

I was allocated a target towards the middle of the line of twenty, and lay down behind my sandbag. A little, weaselly corporal, carrying a telescope on a tripod, came and lay down beside me.

" 'morning, Sir," he said in a high voice. "I'm your spotter. My name is MacNamara, but they call me Corp; I been one a long time ..."

"All right, Corp," I settled myself down and loaded two rounds. "This should not take very long. Just tell me where they land."

There was a gusty wind blowing across the ranges. It was overcast.

"Aim off to the edge of the target into the wind," said Corp, "and give her an extra thirty yards for overcast."

The Sergeant-Major in charge of the butts shouted:

"Attention! Open fire!"

I fired my first sighter, according to Corp's instructions. A disk appeared in front of my target and twirled round. The target disappeared downwards.

"A 'magpie' at nine o'clock," said Corp. "Good sighter. Move a little to the right."

I was quite pleased. A 'magpie' was between the inner and outer rings of the target. The hole was patched and the target rose again; I could just about make it out. I aimed a foresight width to the right and fired.

The disk rose and was placed against the middle of the target. "A 'bull', a 'bull'," chortled Corp. "Good shooting, Sir."

There was firing all round me, with bullets kicking up little spurts of dust all round the row of targets. Then it became quiet.

"Right," shouted the Sergeant-Major. "Sighters are finished. Now you shoot properly and it counts." He paused. "Ready ... Fire!"

"Steady, now, Sir," Corp said quietly. "Let them go first."

There was a scatter of shots on both sides of me. I took a deep breath, aimed and gently squeezed the trigger. A 'magpie', not particularly good.

The wind was very gusty and it was difficult to aim properly. My next three shots were a 'bull', an 'inner' and another 'magpie'. Not bad. A lot would depend on the last shot.

The wind died down and I took aim. I held my breath. Corp sneezed loudly, startling me just as I fired. I was about to shout at Corp when he suddenly stood up and capered round. "A 'bull', a 'bull', good shooting, Sir. Great shot "

"Nonsense," I said loudly. "You sneezed, you fool and I missed the target."

But I had indeed hit the bull.

I was proclaimed "runner-up, rifle, 600 yards" and took a silver medal back to camp, to the disbelief of my colleagues and sour pleasure of the OC, who gave me a bottle of port. We drank this, and some others, in celebration that night and I was put to bed by Myrtle and Flunkey as the sun rose. I remember little of the evening.

Time passed. The routine was unvaried and became rather

boring. The time for my demob approached; I was told I had been granted early release from my National Service in order to go up to Cambridge in October, instead of having to waste a year.

Then there was what became known as 'The Daimler Incident'. Among the luxury cars we had for the use of the War Office and Southern Command, there was a breathtakingly beautiful 1937 Daimler sports coupé allocated to General Templer, GOC Southern Command. It was some twenty feet long, with a bonnet of nine feet, a huge twelve cylinder engine – a gleaming black monster, weighing more than two tons.

It had many strange extra fittings, including a built-in system of four hydraulic jacks, controlled from the dashboard, which could raise the car completely off the ground for changing flat tyres, working on the exhaust and so on.

One day, when I was Orderly Officer and had to show that I was busy, I was walking around the parade ground near the workshops. I suddenly became aware of a muffled bellowing not far away. I hurried towards it and discovered that there were legs projecting from under the rear of the Daimler, and that they were thrashing about, while the bellowing came from under the car.

The built-in jacks were hydraulic and there were standing instructions that blocks of wood should be inserted under the car for safety if there was work to be done. The jacks were notorious for their leaks and the car would gently and imperceptibly settle down to the ground, without the blocks.

The wheels were off and the man underneath, George Pornock, a particularly stupid mechanic well known for his laziness and corner-cutting, had failed to put in the wooden safety blocks. As a result (he was absorbed in working on the prop-shaft) the car had gently settled, with the differential pressing on his chest. He was trapped and about to have his rib-cage crushed by the monster.

I gave a yell, and shouted for help. A couple of passing privates ran up with me and we grabbed the rear bumper to try to block its inexorable and deadly descent or, at best, to lift the car.

We strained and heaved but to no effect. The car went on sinking.

Suddenly a voice said: "Let me do this!" I looked round and there was Alun Thomas, a Corporal in the REME platoon. He was known as Big Taf, since he was very Welsh, stood six foot eight in his socks, weighed more than 260 pounds of muscle and was as gentle as a lamb; that is, when he was sober. When he was not sober he was a good man to avoid.

He elbowed us aside, bent at the knees and took the bumper in his huge hands. I shouted for someone to bring the wooden blocks.

Big Taf took the strain. The veins on his neck, as thick as my thumb, stood out with the effort. He grunted and began to straighten his legs and, as he did so, the back of the car began to rise. He went on lifting and George was free.

I immediately seized his legs and dragged him from under the chassis while someone put the wooden blocks in place. Big Taf lowered the car onto them and straightened up with a grunt.

"Well done, well done, Corporal," I said. "You saved his life. Two tons of Daimler would have squashed him flat. A great effort."

Big Taf grinned. "Ay," he said in his soft Welsh voice. "I had to do it, look you. He owes me three shillings and eightpence and I mean to collect."

The story went round the camp, and Southern Command like wildfire, and entered the collection of legends of the Corps.

Eventually the time came to leave. I said a fond farewell to my sergeants, corporals and drivers. The girl drivers all lined up and shook hands. Flunkey cried.

The Mess gave me a send-off, at which we all got a little drunk and very sentimental. I was given a lighter and Myrtle said a few kind words, while the girls kept kissing me.

The following morning, with a mild hangover, I strapped my guitar case on my back, fastened the suitcase containing all my worldly possessions on the pillion, climbed on my motorcycle and set off for Jesus College, Cambridge, marriage, a career first in journalism, and then working for an oil company all over the world; this would take me back to the desert, and that plane with the gibbering madman. But for the moment, I was heading for Cambridge.